Wiehler   Mobility, Security and Web Services

Mobility, Security and Web Services

Technologies and Service-oriented Architectures
for a new Era of IT Solutions

by Gerhard Wiehler

Publicis Corporate Publishing

Bibliographic information published by Die Deutsche Bibliothek

Die Deutsche Bibliothek lists this publication in the Deutsche Nationalbibliografie;
detailed bibliographic data is available in the Internet at http://dnb.ddb.de

This book was carefully produced. Nevertheless, author and publisher do not warrant the
information contained therein to be free of errors. Neither the author nor the publisher can
assume any liability or legal responsibility for omissions or errors. Terms reproduced in this
book may be registered trademarks, the use of which by third parties for their own purposes
may violate the rights of the owners of those trademarks.

http://www.publicis-erlangen.de/books

ISBN 3-89578-229-7

Publisher: Publicis Corporate Publishing, Erlangen
© 2004 by Publicis KommunikationsAgentur GmbH, GWA, Erlangen

This publication and all parts thereof are protected by copyright. All rights reserved.
Any use of it outside the strict provisions of the copyright law without the consent of the
publisher is forbidden and will incur penalties. This applies particularly to reproduction,
translation, microfilming or other processing, and to storage or processing in electronic
systems. It also applies to the use of extracts from the text.

Printed in Germany

Foreword

The definition and realignment of business strategy is crucial for enterprises whose primary objective is to achieve sustainable success and profits in a world of steadily changing market requirements. In this context, the core business processes are the backbone of enterprises' business activities. Enterprises must focus more and more on these processes and key strategic competencies in order to stay competitive, which in turn will lead to greater specialization and elaboration of their value chain. The conventional concept of the value chain is now being expanded to include the value network, where on the one hand components are bought in and on the other hand processes such as purchasing, financial services, and personnel services are outsourced to specialist partner companies.

The support provided by IT services, and their underlying architectures, applications, platforms and infrastructures are increasingly crucial if companies are to meet these new challenges, while at the same time ensuring more efficient business operations. IT services and solutions are more than ever required to ensure a quick response to changing business priorities and activities, while also enabling consolidation of processes, adoption of the latest technologies and operational cost savings.

In view of this changing business environment and IT challenges, the subject of this book – *Mobility, Security* and *Web Services*, embedded in service-oriented architectures – are of topical interest for IT organizations. From the solution perspective, line managers need to be aware of the driving forces of these technologies and the resulting business opportunities. However, they must also carefully consider the inherent risks.

Mobility, Security and *Web Services* will have a far-reaching impact on IT infrastructures and solutions. Though they are disparate technologies with independent technical implications and histories, they must be considered jointly in the context of overall paradigm shifts and business needs that will be witnessed over the next decade.

The author, who has many years of experience in the IT sector, describes the complex interrelations of the latest technologies in a clearly comprehensible way. He points the way ahead towards a new era of IT solutions that are capable of meeting future business requirements.

Johann Breidler　　　　　　　　　　　　　　　　　　　　　　　Siemens Business Services
　　　　　　　　　　　　　　　　　　　　　　　　　　　Vice President, Systems Strategy

Foreword

After a long process of convergence and evolution, traditional communication systems, the internet and mobile communication networks have developed into a strong innovative force in our society. The continuing dynamic developments are characterized not only by exciting technical innovations, but most of all by the growing importance of social and particularly of economic aspects. Modern information and communication technology ("IT" for short) is fundamentally changing the world. Being mobile and able to communicate securely and in every conceivable way and to use services efficiently and flexibly – that's what people want today.

As an international forum for communication research, the MÜNCHNER KREIS [F1] has focused on the development of telecommunications and related technological, social, economic and political questions for more than thirty years. The group pays particular attention to the conditions under which innovative steps can be carried out successfully, with a special focus on interdisciplinary analysis so that trends or paradigm shifts can be recognized early and their ramifications properly assessed.

This book – 'Mobility, Security and Web Services' – examines subjects that have recently been the subject of intense discussion at conferences of the MÜNCHNER KREIS. One of the resulting insights is that IT will play a key role as the common link between a slew of innovative communication and application scenarios. As a result, infrastructures and platforms that have grown over time will change fundamentally. New mobile applications and service-oriented solution approaches will affect our leisure time and private life just as much as future business solutions. While remaining security gaps and related risks have been recognized among experts, the explosiveness of these problems is often underestimated.

Our society must master this change. Wider education and greater awareness are called for. With the help of numerous examples, this book explains how communication and information technologies are converging. It applies structure to the complex interactions and uses descriptive illustrations to make them understandable. The author explains key evolutionary steps, focuses on corporate solutions and application architectures, and provides useful recommendations for IT organizations.

This fascinating yet practical outlook toward a new IT era opens up many new and interesting perspectives for the reader. Let's hope that this book will help us to not just cope with this change, but to actively manage it!

Prof. Dr.-Ing. Jörg Eberspächer   Institute of Communication Networks
Munich University of Technology
and MÜNCHNER KREIS

Content

1	**Introduction**	9
2	**Evolution of information and communication technologies**	14
2.1	IT paradigm shifts	14
2.2	Network evolution	16
2.3	Mobile device evolution	25
3	**Forward-looking e-business solution architecture**	28
3.1	Application development	28
3.1.1	Component-based software development	29
3.1.2	The two camps	30
3.1.3	XML – the Lingua Franca of the Internet	32
3.2	Multitier application architecture	35
3.2.1	Portal server	38
3.2.2	Application server	42
3.2.3	Integration server	44
3.3	Cross-enterprise solution architectures	46
4	**Mobile applications and platforms**	50
4.1	Mobile application categories	50
4.2	Value of mobile applications	53
4.3	Mobile application platforms	57
4.3.1	Generic WAP architecture	58
4.3.2	Integration in existing application platforms	60
4.3.3	Mobile device platforms	63
4.3.4	Examples of forward-looking mobile application platforms	69
4.4	Example applications	75
4.4.1	B2E applications	77
4.4.2	Other mobile applications	83
4.4.3	Prospects involving UMTS	84
4.5	Summary and recommendations	86

5	**Web services**	88
5.1	Web services paradigm – SOA	89
5.2	Web services standardization	95
5.3	Web services impacts	101
5.4	Forward-looking SOA-based application platforms	108
5.4.1	SAP NetWeaver	108
5.4.2	Other vendor's platforms	116
5.5	Summary and recommendations	119
6	**Security focus areas**	121
6.1	Dangers and vulnerabilities	122
6.2	Security embedded in e-business solutions	124
6.2.1	The house of e-business security	124
6.2.2	The holistic security solution	129
6.2.3	Relevant focus areas	137
6.3	Mobile end-to-end security	139
6.3.1	Network channels	140
6.3.2	End-to-end secure application platform	143
6.3.3	Summary and recommendations	151
6.4	Authentication, single sign-on	152
6.4.1	Definitions	152
6.4.2	Authentication techniques and building blocks	154
6.4.3	Microsoft .NET Passport	161
6.4.4	Liberty Alliance project	166
6.4.5	Entrust GetAccess	171
6.4.6	Other SSO services	177
6.4.7	Summary and recommendations	178
6.5	Web services and security	180
6.5.1	Web services security standards and specifications	181
6.5.2	Web services security scenarios	190
6.5.3	Web services deployment example	192
6.5.4	Vendors and products	193
6.5.5	Summary and recommendations	196
7	**Outlook**	198
7.1	Trends in information and communication technology	198
7.2	Relationship with mobility, web services and security	201
7.3	Summary and conclusion	208
	References	210
	Index	213

1 Introduction

Information and communication technologies have been developing at a breathtaking speed, their evolution accelerating despite the recent slow-down in the economy. Experts are convinced that this development will continue throughout the next decade and we may expect it to result in changing business requirements, new business opportunities, and changes in the behaviors and wishes of consumers who inhabit what will hopefully be a wealthier, prospering society. These are trends that will influence virtually every area of human activity.

Mobility, *Security* and the recently introduced *Service-Oriented Architecture* based on *Web Services* technology number among the most exciting of the emerging orientations that will bring about significant changes in every aspect of IT infrastructure, accompanied by the development of so-called *Middleware* and securitized methods for implementing business solutions.

This book will explain why these issues are crucial. It will highlight the consequences, in particular as they impact medium-sized and large enterprises and will describe the effects on such business's information and communication infrastructures and e-business solutions.

Mobility

The power of web technology has ushered in a new business age. The world of e-business has its roots in the ability to leverage and integrate the various data sources and processes that constitute an enterprise's business assets and deliver them to consumers, employees or partners via web portals. Where companies were once limited to only those customers they could contact in person, the Internet now moves millions of connected consumers within their reach.

In the future, the world of wireless connectivity will give people the flexibility to do business wherever they are. Mobile phones, PDAs and wireless handheld computers will liberate professionals and consumers and enable global connectivity anywhere, anytime. Instead of being tied to a desk, individuals will be contactable wherever and whenever there is a sign of interest and, conversely, they will be able to access their personal resources via any network, whether fixed or wireless.

The decreasing cost and increasing speed of wireless networks are driving the move to wireless communication. Technological developments are now converging to enable wireless devices to act as clients in tomorrow's e-business world. Mobile technology, commercial and business needs, coupled with network and device availability, are all combining to drive the evolution of mobile business.

New types of application will arise as mobile technology becomes more affordable. Mobile phones will be taken up by very nearly all economically active consumers. The Internet and the evolution of mobile devices and networks are both considered to be major trends. Their convergence signifies the birth of a new era.

Developments in the mobile business sphere over the next five years will be dominated by the transition from e-business to mobile business solutions. This move will be fuelled by the emergence of new technologies. Combined web/mobile portals endowed with considerable functionality will be crucial for the integration of e-business and mobile business.

Very significant progress will be achieved as a result of end-to-end secured transactions, always-on applications and location-based services in GPRS networks, flexible broadband services with WLAN technology at high-demand venues such as airports, hotels, or exhibition centers, *ad hoc* networks enabled by Bluetooth technology; and, finally, rich multimedia applications vehicled by third-generation UMTS networks.

Mobile business architectures will be based on the same n-tier models used in today's e-business solutions. The integration of mobile business into existing e-business architectures will constitute the mainstream for the foreseeable future.

However, there are a number of inherent aspects such as the limitations of today's mobile device technology that not only differentiate the mobile Internet from the traditional Internet environment, but also complicate application development and the prospects for progress.

It is important to recognize that building mobile solutions is not just a matter of integration but also of understanding this emerging mobile environment. Enterprises therefore frequently need to call on consultants in their efforts to assess the value of mobility as it relates to their organization and business processes.

Web services and the service-oriented architecture

Another important area of change is the evolving web services paradigm. This new paradigm may prove to be the most significant avenue of progress for electronic business solutions during the current decade.

It is comparable to the shift from the unitary manual production of parts to the assembly or production line approach introduced in the automobile industry decades ago. Today, production lines are fully automated thanks to the use of dedicated robots for the majority of production processes. By analogy, *workflow engines* will control the process flow of e-business solutions, while web services will constitute the process steps performed by robots in an assembly line.

Web services are structured within a Service-Oriented Architecture (SOA). This constitutes a distributed computing environment in which applications call functionalities from other applications either locally or remotely over a network in a loosely-coupled way.

The SOA is characterized by the ability to *publish* a service in a network, with two other significant capabilities being provided inherently: *discovery,* i.e. the ability to find a required functionality (service), and *binding,* i.e. the ability to connect automatically to this functionality.

The IT industry has been talking about SOA and web services for a number of years. The benefits of having a loosely-coupled, language-neutral, platform-independent method of linking applications within organizations, across enterprises, and across the Internet are becoming increasingly evident as web services come to be employed for large-scale production purposes.

Web services are autonomous, self-contained, self-describing modular applications that can be deployed either within an enterprise – where they offer a simpler way of achieving modular and/or distributed computing aims – or that can be published, located and invoked across the Internet.

When discussing new technological trends, analysts have remained adamant about the significance of web services and stressed the very committed involvement of all of the major software vendors such as IBM, Microsoft, SAP, BEA, Sun, HP and Oracle. They predict that web services are going to be critical to IT infrastructures for the next 20 years. They see an *extended web* as a way of allowing businesses to become more agile, sense trends and respond more quickly.

The revolutionary nature of web services technology is that enterprises now create and deploy distributed applications without regard to the hardware platform, operating system, programming language, or network topology of any party wishing to communicate with the chosen web service application.

In the past, security concerns were the main factor inhibiting the widespread deployment of web services. Professionals in the IT industry have spent more than 20 years developing methods for enabling secure communication between applications in a corporate, leased-line, distributed WAN environment. Companies now expect the use of web services over the Internet to be based on secure foundations.

Provided that the security issues are solved, the vision that, thanks to SOA and the widespread deployment of web services, the Internet will evolve into a *Business Web* in which web services may be dynamically combined very flexibly and efficiently to represent any kind of business process may yet become a reality.

Moreover, the vision of the *agile enterprise* and the *real-time enterprise* implies the seamless integration of all business processes. Real-time enterprises will support not just individual business processes, suboptimized via IT systems and applications, but will also achieve the flexible, consistent integration of business processes with suppliers, partners and customers across enterprise boundaries. Real-time enterprises will be able to respond flexibly to customer needs and market changes while focusing on their core competencies, leaving extensively integrated strategic partners to concentrate on other selected activities.

The question remains: is this another high-tech bubble that can soon be expected to burst, similar to the dotcom phenomenon? Or will it become a reality in the foreseeable future? Although no definitive answer is possible at present, the paradigm shift is already underway.

Security

Beside the trend toward increased mobility, enterprises have undergone a dramatic transformation in recent years – enterprises are now operating in a global economy and increasingly run offices in multiple locations with growing numbers of remote workers who all need to communicate and share information in real-time. Communication and information sharing between different offices in the same company or between supply chain partners are now imperatives, no matter where the various offices are located or what time of the day it is. It is essential for communication and information sharing to be guaranteed by secure business processes, regardless of whether or not the different business partners have access to protected Intranet data and applications.

Nowadays, everyone expects the required information or services to be available in real-time. Customers will no longer wait for the information they need to make business decisions. Enterprises today have to meet these expectations and to provide the services their customers require.

However, there is an increasing conflict between the security an infrastructure can genuinely provide and its users' need for extended real-time access. The challenge facing organizations is to strike a balance between accessibility to corporate resources and the maintenance of a security level that is sufficient to ensure that the company's assets and sensitive business processes are not put at risk. This is a delicate balance that can only be assessed accurately by examining the specific business context and calculating the threat to the various business processes. It is difficult to strike the correct balance at any given time, a fact that may explain the tendency of many enterprises to remain with their existing security infrastructure. CIOs worry about how to maintain security while at the same time supporting innovative e-business solutions with the associated increase in access requirements.

Security has always been a top priority, especially where e-commerce and sensitive e-business processes are concerned. The new challenges of wireless Internet access and the greater integration of mobile employees, partners and customers make potential shortfalls significantly more probable. Moreover, web services and SOA will add a new dimension to the challenge posed by security, in particular in cases involving the dynamic interaction of partners who have never done business together before.

However, a more or less comprehensive framework of security standards for web services has now been elaborated, and although the task is not yet complete, appropriate products are now available. The good news is that the new security standards for web services have been designed to interact with and deploy existing basic security techniques such as Kerberos, Secure Socket Layer (SSL), Digital Certificates and Public Key Infrastructure (PKI).

An analogy may make it easier to understand the concept of web service security. It acts as a security guard who accompanies the information to ensure that it arrives unmanipulated at its destination. The guard not only makes sure that the information travels securely from the sender to the recipient, traversing bridges, boundaries and intermediate stages, but also protects the data and takes into account the identity of the sender. It is the fulfillment of this combination of tasks that makes for secure business processes.

All businesses need to address these unavoidable challenges, and security is consequently now an issue that requires the involvement of the executive board. Security awareness at the board level is the first step in recognizing the real risks associated with e-business processes and provides the basis for the development of an appropriate security strategy which balances security needs with affordable costs and acceptable risks.

Moreover, confidence is the single most important thing that is needed for businesses to compete successfully. Confidence is a great enabler, making it possible to exploit new opportunities through e-business – reaching more customers, working more closely with suppliers, empowering employees and driving new revenue streams. However, confidence is only possible when every participant knows that every business-related interaction is totally secure. Thus the implementation of a reliable and secure infrastructure will add real value to enterprises, which will stay competitive by defining standard e-business processes.

Issues not considered here

One key future topic in the IT sector which is very closely bound up with the question of web services is not covered in this book: *grid services*. The combination of *grid computing* – middleware that has already been developed for scientific computing – and web services to form *grid services* is a challenging development that is the subject of intense discussion among IT experts. Collections of grid services are required to perform more complex functions that cannot be offered by individual services. Grid services constitute a central building block for tomorrow's computing paradigm: *On-demand computing*. On-demand computing possesses the potential to transform computing into a utility provided in the same way as water, power or telephone services, which is why this paradigm is also referred to as *utility computing*.

The examples used in the following chapters frequently refer to proven products and platforms. Open source platforms will undoubtedly play an increasingly important role in modern e-business solutions. However, any reasonably detailed consideration of open source software would go beyond the scope set for this book.

The author placed great emphasis on ensuring that the information provided in this book is up-to-date. However, the products or standards referred to may change over time. As an example, the product cycle of mobile phones is currently only nine months. The author therefore apologizes if, on occasions, a reference fails to cite the most recent version of a product.

2 Evolution of information and communication technologies

Over the last two decades, the application scenarios mobilized by business solutions have changed significantly, as evidenced by IT architectures and paradigms, networks and communication technologies as well as by the classes of mobile devices.

This chapter highlights some of the past developmental phases within a historical context and points to the directions development might take in the future.

2.1 IT paradigm shifts

Business processes in enterprises are supported by an underlying IT infrastructure and applications. These control and optimize enterprise resources and support purchasing processes, supply chain management, customer relationship management and other processes. As figure 2.1 illustrates, two application paradigm shifts constitute the most profound changes to IT infrastructures and business solutions that have arisen since the eighties.

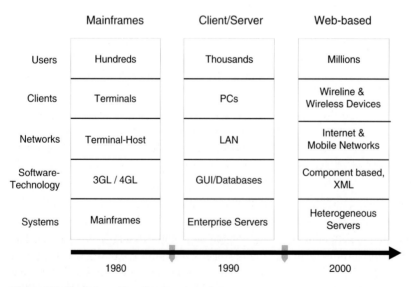

Figure 2.1 Evolution of application scenarios

2.1 IT paradigm shifts

In the late eighties, the old *monolithic application paradigm*, characterized by unstructured and inflexible applications, designed using 3rd and 4th generation programming languages, running on mainframe (host) systems, and supporting dumb, text-oriented terminals has been replaced by a 2-tier client/server application paradigm.

Paradigm shifts do not usually come about due to the evolution of a single technology or as a result of a unique invention, but rather through a complex of mutually complementary, emerging new technologies, ideas and business needs that combine to create added value.

The shift to the *client/server paradigm* represents a clear demonstration of this hypothesis.

The business needs: competitive companies in the eighties needed to get more users online, distribute applications to different locations and facilities, generate separate databases from their applications in order to use and manage them independently of the application and, finally, wanted to work with more comfortable graphical user interfaces.

The technological developments: PC and LAN technology can be considered to be the main evolutions that made this paradigm shift possible. However, other developments such as the power of the emerging Unix server platforms, graphical user interfaces and rich database management systems have complemented one another and combined to make the paradigm shift a reality.

The idea: Give the client processing power and intelligence in order to distribute the workload to more economic platforms. In addition, provide users with a more convenient user interface and with office tools that support their daily tasks more efficiently.

10 years later, another paradigm has started to establish itself as the result of significant technological developments and emerging business-related requirements: *web-based e-business*.

The business-related factors include globalization, shorter product cycles, more flexible corporate structures, virtual organizations, the creation of closer customer and partner relationships and, finally, the increasing demand to do business anytime, anywhere in the world.

It is without doubt the development of Internet technology that has acted as the principle driving force in shifting the IT world towards today's state-of-the-art, multitier architectures – described in chapter 3 – and the new web-based, e-business application paradigm. The Internet and e-business have now become part of everyday working life and, regardless of the dotcom hype and ensuing crash, new business opportunities such as e-commerce and e-auctioning with millions of users have been seized on successfully.

Another significant evolution which, in combination with those mentioned above, has permitted the shift to the web-based, e-business paradigm, is the establishment as a standard of *XML (eXtensible Markup Language)*. XML, which evolved jointly from the document-oriented *SGML (Structured Generic Markup Language)* and the presentation-oriented *HTML (HyperText Markup Language)*, may now be considered to be the *lingua franca* of the Internet.

XML, as an open standard which is widely accepted by industry, underpins interoperability. It permits the description of data, documents, information, content of all types, protocols and programs. It makes it possible to separate data/content and presentation, and acts as a single source for the generation of diverse presentation formats for workplaces and mobile devices. It greatly facilitates data exchange across industries and between business systems regardless of platform, operating system or the underlying technology. Finally, XML is the technology underpinning remote function calls and web services.

As a second stage in the emergence of this web-based paradigm, another development – wireless Internet access using a variety of innovative mobile devices to exploit Internet services via mobile access networks – will increasingly change both individual lifestyles and business operations. A number of mobile business solutions has now been successfully implemented, optimizing business processes by, for example, reducing travel costs and creating new value for customers, partners, employees and enterprises.

The technologies and architectures involved in this web-based, e-business paradigm – including the question of mobile access – are discussed in more detail in chapter 3. Moreover, chapter 3 also looks at the architectural changes apparent in forward-looking, e-business application platforms in terms of the deployment of web services and the increased integration of mobile applications.

2.2 Network evolution

During the last three decades, the Internet has developed to become a unique global network infrastructure providing unlimited access to information and new commercial opportunities.

In the seventies, its function was to ease military deployment and provide expert university networks. In the eighties, it became a showcase for the pioneers of new technologies while the nineties represented the dawn of the e-commerce era. This evolution is illustrated in figure 2.2.

The Internet and the evolution of mobile devices and networks are both considered as megatrends. The convergence of the two will lead to a new era – the *Mobile Internet* era. Within the next decade, the number of Internet subscribers will again increase substantially, with the majority of users employing mobile devices. The use of mobile devices makes the Internet an *Everywhere Marketplace* and provides the impetus for the development of innovative business models.

The technological evolution of the wired Internet in the last few years has been impressive. The development of optical network and switching/router equipment gives the Internet core network literally unlimited bandwidth capacity. The capacity of optical fibers has increased by a factor of 200 over the last decade and the deployment of

2.2 Network evolution

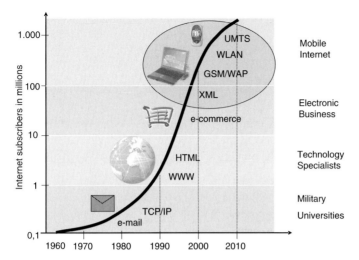

Figure 2.2 Internet evolution

Dense Wavelength Division Multiplexing (DWDM) technology makes transmission speeds of more than 1 Tb/s theoretically possible.

Nonetheless, the most exciting developments have taken place in the field of radio frequency networks. The following brief outline illustrates the variety of new mobile network technologies and indicates how rapidly they have developed. Some of these technologies were not even known just 5 years ago.

GSM

GSM (Global System for Mobile Communications) is a representative of the 2nd generation of mobile communication systems. While the 1st generation was based on analog technology, the 2nd uses digital technology which brings about significant advantages in terms of the total costs, the quality and the size of mobile devices.

Introduced in 1996, GSM [2.2.1], a European standard, is the most successful of the mobile phone network technologies with a global market share of about 70% and network providers offering GSM networks in more than 200 countries worldwide including 100% coverage in Europe. In the near future, more than 1 billion subscribers will use GSM networks. GSM networks will remain in use at least up to 2010, though GPRS and 3rd generation networks will offer much larger bandwidths, improvements on existing services and a range of innovative services.

GPRS

Growing out of GSM, *GPRS (General Packaged Radio System)* networks provide voice and data services. GPRS has been available since 2002 in most GSM networks and offers three key benefits for the providers and users of data services:

- It reduces the costs of providing connectivity in comparison to circuit-switched technologies like GSM. GPRS constitutes a connectionless technology that uses network resources more efficiently since applications occupy the network only when data is actually being transferred.
- It provides greater bandwidth – roughly comparable to ISDN bandwidth with approximately twice the burst transmission rate.
- It also provides transparent IP support. By transparently tunneling the IP protocol from the mobile device to the Internet or Intranet and giving the device the same status as an IP server on a LAN, GPRS provides seamless mobile access to the Internet and corporate Intranets.

GPRS is the first mobile network that allows always-on connectivity. The combination of always-on/packet switching with volume instead of time-based pricing and data transmission rates comparable to those available with ISDN has the potential to boost mobile data access.

SMS/MMS

The *Short Message Service (SMS)* is a wireless network service initially used in GSM networks where it constituted the first data service. It allows the asynchronous transmission of up to 160 characters in one message. Today, every GSM phone supports SMS. It has developed as the GSM killer application, with more than 20 billion messages being sent every month.

MMS (Multimedia Messaging Services) is a combination of SMS, Audio Message Services, Photo Message Services, Video Message Services and Group Message Services. As a result, a mobile phone supporting MMS can send a message that contains one or any combination of the above-mentioned elements: text, audio, photos, graphics and video. In a work context, for example, speech or written comments can be added to a photo or video clip of a machine in order to provide maintenance instructions. The Group Message Service makes it possible to send an MMS to a user-defined group of recipients in a single operation, thus reducing transmission costs. MMS is supported in GPRS networks but may be widely deployed in 3rd generation networks because of the need for additional bandwidth.

WAP

The Wireless Application Protocol (WAP) is a protocol for synchronously delivering data over mobile networks to the Internet and receiving data from it. It specifies an application framework and network protocols for wireless devices, mainly mobile phones but also optionally PDAs. It takes account of the current constraints of wireless networks and devices, such as limited bandwidth, less powerful CPUs, memory capacity, and limited input/output capabilities.

The framework was elaborated by the *WAP Forum*, with the first version making its appearance in 1999. Since then, the WAP Forum has been integrated in the *Open Mobile Alliance* [2.2.2]. Although its launch did not prove to be a success, WAP is now an established Internet access standard for mobile devices worldwide and particularly in Europe. Today's mobile phones usually support WAP.

The WAP protocol model is derived from the web model. It allows network operators, software vendors, service providers and enterprises to build applications and services that can reach a variety of different mobile platforms efficiently and effectively. It also includes a microbrowser environment containing the following functionality:

- *Wireless Markup Language (WML)* – a lightweight markup language similar to HTML but simplified
- *WML Script* – a lightweight scripting language similar to JavaScript
- *Content Formats* – a set of defined data formats, including images, phonebook and calendar
- *Wireless Telephony Applications (WTA)* – telephony services and application interfaces.

The Wireless Session Protocol (analogous to HTTP) constitutes the WAP application layer and offers consistent interfaces for both connection-oriented and connectionless services. The Wireless Datagram Protocol (partially analogous to TCP/IP) provides the general transport services and decouples the upper layers from the different bearer services, which may take the form not only of GSM and GPRS but also of other networks provided in Asia and America.

More details of WAP are provided in chapter 4 (architecture) and chapter 6 (security).

i-mode

A proprietary protocol and mode to obtain Internet access from mobile phones, *i-mode* was introduced in Japan in 1999 by the country's largest network operator NTT DoCoMo. Unlike WAP, it has enjoyed great success ever since the time of its launch.

Instead of WML, i-mode uses a presentation language known as *cHTML (compact HTML)* which is more similar to HTML. i-mode is based on packet transmission, i.e. utilization costs are priced by packet, regardless of usage time. The use of packet transmission and the pricing model have undoubtedly been crucial factors in i-mode's business success. In addition, widely appreciated services coupled with a win-win business model that embraces content providers and business partners have been reasons for i-mode's rapid take-up in Asia.

i-mode is now also offered by a number of network operators in Europe. However, as it is not an open standard it is not supported by the majority of mobile phones supplied in Europe. In competition with WAP, i-mode will probably not play a dominant role either in Europe or in North America.

i-mode and WAP can both be considered as interim technologies. In the near future, technological solutions will be found to the above-mentioned technical limitations that constrain both devices and mobile networks, thus providing pervasive Internet protocols for implementation in devices as well as in wireless and wireline IP networks.

Migration to 3rd generation mobile networks

The 3rd generation (3G) mobile telephone system in Europe is known as *UMTS (Universal Mobile Telecommunication System* [2.2.3]) and was standardized by the *ETSI (European Telecommunications Standards Institute)*. UMTS is based on *W-CDMA (Wideband-CDMA)* technology, which is a broadband evolution of *CDMA (Code Division Multiple Access)*. UMTS will offer both real-time (e.g. for speech) and non real-time modes (e.g. for e-mail) using common mechanisms capable of providing reliable transport for voice, message, files and stream-type data. UMTS allows connection-oriented (circuit-switched) as well as connectionless (packet-switched like GPRS) communication.

Although UMTS is associated with transmission speeds of up to 2 Mbit/s, this will be achieved only in fixed locations. Pedestrians will be offered a speed of 384 kbit/s and users in moving vehicles 144 kbit/s.

UMTS services have started to be introduced by carriers in European countries from 2003 onwards.

It is a well-known fact that carriers have paid huge amounts to obtain UMTS licenses in certain European countries (e.g. € 50 billion in Germany). The carriers will also need to make additional investments on a similar scale to build the required infrastructure. As a result, only metropolitan areas will be covered by UMTS networks during the initial phase.

UMTS will open up new business opportunities and scenarios and create a bouquet of innovative applications such as video conferencing, video streaming, and video on demand. Thanks to 3G systems, users will be able to determine the quality of the voice, data or video call at the moment it is set up and pay accordingly. Further properties of UMTS with regard to mobile business applications are discussed in chapter 4.

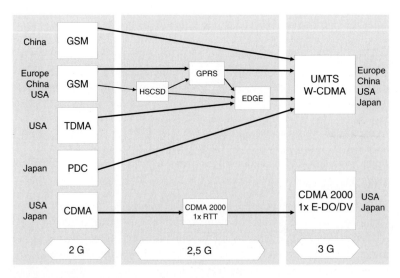

Figure 2.3 Migration path to 3rd generation mobile networks

The migration path from GSM (2G) to UMTS (3G) is provided by the so-called 2.5 generation (2.5G) technologies. In most European countries, GPRS has been chosen as the natural path to 3G. However, as illustrated in figure 2.3, two other wireless technologies – *HSCSD (High Speed Circuit Switched Data)* and *EDGE (Enhanced Data Rates for GSM Evolution)* – will constitute future developmental steps. However, these will not have as significant an impact as GPRS – at least not in Europe.

HSCSD, which is purely a connection-oriented technology with a bandwidth similar to ISDN, has been available from some network operators for several years. It may be useful for some niche applications, for example when enhanced security requirements are involved. It nevertheless remains an interim technology.

EDGE will permit data rates of up to 384 kbit/s (connection-oriented as well as connectionless). Widespread deployment is not expected in Europe (with the exception of certain countries), since the technology requires considerable investment and came on stream only shortly before the advent of UMTS.

The situation is different in North America where GSM networks are currently growing faster than anywhere else. Here, EDGE networks, deployed as a further development of GSM and *TDMA (Time Division Multiple Access*, currently used in North America), make a lot more sense, because 3G networks will arrive later than in Europe.

CDMA networks are primarily employed in North America and Asia (Japan, Korea) and will have no impact on Europe's mobile networks. They will evolve via CDMA2000 1xRTT (2.5G, bandwidth up to 300 kb/s) to CDMA 1xE-DO/DV (3G, bandwidth up to 5 Mbit/s).

3G networks were first introduced in Japan. NTT DoCoMo introduced the *FOMA (Freedom of Mobile Multimedia Access)* network in 2001. From the very outset, Asia has played a leading role, with the 3G networks deployed in Japan, Korea and Hong-Kong now numbering several million subscribers.

The standardization of 3G networks is promoted by the *3rd Generation Partnership Projects (3GPP)*. The 3GPP [2.2.4] is responsible for W-CDMA technology and the 3GPP2 for CDMA technology. The 3GPP is a collaboration agreement, established in 1998, that brings together a number of telecommunications standards bodies.

The consolidation of mobile network carriers by acquisitions and forming alliances is still in progress due to the huge investments for network infrastructures and innovative applications. Just two recent examples are the acquisition of AT&T Wireless by Cingular Wireless LLC in USA and the foundation of the Starmap Mobile Alliance (comprises 9 smaller carriers) in Europe.

Mobile location technologies (GSM, GPRS, UMTS)

The ability to locate the position of a mobile device is crucial for the provision of geographically specific value, i.e. added information that stimulates mobile business. Various technologies will be available to provide these services.

The simplest of these technologies, and one that is available now is the *COO (Cell of Origin)* method. Network operators can correlate phone numbers with the network cell in which the device is transmitting. Depending on the cell size, the sensing accuracy is between several hundred meters and a few kilometers.

Some more accurate *Location Fixing Schemes* (LFS), such as *GPS (Global Positioning System), TDOA (Time Difference of Arrival)* and *E-OTD (Enhanced Observed Time Difference)* will penetrate the mobile market in the near future. These methods provide location sensing accuracy of between 20 and 200 meters.

Besides these technologies, which require a greater or lesser extent of device and/or network modification, other approaches have been developed which are handset-based and work in standard GSM/GPRS networks where they offer a precision in the range of 100 meters.

There is a high probability – at least over the next 2 years – that only the network operators will own location-dependent information. They will therefore be in a prime position to promote location-dependent services.

The challenge now is to bring together the content providers with the geo-coded information that makes it possible to exploit this technology. Applications that make use of mobile location service technologies include fleet management, vehicle tracking for security purposes, tracking for recovery in the event of theft, telemetry, emergency services, location identification navigation, route tracking location-based information services and location-based advertising.

WLAN

WLAN (Wireless LAN) technologies are designed to transmit and receive data over the air, thus minimizing the need for wired communications over short distances. WLAN may either take the form of an extension to an existing LAN or act as a substitute for a wired LAN. WLANs have the benefits of reduced costs due to the elimination of unnecessary cables while also offering easy, flexible network access.

Because WLANs can provide high data rates (theoretically up to 54 Mb/s), at a cost lower than that available using mobile networks, they will complement mobile networks and even have the potential to supplant them in certain specific data application areas. The typically cited example is that of the business traveler in an airport. Because of their limited range of approximately 100 meters, WLANs are not, however, in general suitable for wide area coverage.

To date, WLANs have been installed in several tens of thousands of hotspots and other locations worldwide, including airports, hotels, cafes, malls, exhibition centers, conference centers and others. Even some cities are considering providing WLAN-based wide area coverage. Increasing numbers of businesses are installing WLAN hotspots in libraries, conference rooms and customer information centers. Moreover, WLANs will play a significant role in mobile business solutions, offering an additional communication network for workforces, customers and partners alike. In such applications, however, the security issue is crucial and must be considered carefully.

The WLAN standard is based on the *802.11 LAN standards*. The institute of *Electrical and Electronics Engineers (IEEE)* formed its 802.11 WLAN working group in 1990.

This was set up with the aim of developing a global standard for wireless LAN. However, since then, many different and sometimes partially incompatible variants have emerged.

The first standard to be introduced and the one in most widespread use is 802.11b. This operates in the license-free 2.4 GHz frequency spectrum, providing a maximum data rate of 11 Mbit/s. A further evolution within the same frequency spectrum which offers upward compatibility to 802.11b is the 802.11g standard with a maximum data rate of 54 Mb/s. Its deployment level has grown ever since it first arrived on the scene and most vendors today deliver WLAN network cards and access points which offer compatible support for both standards.

The more recent 802.11a standard (products available since 2002) operates in the license-free 5.2 GHz frequency spectrum. Although it also provides maximum data rates of 54 Mb/s, it is incompatible with the 802.11b/g standards. This standard has the advantage of providing more non-overlapping channels, thus resulting in higher bandwidth capacity with multiple concurrent users in one WLAN cell. However, the disadvantage is that the corresponding frequency bands have not been released in some countries.

It is important to note that the maximum data rates cannot be achieved in the real world. Depending on the distance separating the device from the access point and on the number of concurrent users (should be less than 20) in a cell, the actual transmission rates may well be only 10% of the maximum rates.

There are other important WLAN standards, such as WEP, WPA and 802.11i. These address security issues and are discussed in more detail in chapter 6.

The *Wireless Ethernet Compatibility Alliance (WECA)* [2.2.5] tests 802.11 products to ensure interoperability. Products that comply with the specification feature the *'WiFi'* logo.

Bluetooth

Bluetooth was initiated in 1994 by a study conducted by Ericsson and has been actively promoted from 1998 onwards by the *Special Interest Group (SIG)*. The SIG was set up by Ericsson, Nokia, Intel, IBM, and Toshiba. Since its inception, several hundred other companies have become members.

Bluetooth, which has been in more widespread use since 2002, is a low-power radio technology that is being developed to replace cables and infrared links over distances of up to 10 meters. Devices such as PCs, printers, mobile phones and PDAs can be linked together to communicate and exchange data via a wireless transceiver that fits on a single chip.

Key Bluetooth applications include the synchronization of different items of equipment, e.g. mobile phone, PDA, and PC. This will make it possible to enter data at any one of the devices used and then synchronize the others with it. Additionally, data exchange (for example, with POS (Point of Sale) terminals), ticketing or e-wallet applications for mobile commerce might also boost the success of Bluetooth. Bluetooth technology enables any device with a chip to communicate seamlessly even through non-metallic walls or other intervening objects.

Using Bluetooth, it will be possible to separate a mobile phone's transceiver unit from the earpiece and the display. Thus, the transceiver could be housed in the user's belt buckle and the display in the watch with no wires needed. Bluetooth provides some of the key functionalities required in order to transform a mobile phone into a comprehensive lifestyle tool.

Since Bluetooth has a throughput of up to 1 Mbit/s (in real operation, 400 - 700 kb/s) and is not limited to point-to-point links, it might also be used in wireless LAN applications. Easy connections make it possible to set up *ad hoc networks*. For instance, participants at a meeting can create a so-called piconet in order to share documents. Moreover, a Bluetooth device can serve as a short-range (about 10 meters) Internet bridge that enables others to connect to it in order to access Internet content.

Different Bluetooth profiles have been defined in order to provide interoperability between devices. Profiles indicate which functionalities are supported by a device, and devices that possess the same profiles can communicate.

Nonetheless, compatibility and security issues still hinder wider deployment of the technology in business solutions. (For more details, see chapter 6).

The Bluetooth standards are specified by the Bluetooth Special Interest Group [2.2.6].

Scope of mobile network technologies

The mobile networks that have been outlined above constitute a comprehensive set of complementary network technologies that cover the full spectrum from short-range technologies (Bluetooth, WLAN) through to globally deployed technologies (GSM, GPRS) as illustrated in figure 2.4.

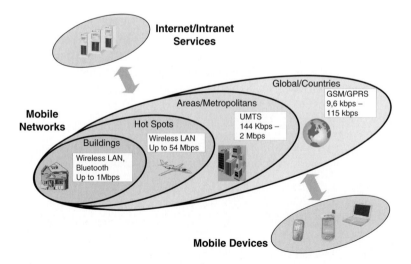

Figure 2.4 Scope of mobile network technologies

The foregoing should have made it clear that all of the network technologies that have emerged in recent years are characterized by different focuses and parameters in terms of bandwidth, quality of service, standards, range, costs, and services. Though some technologies may compete with others and their areas of application may overlap, for example Bluetooth and WLAN deployment in buildings or UMTS and WLAN in metropolitan areas, complementarity is the keyword. This means that all of these technologies will remain established for the foreseeable future.

Moreover, we can identify a clear tendency towards convergence on IP networks and Internet protocols for these networks. This convergence is the only answer to increasing network complexity and is driven primarily by considerations of economy and the advantage of seamless communication. The digitization of any content, such as text, data, voice, graphic, picture, video, multimedia, is an important step towards a unified network and will help drive the convergence process. Technologies such as voice over IP and the implementation of IP protocol stacks within a variety of access technologies will make this development unavoidable.

Although the goal of seamless communication with any device over any network to access any service is a greatly prized objective, it will not be achievable in the near future. However, the different network protocols, shortcomings in roaming capabilities, and device limitations may be overcome in the longer term.

Readers who want to find comprehensive coverage of the topic of mobile networks in order to learn more about their technical basis are recommended to refer to the book: GPRS and 3G wireless applications: Professional developer's guide [2.2.7].

2.3 Mobile device evolution

The development of mobile devices has a number of predecessors: pagers, unwieldy analog mobile phones, portable PCs and others where development has been accelerated by the availability of network infrastructures and the miniaturization of electronic components.

Nowadays, mobile devices such as mobile phones, smartphones and PDAs count amongst the technologically most highly advanced products because they integrate a range of the most recent developments, such as processor, radio frequency, memory, display, battery, voice recognition and software technologies. The software input is particularly impressive, now accounting for approximately 70% of a mobile phone's value chain. In less than three years, the lines of code implemented in a typical mobile phone have quadrupled from around one million to over four million.

The combination of these rapidly developing technologies coupled with the increasingly exacting wishes and demands of leisure and business users has resulted in the appearance of a huge range of new devices over the last two years as the examples in figure 2.5 demonstrate.

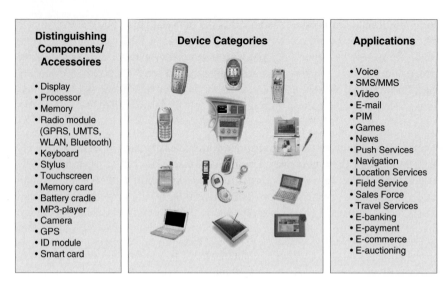

Figure 2.5 The wide range of new mobile devices

The list of device categories stretches from fashion mobile phones, via simple mobile phones (WAP), business-oriented smartphones, PDAs, clamshell handhelds, laptops, tablet PCs, webpads to car navigation systems.

The most exciting developments in the near future will be seen in the field of fashion phones, smartphones and PDAs.

An example of the fashion category is the Siemens' Xelibri family. These handsets are designed to appeal to fashion-conscious users and to be displayed as items of personal jewelry rather than traditional mobile telephones. Typically, such devices feature 4096 color screens, voice dialing technology and polyphonic ringtones. They dispense with a keypad altogether, relying on voice dialing and navigation buttons to operate the phone's features and FM radio equipment. Some are shaped like a clip, allowing them to be fastened to an item of clothing; others are supplied with a 'cargo-style' clip to be attached to the waistband of the user's trousers.

In contrast, smartphones and PDAs will play a significant role in future business solutions.

Smartphones like the 6600 from Nokia or SX1 from Siemens use the open Symbian-based Series 60 operating system which offers the downloading of mobile applications, enhanced XHTML browsers for integrated access to web and WAP sites, and advanced PIM (Personal Information Management) applications. Usually such devices possess additional multimedia features, such as video download and play capabilities, and camcorder features. Moreover, these devices boast integrated Bluetooth as well as multi-band capabilities, e.g. GSM, GPRS and HSCSD or GSM, GPRS and UMTS.

The competition in this device category will remain intense, involving vendors from Europe (Nokia, Siemens), the USA (Motorola) and Asia (Samsung, SonyEricsson) to

2.3 Mobile device evolution

name only the leading companies. Series 60 is the dominant operating system in this smartphone device class with a market share of about 75%. The other player whose importance in this sector is probably growing is Microsoft with its Windows Mobile (for smartphones) operating system (More details can be found in chapter 4).

As a device class, PDAs have developed in two main areas: networking and the expansion of interfaces and features. Unlike their counterparts of two years ago, today's PDAs possess integrated network modules, mostly Bluetooth and WLAN or GPRS, or can accommodate network interface cards. Newer models are capable of communicating via Bluetooth, WLAN and GPRS networks. An increasing number of devices, such as Toshiba's e800 series, provide Voice over IP capability, which enables users to place phone calls over a high-speed WLAN network, thus reducing the cost of long-distance calls.

Thanks to the availability of a variety of interface cards such as network interface, GPS (Global Positioning System) or camera interface cards, memory cards, smartcards, SIM cards, keyboard interfaces, MP 3 player interfaces, etc., PDAs may be configured in many ways for various leisure and business purposes.

This category has also been characterized by keen competition for a number of years. The leading vendors are HP, Palm, Handspring, Sony, Toshiba, Fujitsu Siemens, and Dell. The dominant operating systems are Palm OS from Palmsource and Microsoft's Windows Mobile (for Pocket PCs). However, alongside Linux, RIM (Research in Motion, a Canadian company) is also attempting to boost the market share claimed by its Blackberry operating system (For more details, see chapter 4).

It is interesting to observe the increasing rate of convergence of the functions and features of smartphones and PDAs. Undoubtedly smartphones currently offer better voice capabilities. On the other hand, however, PDAs provide a larger number of interfaces. In fact, smartphone growth has outstripped that of PDAs. As component integration intensifies, the more likely it is that attractive smartphones with different form factors will emerge.

Within the context of mobile business solutions and the access to sensitive enterprise resources from mobile devices, appropriate security features will play an increasingly vital role. Security considerations are discussed in chapter 6.

3 Forward-looking e-business solution architecture

Enterprises today run their businesses on the basis of architectures and applications that usually consist of a mix of heterogeneous software and hardware technologies sourced from different vendors. Today's applications therefore offer only very little capability in terms of interoperability.

In the past, enterprises made large-scale investments in best-of-breed products to support the functional requirements of their business processes. In the meantime, however, they have grown disillusioned and have increased the pressure on their IT organizations to reduce costs, increase flexibility and, in the final analysis, create value for their business.

This situation forces IT organizations to manage a high degree of heterogeneity in order to meet their companies' requirements. In addition, CIOs need to migrate enterprises' IT infrastructures to forward-looking e-business solution architectures if they are to make their businesses adaptable and capable of developing new and innovative cross-functional business processes.

The good news is that vendors have recognized the seriousness of this situation and, more than ever before, are now driving the development of technical and business standards to reduce the friction between products.

The following sections provide an overview of the fundamental elements of a forward-looking architecture and the way they work together in modern business solutions.

3.1 Application development

Application development is an important facet of the design and development of business solutions. Visual *GUI (Graphical User Interface)* builders are available for developing user interfaces. These permit the definition of the layout as well as the control and output elements based on drag-and-drop mechanisms without the need for explicit coding. Technologies that support mobile terminals are starting to play an increasingly important role in this context. Visual tools are also available to support the implementation of database accesses or web services.

Development environments are frequently optimized for specific operating systems. Suitable development environments are also available for special middleware, such as Microsoft's .NET and IBM's WebSphere. *IBM's Eclipse* development environment has been available as an open source framework since 2003. Taking Eclipse as their basis, other software vendors have now optimized their development tools for their specific environments. A well-known example is SAP's decision to use Eclipse as the Java development tool for its NetWeaver platform. As a result, Eclipse can now be considered more or less to be the standard development environment in the Java world.

In contrast, Microsoft offers the proprietary *Visual Studio.NET* development environment which is designed for Microsoft platforms only. However, it is rated by experts as the best and most efficient development tool available today.

Modern development environments can generally be integrated easily with software modeling and test tools in order to provide a standard environment that offers consistent support for the application development process.

3.1.1 Component-based software development

In the late 1980s, programmers and information technology (IT) professionals began to realize that large software development projects not only entailed excessive overhead but were also inflexible. Most enterprise applications were written for a specific set of tasks and the resulting code could not be repurposed for other jobs. Consequently, even related applications had to be coded from scratch.

Design experts and programmers therefore began to turn to *object-oriented programming*, a modular approach that formalized the idea of reusable code. Object-oriented programming enabled programmers to link reusable code objects together within a single application for the first time. The introduction of *component software models* followed. Component software models applied object-oriented programming principles between applications with the result that developers could create applications by assembling discrete components.

These models made it possible to achieve the main objective: the modularization of complex applications in order to boost flexibility and efficiency.

Component technology allows application development to be tailored in a concrete way to business processes. Functionalities are encapsulated in components and these are assembled in an application as illustrated in a simplified way in figure 3.1.

To support a specific business process, an application executes and controls a sequence of components, named business objects. The way the business objects are deployed is defined by the deployment description associated with each of them. They are stored and administrated in a business object directory and processed in the runtime system's business object container (part of the application server).

Components from existing applications can also be used for new solutions. The presentation and business logic as well as resource management are strictly separated from one another and no longer bound to any specific application. The strict separation of components means that parts of applications can be combined or extended in different

3 Forward-looking e-business solution architecture

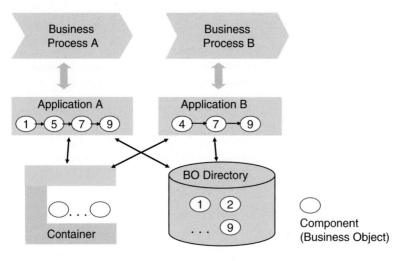

Figure 3.1 Component-based application model

ways. Communication is performed on the basis of a small number of standards and interfaces that are accepted industry-wide.

Component technology offers some significant advantages:
– Reduced time and costs due to the reusability of components
– Reduced complexity by splitting complex applications into modular functional components
– Reduced development risk thanks to the possibility of creating and then subsequently extending partial solutions
– Better quality through the use of proven components
– Increased flexibility through the substitution of components within a system environment

For more information about component-based application development, readers are recommended to consult the book 'IT-Lösungen im e-Business' [3.1.1].

3.1.2 The two camps

Ever since the advent of component technology, two camps have led the market. The resulting competition has proved to be of great value by motivating alternating enhancements of the competing concepts.

The camps are, on the one hand, Microsoft with the *.NET framework* and, on the other, the *Java world* with the *J2EE (Java 2 Platform, Enterprise Edition) / Enterprise Java-Beans (EJBs)* model. This second camp is headed by Sun and supported by major software vendors such as IBM, HP, BEA, Oracle, SAP, to name only a few.

The Java camp's goal is to allow customers to choose between vendors' products and tools and to encourage best-of-breed products to emerge through competition. Sun initiated the *Java Community Process (JCP)* in order to solicit new ideas. Java technology is based on open specifications for which various vendors then supply the necessary products. In this way, the Java standard offers companies independence from individual vendors. The *J2EE architecture* is based solely on the *Java programming language* and, once written, Java code can be deployed on any J2EE-compliant platform.

Microsoft .NET, on the other hand, is a proprietary technology. However, Microsoft has the advantage that it does not have to compromise with others and can closely couple various functions of the .NET runtime environment with the Windows operating system. Because optimum use can be made of the underlying operating system (Windows), it is believed that comparable applications would run more efficiently under .NET.

Conceptually, the J2EE and .NET application environments are very similar as figure 3.2 demonstrates.

Both are based on a virtual machine, a neutral intermediate code and a uniform class library. In terms of architecture, both technologies are designed for server-based processing for different front-ends such as web browsers, GUI clients and mobile terminals. Support is provided for GUI (*Swing* versus *Windows Forms*), for HTML generation (*Java server pages* versus *ASP.NET*), data access (*JDBC* versus *ADO.NET*), XML, and web services. The respective application servers offer parallel processing, session and transaction management, as well as adapters for databases and third-party systems.

When developing the .NET technology, Microsoft had the advantage of being able to use proven Java concepts, thus resulting in the creation of a technically more modern solution. This can be seen both in the C# programming language and in the consistent integration of web technologies and XML. Furthermore, as far as data access is concerned, Microsoft's ADO.NET offers a greater level of comfort than is available with JDBC. On the other hand, the Enterprise Java Beans (EJB) component model is methodologically more advanced than COM+, which was adopted in Microsoft .NET for the provision of enterprise services and managed components. As mentioned above, the

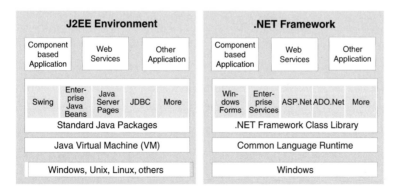

Figure 3.2 Java/J2EE environment versus .NET framework

competition between these two concepts has been of benefit to users and the best features have been offered in new versions alternatively in both the .NET and the Java model.

The real differences between Microsoft's .NET and J2EE tend to lie at the strategic level. Java is an open technology platform which both extends over all operating systems and embraces a variety of alternative vendors. It is important here that there are attractive open source products available for all components of Java technology. These products, for example from the Apache Group, are not only cheap but also powerful and stable. In the case of Microsoft .NET, the fact that the technology comes from one source means that new functions can be developed quickly. However, dependence on the vendor is absolute.

3.1.3 XML – the Lingua Franca of the Internet

The emergence of *XML (eXtensible Markup Language)*, which developed out of HTML and the document-oriented *SGML (Structured Generalized Markup Language)* and which permits information-oriented data processing on the web, will be one of the most important technological developments for future business solutions.

XML is a unique attempt to provide the comprehensive communication, presentation and processing of any data. It is an attempt to standardize, packetize, structure, and translate information so that it can be presented on different devices and make the storage, retrieval and exchange of all types of information more efficient and more responsive to real human and organizational needs.

As a meta-language, XML is more than just a tool for the semantic structuring of information in documents. With XML, it is also possible to create languages which standardize the processing of all types of information, such as the presentation of data (style), data transfer, access by applications to the information structure, the description of relationships between data and data modules (hyperlinks, addresses), or communication between applications. Many languages that support the processing of XML data are derived from XML itself.

XML is the future of the web and is often referred to as its *lingua franca*. The decisive factor is that XML can be tailored completely to respond to users' needs, the characteristics of the information they want to work with and, finally, the specific objectives of the application.

At the same time, this huge potential represents a great threat to the success of XML. XML is not a solution but rather a tool for developing solutions. These solutions are as good or bad as the concepts behind them.

Development is proceeding rapidly and gathering pace. For many sectors and branches of industry, specific formats (Document Type Definitions, schemes) have already been established which enable and optimize the access to and interchange and processing of homogeneous information. Examples of some of the important bodies engaged in this work are *ebXML* [3.1.2], *OASIS* [3.1.3] and *RosettaNet* [3.1.4].

3.1 Application development

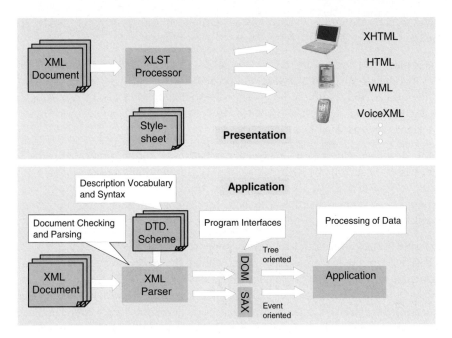

Figure 3.3 XML deployment scenarios

XML is a globally recognized industry standard and is recommended by *W3C* [3.1.5]. More information about XML can be found at *XML.Org* [3.1.6].

To illustrate the flexibility of XML deployment, figure 3.3 depicts two scenarios.

The upper scenario shows how different output formats can be generated from a single *XML document* source.

XML has a complementary technology, known as *XSL (eXtensible Stylesheet Language)*, which offers both a method for formatting XML information and altering or even transforming XML documents by means of pattern matching and template-based transformations.

XML stylesheets together with an *XSL processor* can be used to transform any XML document into a presentable form on any device.

A *stylesheet* contains a set of tree-construction rules consisting of two components, the first being a pattern matched against the elements in the source tree and the second a template that constructs a portion of the result tree. The stylesheet contains a template of the desired result structure and identifies data in the source document to insert into this template.

The XSL processor works through the nodes of an XML document tree. First, it examines which rules apply to the root element. It then searches for possible child elements and rules that might apply to each child and continues this process through the tree.

33

The lower scenario in figure 3.3 shows how an XML document can be processed by an application.

The vocabulary and syntax are defined in *DTDs (Document Type Definitions)* or schemes that may form an industry-specific vocabulary and can also contain program type definitions for the data. In order to reference a publicly available *XML scheme*, a reference URL may be inserted in the XML document. This URL points to the referenced schemes and functions as a dictionary.

The XML document can then be analyzed, evaluated and further processed using a software parser. Furthermore, XML technology is currently being enhanced by programming APIs such as *DOM (Document Object Model*, tree-oriented) and *SAX (Simple API for XML*, event-oriented) as well as by further concepts such as *XLink, XPath, XPointer* [3.1.7].

One example of such a scenario would be a situation in which an electronics company has to design a new component for a product, with all the product-related information being stored in a database. The product information now has to be made available to all the partners, each of which possesses a different merchandise system. The solution can be implemented by means of an SQL statement that extracts the data from the product database, uses the table column headings as tags and thus automatically generates an XML document. The XML document is then transferred to a document conversion program that can use mapping rules to generate other document formats.

XML Web Services

From the very outset, the creation of XML has been a vendor-neutral, standards-driven effort to define a markup language that can be used for a multitude of purposes, including the exchange of data between multiple systems.

Taking the XML standard as the starting point, the modular nature of *XML Web Services* can be seen as the next logical step in application development.

To enable the program-to-program communications that define web services, additional specifications were needed in order to define the services, the interfaces to the services, and a mechanism for invoking the services.

Although advanced component models such as *J2EE/EJB* and *Microsoft's .NET Object Model* have enjoyed widespread acceptance within companies, extended component models that enable components to work across networks have been less successful. This is mainly due to two factors:
- The incompatibility of the two camps' frameworks. The two component-based frameworks use different platforms and a different scheme to communicate. An J2EE application cannot communicate easily with one based on the .NET architecture.
- Given that companies' security policies usually require that their firewalls block the type of network services used by software components, the two component-based frameworks cannot be used successfully on an inter-enterprise basis.

To overcome these problems, IBM, Microsoft, Ariba, HP, and Sun started to lay the groundwork for web services in the late 1990s. The companies embraced two established standards, XML running on top of HTTP, as the foundation for inter-component communication and defined additional specifications that describe the services, the interfaces to the services, and a mechanism for invoking the services. In acknowledgment of the XML standard, these services often are referred to as *XML Web Services*.

The three XML standards crucial to XML web services are the *Simple Object Access Protocol (SOAP)*, the *Web Services Description Language (WSDL)*, and *Universal Description, Discovery, and Integration (UDDI)*. Microsoft and IBM have led the development of all three. All the protocols are multivendor specifications upon which vendors base their XML web services frameworks. An XML web service may be written in any language and run on any platform, as long as it conforms to these basic XML web service standards. More details about web services standards and the service-oriented architecture (SOA) can be found in chapter 5.

3.2 Multitier application architecture

The objective of an enterprise-wide application architecture is to develop applications in conformity with guidelines that enable them to communicate and cooperate with each other more efficiently, have a common look and feel, and can be deployed on different platforms.

As depicted in figure 3.4, modern application architectures are subdivided into four layers: the *communication/presentation tier*, the *business logic tier*, the *integration tier,* and the *services/resources tier*.

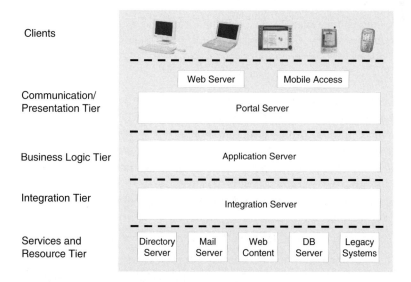

Figure 3.4 Multitier application architecture

Applications developed on the basis of this four-layer model have a modular structure and are distributed, open, flexible, adaptable and extensible. Consequently, they can be adapted more easily to the structures of modern business processes, i. e. it is possible to respond quickly to new requirements.

However, such a *multitier application architecture* requires careful application and system design. Monolithic programs are replaced by groups of specialized, loosely coupled, interaction-capable components that can be placed on different systems and platforms while taking account of technical and operational aspects.

Some of the essential attributes of a modern, enterprise-wide application architecture for the design and implementation of business solutions are:

- The separation of the application into different layers: for presentation; business logic; integration; and enterprise resources, services and data storage (multitier architecture)
- The use of web browsers and micro-browsers (for mobile devices) as primary user interfaces that support the relevant standards such as HTTP/HTML and WAP/WML
- The use of protocols and data formats based on *de facto* standards and/or Internet standards
- The use of XML as a universal format for data interchange and as the basis for business process communication between companies in the form of XML web services
- The use of component technologies
- The deployment of dedicated, function-optimized server technologies such as web servers, portal servers, application servers, integration servers, database servers and directory servers
- The integration of mobile application technologies

The communication tier (often called presentation tier) is primarily responsible for the terminal-specific communication and presentation of information contents. It must make the information volume available in a suitable form to the user and must respond appropriately to input from the user. The communication/presentation tier covers the system building blocks *Web Server* and *Mobile Access*.

Web server

A *Web Server* typically transmits web pages on demand via HTTP to a web browser (PC client). In order to perform this task, a web server possesses special, system-related software modules, such as a module for monitoring communication channels and for analyzing and interpreting the incoming URL command line. The primary tasks of a web server include:

- Implementing simple business logic with server-based scripting technologies, such as Microsoft Active Server Page (ASP) or Java Server Page (JSP)
- Accessing business data (e.g. database)
- Preparing HTML data streams and transferring the web pages that are to be displayed for interpretation by the web browser (client). Program code can also be optionally transferred for execution at the client.

The technologies used most frequently for generating web pages include:
- Java Server Page (.jsp) and *Java Servlets* within the J2EE environment
- Active Server Page.NET (.aspx) within the Microsoft environment

The web applications running on web servers do far more than just return information in HTML format. They may also contain business logic, access databases, prepare data for specific browsers and/or deliver components to the client to enable part of the business logic to be executed at the terminal (e.g. in a Java virtual machine).

Mobile access

A range of protocols has been developed for mobile terminals in parallel with those that characterize the Internet. WAP stands for Wireless Application Protocol and is an open standard for data access and communication with mobile devices. The protocol is independent of the transport network and the actual terminal. It takes account of different displays, optimizes the presentation format and communicates with WAP browsers (micro-browser) in the mobile device. In addition, WAP ensures effective communication within a limited bandwidth and supports mobile radio networks such as GSM, GPRS and UMTS. WML (Wireless Markup Language) was developed as a description language for presentation.

A *Mobile Access* building block usually contains a WAP gateway that is responsible for the content of the information that is to be exchanged with mobile terminals such as mobile phones. It converts HTML or other data formats and stores or creates WML data formats. WML documents may either be retrieved in this format from storage, or may be generated at runtime from XML documents in a form appropriate for the terminal in question, for example through transcoding procedures or by means of the XML Stylesheet Language (XSL).

A WAP gateway represents the point of connection between the mobile radio and Internet worlds and is responsible for converting the mobile radio protocol to the Internet protocol and vice versa.

Thus, for example, it converts input from WAP terminals, which is available in a binary/compressed protocol, to the HTTP protocol and converts the Wireless Datagram Protocol (WDP) to the Transmission Control Protocol (IP/TCP). Nowadays, WAP gateway functions are often included in portal server products and represent an important part of the communication/presentation tier.

Other mobile devices such as PDAs and smartphones sometimes implement the WAP protocols but frequently use only HTML and TCP/IP. Furthermore, certain other mobile phones support the i-mode protocol which is based on packet transmission and uses a kind of compact HTML.

The core building blocks

The services and resource tier comprises the legacy systems, corporate services such as e-mail and directory services, and the enterprise's databases and web content servers.

These resources are based, to a greater or lesser extent, on established technologies and are not discussed in more detail here.

In contrast, the *Portal Server, Application Server* and *Integration Server* – i.e., the core building blocks of forward-looking application architectures – have undergone significant developments over recent years. Their underlying architectures and features will therefore be highlighted in the following sections.

3.2.1 Portal server

In many enterprises, portals are developing into the central entry point for all business-relevant information and workflows, including the handling of transactions across a very wide range of business processes. The users of such portals are customers, business partners, vendors and the enterprise's own employees.

Enterprise portals frequently combine different enterprise tasks within a single portal, such as customer portal, broker portal, field service portal, internal services portal, supplier portal, editor portal, etc. They have also become a key element in enterprise-wide integration (people integration) and have acquired interoperability with other vendors' platforms and applications.

Portal servers suitable for use as enterprise portals must be capable of continuous adaptation to a very wide range of enterprise and user requirements. Consequently, this key building block in modern solutions demands, in particular, a modern, flexible, forward-looking architecture. The basic requirements for suitable portals are a scalable infrastructure, high availability and flexible presentation services, as well as support for mobile terminal devices. Other important portal functions are the assurance of a high level of security through adequate authentication and access control mechanisms, together with easy-to-use personalization facilities which permit optimization both for

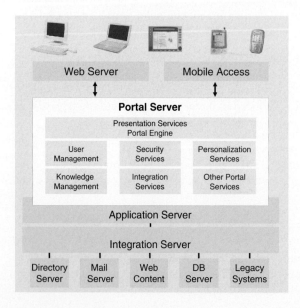

Figure 3.5
Portal server architecture

the enterprise and the users of the portal. Portal servers are embedded in the existing IT environment and comprise services as shown in figure 3.5.

In the actual product variants offered by the various vendors, the portal server is frequently a component of an application server family, with the application server acting as both runtime environment and backbone for the transaction processing carried out over the portal. Existing implementations from leading vendors are all based on Java standards (J2EE, EJB etc.) and are largely independent of hardware and software platforms (with the exception of Microsoft).

Today's most successful portals offer the technologies and generic services described below.

Portal engine, presentation services

The technological kernel of a portal server is the *portal engine*. The portal engine analyzes incoming requests and starts up appropriate components, whose function is to provide the results in the form of portlets. *Portlets* are the visible components which users see on their portal pages. On the basis of the page layout, the portlets are grouped together in the assigned frames and then displayed. The page structure is normally defined in template files (Java Server Pages Markups) which can be flexibly adapted and modified. The pages are built by the *presentation services*, which take account, wherever appropriate, of the requesting user's authorizations and personal parameters as well as of the characteristics of the terminal device in question.

Users prefer to work with a simple, web-based user interface, if possible with intuitive navigation and access to all the applications they need to perform their tasks. Separate web servers or servers integrated in the portal supply the corresponding portal information in HTML format to browser-based devices. Frames containing the requested or configured content (portlets) are typically supplied with a navigation bar and links to lower-level pages. Portal contents may be drawn from different sources, e.g. catalogs, documents, sales reports, address lists, appointment diaries, worklists and ticker bars.

The use of mobile terminal devices (laptops, PDAs, Internet-capable mobile phones) in business processes (especially B2E and B2C) will increase sharply in the future. Modern portal servers take account of this trend through integrated transcoding and rendering procedures (part of the presentation services) which manage the device-specific processing of the presented content. Portals must thus be able to identify device classes, and possibly also device types, in order to ensure the required presentation and interaction.

User management

The *user management* function has the task of administering the various user groups together with the assigned roles and authorizations. User administration stores the user and role-specific information that is needed for each business process. Users are able to log onto the portal and administer their preferences and account information themselves. Alternatively, existing information can be integrated into the portal server. Users and roles are normally stored as information in the portal server and are synchronized with existing directories via LDAP. These directories often also contain access privileges and certificates which are monitored and administered by a CIO and used by the security systems. As organizations, roles and authorizations change frequently, it is important that the relevant management system should be administratively simple, flexible and secure.

Personalization services

The *personalization services* make a considerable contribution to the usefulness of enterprise portals. From the user's point of view, settings regarding portal content and device-specific settings play an important role, as do also preferences of various kinds, the selection of information channels, the enabling and disabling of notification services, etc. From the enterprise's point of view, user profiles, rules and authorizations play an important role in various situations. From the information provider's perspective, customer profiles can be generated from customers' navigation and purchasing behavior and items that are of interest to individual customers can be displayed to them at runtime.

Personalization and simple menu guidance are of particular importance in the case of mobile devices since the constraints limiting these devices (small display screen, limited interaction) mean that users must be guided directly to the information that is relevant to them.

Security services

Since the portal represents the central entry point for users with very different authorization levels, *security services* form an essential component of enterprise portals. The security system monitors the authentication and authorization of portal users and enables encrypted and/or authenticated data transmission on request. It can also ensure that transactions are of a binding nature.

In most applications today, *authentication* is performed by means of a *user ID* and *password*. However, leading portal suppliers also offer *public key infrastructure (PKI)* support coupled with the use of *digital certificates* for authentication and to ensure the non-repudiability of transactions. As users have access to several independent applications via the portal servers, single sign-on functionality can be extremely useful. Here, the user is given a ticket that is digitally signed by the portal server. Applications (including 3rd party applications) can check this ticket against appropriate portal libraries before allowing access. Portal servers also often provide interfaces to independent authentication products (See chapter 6 for more details on single sign-on).

Access by users and user groups is controlled through to portlet level by *authorizations*. The access control lists for the various portlets are defined by administrators who take account of any relevant provisions in the company's security policy.

The complexity of end-to-end security implementation is frequently underestimated. Secure transactions can only be guaranteed if end-to-end security exists. This applies equally to terminal devices, networks, web servers/WAP gateways, portal and application servers, and back-end systems (Chapter 6 provides more details).

Knowledge management

The function of *knowledge management* is to find and selectively read the structured or unstructured information requested by users. Knowledge management covers aggregation, categorization, classification, the distribution of any structured or unstructured information, as well as simple and complex search functions. Company documents can be stored in an appropriate sort order, while version control, procedures and flow control are also of importance in connection with publication.

Integration services

The integration of existing applications and resources in the portal plays a crucial role. The corresponding *integration services* may either be directly implemented in the portal or the EAI components present in an existing integration server may be used. Access to data/information or transactions frequently has to take account of back-end systems and external systems and data sources. The retrieval and conversion mechanisms necessary for this are provided by the integration services. These services provide standard adapters in the form of portlets or remote portlets in order to access frequently used information sources (e.g. Reuters), internal services (e.g. e-mail) or applications (e.g. SAP).

Specific adapters (e.g. to legacy systems) can be added to the development components of an application or integration server (J2EE, EJB, JSP, JCA).

Other services

Even though portal servers generally possess a series of out-of-the-box functions, these must be configured to match the enterprise's task requirements and may be available in a large number of different variants. It often takes several months to arrive at the optimum set-up. Enterprises therefore expect a simple portal development environment enabling them to develop their own portal components and thus react quickly and flexibly to market changes.

Depending on the supplier, other services may be provided by the portal in the form of portal services. Foremost amongst these are the *collaboration services*. They offer businesses improved cooperation across corporate boundaries and give distributed project teams the opportunity to communicate synchronously and asynchronously, and also to administer and edit documents jointly.

Other optional portal services include *publishing services*, alert and notification services and *location-based services*. The latter are particularly important to mobile users of the portal.

As communication and information platforms become increasingly interlinked, a closer interfacing between portal servers and help services will become necessary. Nowadays, customers are contacted both via the Internet and via telephone channels. Multichannel customer contacts, customer profiles and access to back-end applications are relevant to both services, and their close integration is therefore a desirable objective.

Because of their interaction with knowledge management systems and the need to administer web content, portal servers are often closely linked to content management systems. However, content management functions are increasingly being incorporated in portal servers.

3.2.2 Application server

An *application server* forms the centerpiece of a web-based business application. As shown in figure 3.6, the basic function of the application server is to provide the runtime environment for web applications.

The application server provides containers to run the applications' reusable software components. Component technologies such as *Enterprise JavaBeans (EJBs)* or *Microsoft COM+ components* (in DNA environments), as well as *.NET-managed components* in native .NET applications or in mixed environments (DNA and .NET), are in widespread use today.

The container has the task of providing the components with a runtime environment through which they are invoked. Via the container, components indirectly use a set of basic standardized infrastructure services. This model releases programmers from the need to deal with complex system-related security, transaction and communication issues, and hundreds of APIs. Instead programmers can focus on implementing the pure business logic.

This set of runtime services includes access to relational databases and unstructured data, persistent management, management of queues for asynchronous communication on the basis of application-specific messages, transaction management and execution, access and user identification verification, and the auditable recording of all actions.

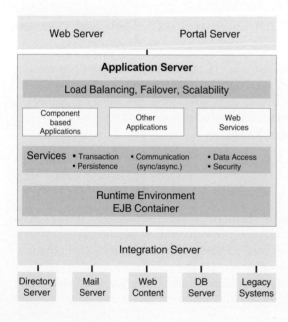

Figure 3.6
Application server architecture

3.2 Multitier application architecture

In addition to these runtime services, a professional application platform requires a highly productive development environment, including support for reusable server-side components. The advanced functions as far as application developers are concerned include support for different programming languages, visual programming tools, code debugging across distributed components, configuration management and the integration of third-party tools.

Application servers also provide the runtime environment for other applications such as packaged standard applications. Support for web services is partially implemented in the leading products but is still undergoing development in the light of the standardization process.

Above all, application servers must provide a high level of application scalability because it is not possible to predict the number of concurrent users who will be using the web application. Advanced application services such as dynamic load balancing and automatic failover mechanisms in an application server cluster are therefore valuable features.

On the basis of the two above-mentioned component technologies, two rival application server technologies or platforms have established themselves. These are Java application servers such as *IBM WebSphere* or *BEA WebLogic*, on the one hand, and *Microsoft Windows Server*-based COM applications and/or .NET applications on the other. For older environments (*DNA, Distributed Network Architecture*), the Windows 2003 operating system family contains all the required application server functions in the form of integrated application services. In addition, the .NET framework contains all the required *.NET Enterprise Services*.

Java application servers are based on the specifications of Java 2 Enterprise Edition and make available a range of middleware services and application programming interfaces (APIs) for the implementation of business-critical Java-based web applications. The most important middleware services and APIs in this context are:

- *Java Server Pages (JSPs)* for creating simple web applications (HTML instructions are generated for the browser by means of a server-side script.)
- *JavaBeans* for programming client-side components such as layout and navigation elements for the user interface (browser)
- *Java Servlets* for communicating with the integrated web server, and for programming and controlling the processing logic
- *Enterprise JavaBeans (EJBs)* for the use of reusable business logic components and system-related runtime services
- *Java Naming and Directory Interface (JNDI)* for address translation and for saving data and attributes in directories
- *Java Mail* for sending and receiving electronic mail
- *Java Messaging Services (JMS)* for asynchronous process communication (message processing) by means of queues
- *Java Transaction Services and APIs (JTS/JTA)* for transaction processing, including the synchronized storage of data records in distributed databases

- *Java Database Connectivity (JDBC)* for access to databases by means of standardized method calls
- *Java Connector Architecture (JCA)* for the standards-based interconnection of custom web applications and application packages such as SAP, Siebel, etc. within the framework of a company's *enterprise application integration (EAI)* strategy
- Java API for parsing XML documents (JAXP)
- Support for synchronous process communication protocols (RMI via IIOP), *CORBA* and *XML web services*.

3.2.3 Integration server

The *integration server* in new business process-oriented solutions represents an important evolutionary step in modern business solutions. Integration servers intergrate functional elements of standard application packages, newly developed business logic (e.g. in the form of components), parts of legacy applications and the necessary data in a way that responds to the needs of the business process that is being created.

The expression *Enterprise Application Integration* (EAI) has become established to cover such issues and has recently been joined by the term *Business Integration* which refers more broadly to the integration issues including business process modeling, execution and management.

The task of business integration is to efficiently combine the various application packages which initially operate in isolation within a company. These packages consist of *Supply Chain Management* (SCM), *Enterprise Resource Planning* (ERP), and *Customer Relationship Management* CRM), as well as user-defined applications and database and host applications. Business integration refers to the integration of business processes at the inter-enterprise level, but also addresses cross-enterprise, B2B business process integration issues, i.e. it deals with business relationships with suppliers, partners and customers and access to electronic marketplaces.

A robust runtime environment in the form of a dedicated integration server is required both for internal and for cross-enterprise business integration. Just as important as the runtime environment is the development environment which, among other things, provides pre-integrated adapters for integrating back-end systems, generic business object definitions, data transformation services and tools for business process modeling and process flow control.

Integration server technologies – as illustrated in figure 3.7 – can be logically subdivided into three functional tiers.
- Within the topology tier, *hub-and-spoke* (i.e. star-type coupling of applications) and *bus-oriented* topologies can be distinguished.
- The communication tier consists of the communication methods used for the integration, distinguished in data, applications and processes. The alternatives here are *message brokers* (messaging, asynchronous, e.g. publish and subscribe), *integration brokers* (RPC of business objects, synchronous, request/response) and *web services* (request/response).

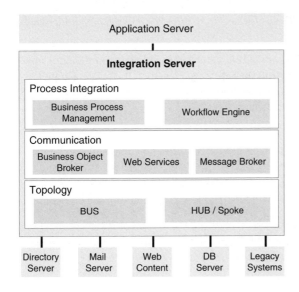

Figure 3.7
Integration server architecture

- The upper tier is concerned with the management and execution of integrated business processes.

Tier 1 and, in particular, tier 2 have a major impact on the suitability of an integration server for different integration requirements. Thus, integration brokers tend to be more suitable for complex process integration. In such cases, however, intensive re-engineering work is usually required. Message brokers require less effort and are especially suitable for message and data exchange as well as for separated, decentralized applications and processes.

To some extent, web services combine the advantages of message brokers and integration brokers and are therefore now playing an increasingly important role in the field of *business integration*. This technology has other obvious advantages: open standards, independence from the application platform and programming language together with the loose coupling of applications run by different organizations and enterprises.

Nowadays, most integration servers contain web services frameworks and therefore take account of this development.

Finally, tier 3, which is responsible for *business process management,* includes a process modeling component and a workflow or business process engine, and constitutes an important process integration function. It now features prominently in the concepts proposed by all the leading suppliers.

Graphics-based process modeling tools make it possible to define workflows in simple steps without any technical background knowledge.

Workflow engines control the execution of individual activities, with web services or incorporated existing applications representing the individual process steps. Activities may also consist of interactions with humans. New processes are far easier to design thanks to the separation of flow control and function execution (applications), while

3 Forward-looking e-business solution architecture

existing ones can be adapted more flexibly than is possible using today's prevalent application structures.

Standards, of course, play a very important role in the field of business integration since efficient integration and interoperability can only be achieved on the basis of standards that are accepted industry-wide. Standardization bodies such as *W3C, OASIS, ebXML* and the vendors (IBM, Microsoft, SAP, Sun, BEA, etc.) are continually extending the range of standards.

IBM and Microsoft are the most prominent motive forces in this field and special mention should be made here of the *Global XML Web Services Architecture* (GXA) and the definition of the *Business Process Execution Language* (BPEL) which is going to be supported by all the relevant software vendors (For more information, see chapter 5).

High-value integration servers are now available from the major software vendors (e.g. *IBM WebSphere Business Integration*, *SAP Exchange Integration*, or *Microsoft Biztalk*) as well as from integration specialists such as *Tibco* and *webMethods*.

3.3 Cross-enterprise solution architectures

The integration of existing and future enterprise-wide and cross-enterprise business processes together with the corresponding applications is currently one of the central challenges facing companies. Whenever CIOs have to make decisions concerning soft-

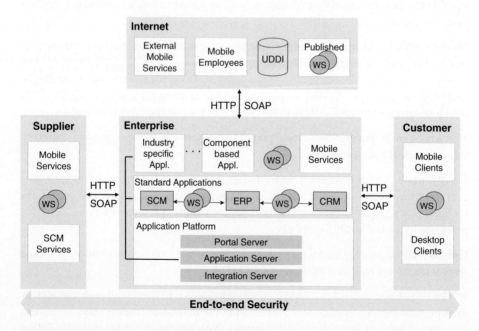

Figure 3.8 Tomorrow's e-business solution architecture

ware investments and changes to their IT infrastructures they should keep in mind the target architecture to which they want to migrate. Figure 3.8 illustrates just such an architecture which includes cross-application, cross-enterprise, flexible and adaptable business solutions.

The cornerstone of this architecture is the application platform including the portal server, the application server, the integration server and the resource and service tier as explained in the previous sections. Running on this platform are standard applications such as SCM, ERP, CRM together with industry-specific applications.

Such an architecture offers added value along multiple dimensions (cost, technology independence, safeguarding of investments, reduced complexity, to name only a few). However, the main advantages that deserve to be mentioned here are the ability to implement pervasive cross-enterprise solutions as well as the capability to increase productivity, flexibility and competitiveness. This will be achieved by building automated processes and by adding services dynamically in order to react quickly to changing market requirements and incorporate mobile services that help achieve process optimization.

The key enabling technologies for tomorrow's business solutions will be *Mobility, Web Services,* and *Security.*

Mobility

Mobile customers and employees using mobile devices can be reached anytime, anywhere and, in turn, may have access to the companies' resources from any location.

Enterprises may provide mobile services in order to streamline their employee-involved processes, keep customers informed or to submit a suitable offer, whenever and wherever appropriate.

Network operators may offer mobile services (e.g. multimedia services, location-based services, administration services) to enterprises via the Internet or mobile networks in order to support these enterprises with enhanced features and reduce costs.

Suppliers may support mobile fleet management services in order to optimize their delivery processes or may provide tracking services to check the delivery status of a shipment or trace missing objects.

These examples are merely a brief illustration of the ways in which mobile applications enable enterprises to increase their competitiveness and secure enhanced benefits. Mobility is dealt with in greater detail in chapter 4.

Web services

Since the advent of XML web services about 4 years ago, most global software vendors have embraced this technology. They now support it in their frameworks and products, such as application servers, portal servers, integration servers, database systems or client middleware, and offer the corresponding development tools. Web services constitute the next stage in the development of component-based applications and have become an integral part of modern application architectures.

Moreover, web services will play an important role in integrating applications within an enterprise and this has been their primary task to date. The next step, however, will bring about the integration of today's still separate and, for the most part application-specific, business processes, for example SCM or CRM processes. Web services technology, in conjunction with *BPEL (Business Process Execution Language for web services)*, makes it possible to define composite services which use elementary services (web services) or existing applications, thus permitting the integration of processes or the establishment of new *ad hoc processes* without the need for any knowledge of the technical background.

Based on *SOAP (Simple Object Access Protocol)* and HTTP, web services permit interoperability beyond enterprises boundaries and help collaboration between, for example, supplier's processes and the corresponding enterprise processes. Using SOAP, customers are also able to invoke the enterprise's web services, while customer processes may be built more efficiently by implementing web services at both sites.

The aim of the *service-oriented architecture* is to achieve the most technologically advanced possible deployment of web services including the dynamic discovery, binding and deployment of web services published on the Internet. For more details about SOA and web services, see chapter 5.

Security

Security has always been a top priority for e-business solutions. However, within the framework of this future solution architecture, end-to-end security is not just a key priority. It is a vital precondition for the world of cross-company, distributed applications.

The new challenges posed by wireless Internet access and the more extensive integration of mobile employees, partners and customers imply a substantial increase in the associated risks. In addition, cross-boundary communication based on web services, as well as the invocation of published web services and their integration in mission-critical business processes, opens up a new set of dangers for enterprises.

Security awareness is the first step in recognizing the real risks associated with business processes and constitutes the starting point for the development of an appropriate security strategy which balances security needs with affordable costs and acceptable risks.

It is important to point out that the decisive factor behind the success of any cross-enterprise solution is the trust that exists between all the involved partners. Confidence is the one thing above all that is needed if businesses are to compete successfully. However, confidence is only possible if every participant knows that every business-related interaction is totally secure.

In cross-enterprise architectures, security encompasses communication, messaging and transactional services including confidentiality, privacy, integrity, availability and non-repudiation. For more details concerning security, see chapter 6.

Summary

Tomorrow's business solutions will be based on an open, *cross-enterprise architecture* which includes suppliers', customers' and employees' processes as well as services offered via the Internet. The key elements of this architecture are:

- *Multitier architecture* comprising the communication/presentation tier, the business logic tier, the integration tier and the services/resource tier
- Application platform comprising the portal server, application server and integration server
- Application platform that runs standard software, industry-specific software, home-grown component-based applications, web services and mobile services
- Portal server that handles fixed-line and mobile access by the different user groups
- Integration server that comprises message and integration brokers as well as business process execution and management
- Interoperability with partner processes and services based on SOAP messages and web services technology
- Embedded Internet services in business processes using SOAP and web services technology
- Provision of comprehensive security services in order to achieve *end-to-end security* for business processes

4 Mobile applications and platforms

More than 1.3 billion mobile phones are now in use worldwide and it is expected this number will exceed 2 billion by 2008. However, the definition of future mobile applications needs to be considered much more comprehensively. Usually such applications, which are distinguished from connection-oriented voice communications, are characterized as connectionless, packetized data applications. Data, in this context, refers to digitized data that may comprise structured data, unstructured data, voice and multimedia.

The best-known of these applications, such as *SMS (Short Message Services)*, *MMS (Multi Messaging Services)*, games, news, tickers, stock information, traffic information, e-mail, etc., are currently offered by mobile network operators. An increasing number of enterprises recognize the value of mobile applications for their business solutions. This chapter focuses on mobile applications within an enterprise perspective. It covers the different application categories, the value-added, the application platforms, while also presenting some examples of mobile applications.

4.1 Mobile application categories

A wide range of opportunities will be available for mobile information and services. The use of mobile applications will include *business-to-business (B2B)*, *business-to-employee (B2E)* and *business-to-consumer (B2C)* models. From the user's perspective, some applications will be dedicated exclusively to business while others focus on leisure or entertainment. Nonetheless, a fairly large number of applications will address both the business and leisure sectors.

The various mobile applications of value to users can be subdivided into application classes as depicted in figure 4.1.

The application classes presented on the left of the diagram are typically deployed in business solutions, while those on the right are mainly provided by network operators. However this is a very rough classification and in reality there is a considerable overlap between classes. By way of an example, while network operators offer location services enabling users to find points of interest, e.g ATMs (Automatic Telling Machines), banks may provide their customers with similar or additional services. These may not only include how to find the ATM closest to the customer's location, but may also provide additional information about the specific services offered by the branch at which it is installed.

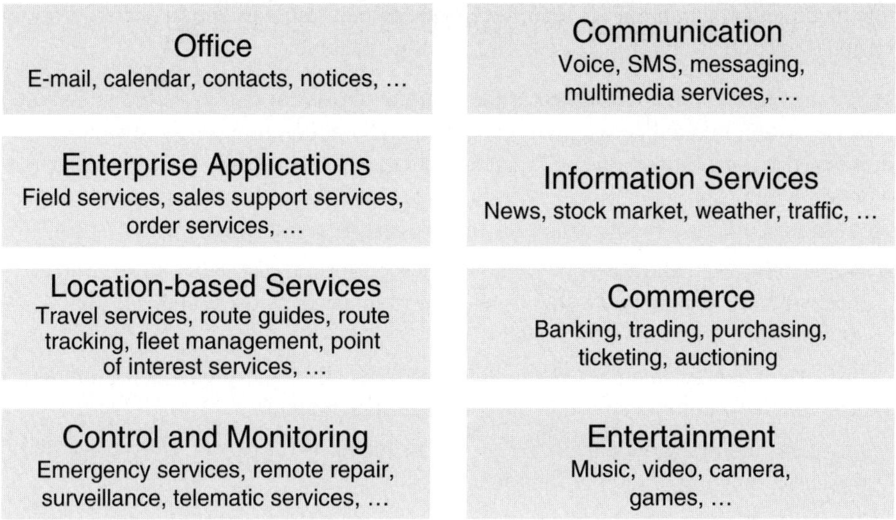

4.1 Mobile application categories

Office
E-mail, calendar, contacts, notices, …

Communication
Voice, SMS, messaging, multimedia services, …

Enterprise Applications
Field services, sales support services, order services, …

Information Services
News, stock market, weather, traffic, …

Location-based Services
Travel services, route guides, route tracking, fleet management, point of interest services, …

Commerce
Banking, trading, purchasing, ticketing, auctioning

Control and Monitoring
Emergency services, remote repair, surveillance, telematic services, …

Entertainment
Music, video, camera, games, …

Figure 4.1 Mobile application classes

Mobile office

is today's most frequently used business application. It includes synchronization and over-the-air access to personal information management (e.g. Microsoft Exchange – Outlook, Lotus Notes) and interaction with back-office systems. Appropriate devices for exploiting such applications tend to take the form of PDAs with wireless connection capability, although smartphones with the required display and input features are becoming increasingly common in this area. The most important application is e-mail with the ability to view attachments such as Word files and Excel spreadsheets.

Mobile Intranet applications

are essential in most mobile business solutions. These provide secure access to corporate applications such as travel management or to applications that employees need in order to perform the tasks assigned to them, e.g. sales force automation. Other business scenarios even allow partners or customers to access enterprise applications, services or resources using mobile devices. The rapid increase in the use of Intranets and Extranets is creating a mobile workforce that expects access to desktop applications, messaging and information retrieval whether in the office, in the car, waiting at transit locations such as airports, staying at a hotel, working at home or visiting a customer location. Mobile workers are increasing at a rate of 60% per year and the number using mobile applications is expected to reach 200 million by 2005.

Location-based services

provide a new generic type of value-added for mobile device users in a variety of different situations, such as leisure (e.g. restaurant finder), emergencies (pharmacy, doctor), commerce (shopping, ATM finder), convenience (route direction), monitoring or business (customer or employee location, fleet management).

While the other applications listed in the diagram above are also available to a greater or lesser extent in fixed network environments and are therefore well-known, the location-based services are unique and specific only to mobile networks. When used in conjunction with push mode, mobile location-based services offer businesses and service providers promising new opportunities for business. A few examples are:

- Points of interest: allow mobile users to request information relating to specific facilities within their immediate environment (e.g. shopping areas, banks, hospitals, cinemas, offices, etc.).
- Instant couponing: matches the mobile user's location and predefined preferences with retailer promotions to send the user an instant coupon.
- Location finding: Mobile users are guided to requested targets or given route directions as a function of their current location.
- Tracking: Mobile objects are tracked and movements are traced in order to coordinate activities and optimize processes.
- Travel services: Mobile users request or are notified of travel-related information (e.g. flight delays, traffic jams) as a function of their current location.

Mobile control and monitoring

includes a wide range of emergency, monitoring, surveillance, remote control, repair and telematics applications which will make a genuine contribution towards simplifying activities such as process control and will also help improve lifestyles, for example by flexibly monitoring people, places, properties, and environments for health, safety and security-related events. Machine-to-machine telematics applications are expected to constitute an important field in the future.

Mobile communication

is undoubtedly a mainstream application area, providing the mobile workforce and consumers with additional options for communication, irrespective of their location and desired contact partner. Options include text, voice, data, multimedia and synchronous as well as asynchronous communication. For example, unified messaging provides users with a communication capability independent of device, time and location.

Mobile information services

can be of a very general, business-oriented or personalized nature. As the web has shown, the range of information that can be provided is unlimited. Obviously, the value of the information to the user increases as it becomes more personalized and localized. Data can be pushed from or pulled to the mobile device. The more urgently information is needed for making a decision (e.g. flight delays), the more users are willing to pay. Other examples of valuable information include events, festivals, attractions, directory services, conversions of currency, weights, sizes, etc.

Mobile commerce

includes all transaction-based applications such as ordering, purchasing, selling, auctioning, trading, payment, banking, money transfer, brokering and ticketing. Mobile commerce has huge potential and should be seen as an extension of e-commerce, but one which will dramatically change both consumers' lifestyles and the way service providers and network operators run their businesses. High-level, end-to-end security is essential for encouraging the use of this promising application.

Mobile entertainment

is an application area which attracts mainly younger and mobile users. Games, for example, are a proven way of drawing users to new applications and devices. Games supplied by mobile devices not only make a wide selection of games available to people but also make interactive games possible with any user around the world. Nokia's N-Gage devices will make this capability available to the mass market. The availability of integrated cameras, MP3 players and video players in mobile devices will encourage Internet-based music and video distribution and revive the debate concerning intellectual property.

It is an observed fact that younger users are early adapters of enhanced technologies. The best example is SMS. It can therefore be expected that the use of video clips in mobile devices will become popular among young people as soon as it is affordable. Deployment for business purposes will follow later, but it is obvious that there are a number of business applications that will make use of video services. Advertisements will play an important role. For example, Coca Cola video ads could subsidize multimedia messages. Another example is providing assistance to a field engineer who has the task of repairing a sophisticated machine. The engineer can obtain instructions about how to mount a spare part from a video downloaded to his mobile device.

Leisure and business are tending to become increasingly intermixed, particularly in mobile scenarios. Infotainment, the mixture of information and entertainment is a new way of attracting people and provides a good example of this trend. E-learning, for instance, can start to become attractive to traveling employees when they use a mobile device to watch a language lesson that features information concerning the major hits currently showing in the city they are staying in.

4.2 Value of mobile applications

The main consideration motivating enterprises to drive the introduction of mobile applications is the maintenance of their long-term competitive position and the generation of new revenue sources.

By way of example, the issue of competitiveness seen from the perspective of mobile banking may be considered: although banks will not gain new customers by offering mobile applications because every bank will be offering them, any bank which did not provide such applications would risk losing customers.

An obvious example of how new avenues of business can generate new revenue is the field of travel assistance where travelers would be willing to pay for location-dependent assistance services which are constantly available to them during their voyage.

Mobile applications support traditional e-business services and solutions and enable participants to do business on the move.

Mobile business therefore means:
- anywhere: in the office, at home, on the road, at transit points
- via any network: GSM/GPRS, UMTS, WLAN, fixed-line
- with any device: mobile phone, PDA, PC
- in any situation: business, leisure, education.

Valuable features

Mobile business solutions will provide valuable features:

Universality

Universality is the most obvious advantage. It fulfils the need for both real-time information and communication that is independent of the user's (device) location.

Reachability

Reachability is important for enterprises who want to be in touch with their employees and customers. Equipped with a mobile device, these can be contacted anywhere, anytime. They can be notified of contacts via push services which simultaneously enable spontaneous business opportunities.

Accessibility

Personal and business resources can be accessed anywhere using any device via any network, whether fixed-line or wireless.

Convenience

Convenience is a characteristic of mobile devices because they not only store personal data but also connect to the services the user needs, are always at hand and are becoming increasingly simple to use.

Localization

The localization of services and applications represents a very significant enterprise value-added. Knowing the physical location of a customer, employee or other traveling individual at any given time will be crucial for the provision of the individually targeted services, can help make business processes more efficient and/or open up new business opportunities.

Always-on

Instant connectivity to the Internet and Intranet from a mobile device is becoming a reality. GPRS and UMTS services will greatly accelerate the development of this capability, thus making new wireless devices the preferred mode of accessing information.

Personalization

Personalization is one of the key features provided by mobile enterprise portals. Thanks to personalization, the mobile device will become an everyday business tool and will permit easy access to selected information on the basis of the user's location and the relevant business scenario.

Value scenarios

Before implementing mobile applications, enterprises are recommended to look carefully at the value scenario. Figure 4.2 illustrates how this scenario can be approached in a systematic way.

An in-depth analysis involving a number of different steps must ensure that the investment in implementing mobile applications will ultimately create real value for the company.

First of all, enterprises must fully understand the mobile features and the generic value of mobile applications as described above and consider how these might be transposed to business processes which could be improved by increased mobility. They need to evaluate the attractiveness of mobility as it relates to their organization. At the very highest level, this not only includes the mobile implementation of existing packaged applications such as web applications, Enterprise Resource Planning (ERP), Customer Relationship Management (CRM), Supply Chain Management (SCM), and Sales Force Automation (SFA). It also means considering new applications capable of improving communications and the flow of information, and facilitating enterprise interaction with employees, suppliers/business partners, and customers.

Unlike the traditional environment in which Internet-based applications are built and developed, the technical issues that are unique to the mobile environment must also be considered in such cases. These considerably complicate the goal of going mobile.

The enterprise must fully understand how mobility differs from the traditional Internet in terms of application development, support, security and evolution. After gaining an understanding of this emerging mobile environment, the enterprise must assess each of the major areas of complexity involved in the development of mobile applications. This assessment will enable businesses to determine how their current infrastructure might support mobility and identify which platform would be most suitable for their specific requirements and overall objectives.

Only after these analyses and investigations have been conducted, the benefits, such as customer retention, increased productivity, new revenue streams, enhanced efficiency, etc., can be precisely identified and the true value of mobility become apparent.

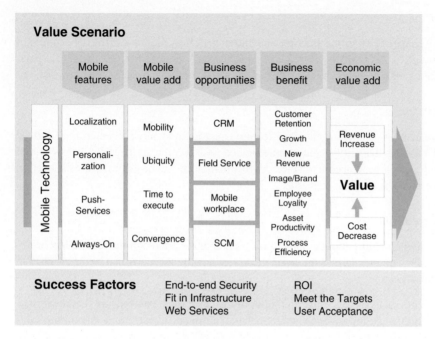

Figure 4.2 The value scenarios of mobile business

As depicted in figure 4.2, there are many technical and non-technical factors which may influence the successful implementation of a mobile business project. The technical aspects include end-to-end security, web services (reusability of services) and the extent to which mobility fits in the existing infrastructure. The latter consideration is important because significant additional costs may arise if the e-business platform is unsuitable for the adoption of mobile applications. The non-technical success factors include ROI, the degree of user acceptance and, last but not least, the achievability of the project targets. This latter factor is frequently the reason for the failure of a mobile project, often due to a lack of thought during the design stage coupled with excessive expectations.

The following checklist may help enterprises to assess mobile business opportunities:

– Identify current mobility-related market developments
– Establish commitment of top management to mobile business
– Assess the company's current e-business activities
– Assess the current technological infrastructure and the changes required
– Identify existing and required mobile business expertise within the company
– Assess the basic business opportunities and the possible mobile business scenarios with regard to cost savings, revenue growth, quality improvements and expanding the existing market
– Identify new and existing corporate processes and the need to adapt these

- Carry out a cost/benefit analysis listing the potential of quantitative and qualitative evaluations
- Identify the main success factors for mobile business within the enterprise
- Identify quick wins
- Draw up a mobile business roadmap as the basis for future activities and the migration plan.

4.3 Mobile application platforms

Modern *e-business architectures* will migrate toward integrated *e-business and mobile business architectures* by supporting devices via traditional wired as well as via wireless networks. The core components of the application platforms – as explained in chapter 3 – are the *portal server, application server* and *integration server*. As illustrated in figure 4.3, the portal server represents the single point of access and provides integrated or separate access components for web devices and wireless IP devices, as well as for wireless WAP devices or even voice devices.

Irrespectively of the type of device involved, portal servers enable users to access the enterprise's services and resources. Nowadays, enterprise portals (including the access components) increasingly tend to support a range of mobile devices and are consequently becoming significantly more complex. The portal must be able to identify different types of devices, process information in a manner specific to each device's

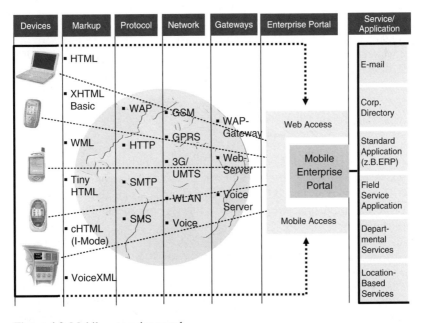

Figure 4.3 Mobile enterprise portal

markup language, handle network and security protocols and communicate over different kinds of gateways or proxy servers.

An enterprise portal provides a single, consistent user interface and point of access to any application, information or network service which a customer, employee or business partner might need in order to fulfill his or her function or task. Enterprises, like the portal users themselves, benefit from portal platforms which are well-designed and, in more general terms, optimized for either the enterprise or the consumer category.

The generic mobile portal platform may be considered as part of an advanced and extended e-business platform.

Some of the main benefits are:
- A new, uniform front-end navigation system which enables the integration of new mobile business processes flexibly and quickly
- Role-based, personalized user experience that provides access to everything needed to get a job done easily, anywhere, anytime
- Single sign-on to all the different applications and services
- Pushed, personalized, relevant, up-to-date information
- Improved collaboration opportunities
- Tracking of behaviors and preferences leading to support optimization
- Centralized access control for decentralized resources
- Centralized administration of systems, devices and applications
- Option of centralized logging that may be utilized by business intelligence applications.

4.3.1 Generic WAP architecture

Though the market introduction of *WAP (Wireless Application Protocol)* in 1999 proved to be anything but a success, most mobile phones that are available today support this protocol and WAP has become a de facto standard. WAP has been designed to operate independently at the lowest level of bearer technology and will be used with GSM, GPRS and UMTS as well as with other similar technologies such as TDMA and CDMA.

Both the latest version, *WAP 2.0* [4.3.1], and the *WAP stack* introduced in WAP 1 provide stack-based support and services in line with the common Internet protocols including TCP/IP, TLS/SSL and HTTP. Although WAP is an interim technology, it must be considered as the standard protocol for the majority of mobile phones sold worldwide, enabling them to access Internet/Intranet resources and services. PDAs, in contrast, usually run only the Internet protocols unless they are equipped with a *WAP browser* that allows them to access original WAP content.

The *WAP architecture* model as illustrated in figure 4.4 was defined by the *WAP Forum* and derives from the WWW model. It takes account of current constraints on wireless networks and wireless handsets. For example, the former demand data compression,

4.3 Mobile application platforms

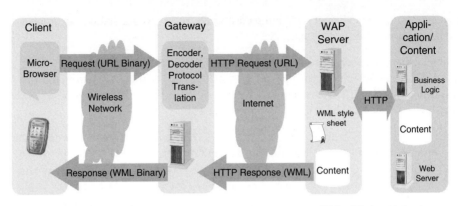

WAP = Wireless Application Protocols
WDP = Wireless Datagram Protocol
WTLS = Wireless Transport Layer Security
WTP = Wireless Transaction Protocol
WSP = Wireless Session Protocol

Internet Protocols:
TCP/IP
HTTP
TLS/SSL

WML = Wireless Markup Language

Figure 4.4 WAP architecture

long latencies and a limited bandwidth, whereas the latter have to do with low CPU and memory capacity, small displays, restricted input capabilities, limited power, etc.

As in the *WWW (World Wide Web)* model, communication is initiated by means of a client request to which the server responds. The WAP model has a WAP server instead of web server. The WAP gateway is intermediately positioned for translation purposes.

The client's request is binary-encoded and compressed to fit in the limited bandwidth of second generation wireless networks and contains the WWW standard URL in order to identify the WAP content.

The *WAP gateway* decodes the request and sends the URL to the *WAP server*. In this process, the gateway's main task is to translate the *WAP wireless protocol stack* to the WWW protocol stack. In this way, *WDP (Wireless Datagram Protocol)* is equivalent to TCP/IP, *WTLS (Wireless Transport Layer Security)* is equivalent to TLS/SSL and *WSP (Wireless Session Protocol)* is equivalent to HTTP.

The WAP server may host the requested URL or transmit it to an application or another website from which the content is then retrieved and returned to the WAP server which handles the session management and end-to-end interaction between the client and the content server. In addition, the WAP server may also transcode the content into *WML (Wireless Markup Language)* if the addressed content is not present in WML.

On the return path, the WAP gateway encodes the WML content into compressed binary form, translates the transmission protocols back from Internet to wireless, and sends the content to the client.

The client software – i.e. the user agent – may be any piece of software, such as a *microbrowser*, that interprets WML and *WMLScript*. The microbrowser coordinates the

4 Mobile applications and platforms

user interface and is analogous to a standard web browser. WMLScript is an extended subset of the JavaScript language.

The user agent software may also implement *Wireless Telephony Applications (WTA)* and a WTA interface for voice applications which resides on a *WTA server* in the wireless network. The WTA server is used to provide WAP access to features of the wireless network operator's telecommunication infrastructure.

Push mode is the key feature differentiating the WWW and WAP models. Because the client in a wireless network has a unique identifier – the MSISDN (Mobile Station ISDN number) – it can be directly addressed by the server. The result is that information, alerts for example, can be pushed in real time if the client is switched on.

The above explanation of a generic architecture does not necessarily correspond exactly to implementations in real products. As described in the next section, the major software vendors have integrated the WAP gateway into the portal server and WAP server functions are provided by the application server. This type of platform is preferred for e-business and integrated mobile business solutions.

4.3.2 Integration in existing application platforms

For the foreseeable future, mainstream mobile business solutions will be created by integrating mobile business into existing e-business architectures.

As shown in figure 4.5, a forward-looking mobile application platform supports both wireline and wireless access to applications, services and resources.

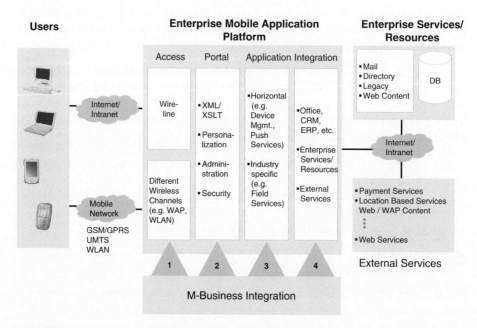

Figure 4.5 Integration in existing e-business solutions

4.3 Mobile application platforms

The transition from e-business to mobile business comprises four integration tasks, i.e. mobile extensions to existing application platforms:

- Support for wireless access (arrow 1 in the diagram)
- Mobile device and mobile user portal integration (2)
- Implementation of new mobile applications (3)
- Application and service integration (4)

Support for wireless access

This dual mode platform can be described as a unified web/WAP platform because it hosts business applications which are common to both wired (web) and wireless (WAP and web) channels of communication. The platform also provides interfaces to enterprise services and resources, to external services, content, and web services regardless of the device the interacting user is employing. For example, the web/WAP platform might connect a user to a banking payment system regardless of whether he or she is sitting at the computer or using a smartphone to shop on the go.

At a more detailed level, four different wireless channels are present. The mobile application platform should support these channels:

- GSM/GPRS/UMTS via WAP gateway located at the mobile network operator's site
- GSM/GPRS/UMTS directly, i.e. WAP gateway integrated in enterprise's platform
- GSM/GPRS/UMTS with Internet protocol stack (laptop, PDA)
- WLAN

These channels use different communication protocols and, it is important to note, possess different *QoS (Quality of Services)* and *security properties*. The security issues are particularly crucial for the proper implementation of mobile business solutions.

One question relates to the way the WAP security issue is handled. The incompatibility of WTLS and TSL/SSL means that, during conversion of the WTLS protocol into TLS/SSL and vice versa in the WAP gateway, the data is briefly unguarded, thus opening up the possibility of a security breach, especially on the part of the staff who are physically operating the WAP gateway system. Even if both the wireless network and the Internet each possess high-performance security mechanisms, additional measures are required to ensure end-to-end security. This is the reason why many enterprises have decided to operate their WAP gateways themselves. This and other security details are discussed in chapter 6.

Portal integration

Integration of the portal is frequently the most challenging integration task. Generic front-end features such as scalability, presentation services, content transcoding, user management, personalization, authentication, and other portal services are required for both web and WAP users. There is a high level of overlapping functionality that requires integration.

An *XML/XSLT engine* performs the content code transcoding from any content source into XML code. Once transcoded into XML, the content can easily be transformed into other languages using the XSLT (eXtensible Stylesheet Language Translation) stylesheets/processor (as described in chapter 3, figure 3.3). Such languages can be interpreted at the different types of mobile devices in the same way as HTML on a web client, WML on a WAP client, tiny HTML on a PDA client, cHTML on an i-mode client, *VoiceXML (Voice eXtensible Markup Language)* on a voice client, and others that remain to be standardized in the future.

The personalization services make a considerable contribution to the usefulness of mobile devices and simple menu guidance is of particular importance since the restricted possibilities of these devices mean that users must be guided directly to the information that is relevant to them.

From the user's point of view, portal content and device-specific settings play an important role, as do the various configurable preferences such as the selection of information channels, the enabling and disabling of notification services etc.

As far as the enterprise is concerned, user profiles and authorizations are of great importance in a variety of situations since they help regulate access to the applications and services that are required for different business processes. As user groups may include customers, partners and employees, user management and administration represent another difficult aspect of the portal integration task in view of the use of multiple devices via different communication channels.

Since the portal represents the central entry point for users, security services form an essential component of enterprise portals. Authentication and single sign-on, role-based authorizations and encrypted and/or authenticated data transmissions must be available for both wireline and wireless clients.

Some horizontal portal services could prove to be useful within mobile applications. Real-life implementation, however, often depends on the business processes in question. An enterprise might expand its search engines or use workflow and collaboration services – such as collaborative forecasting, vendor-managed inventories or distributor/reseller management – that extend business processes beyond traditional organizational boundaries.

New mobile applications

Mobile enterprise applications include application classes as described in section 4.1. Some of these, which are not industry-specific and/or are incorporated as basic features by other applications, may be referred to as horizontal applications. Examples are: mobile office including PIM (Personal Information Management), location-based services, push/notification services, mobile travel services. Others, including security features and downloaded content and applications, are required for the management of mobile devices. Last but not least, there are industry-specific B2C (e.g. location-dependent shopping services, banking services), B2B (e.g. fleet management, tracking services) and B2E applications (e.g. mobile workplace, mobile workforce, sales force automation).

At the technical level, it is advisable to implement such applications on the basis of an existing application server, i.e. the core component of an enterprise application platform. This is not only in order to avoid the need to set up an additional platform but also, and more importantly, to make it possible to integrate and use portal services and optimize business processes.

Application and service integration

The integration with existing business applications and back-end integration are not less important. Enterprises have made huge investments in building applications and transforming their businesses into real e-business solutions.

Enterprises can achieve significant cost reductions, optimize business processes, and attract new customers by adapting mobile devices to existing processes. The integration of existing applications is the prerequisite for mobile interaction, whether – to name but a few examples – this takes the form of a sales person accessing a customer's contract or certain product information while on the road, a field engineer obtaining spare part data while repairing a machine at a customer's site, or a customer consulting necessary information via a particular communication channel. Such integration might comprise the adaptation of ERP, CRM, e-commerce, SCM, Business Information Management (BIM), legacy or other specific Intranet applications as well as access to corporate directories and other data and content.

The integration of external services expands the potential for mobile device use to new areas of application. For example, a traveler might want to obtain traffic or flight delay information at a specified time on his or her way to the airport and would be willing to pay for this valuable information. This new business scenario is growing in importance. Two new, evolving services, i.e. pre-payment or micropayment services and location-based services – which could, for example, be provided by a network operator – will make such highly desirable, innovative solutions possible.

Another example of the valuable adaptation of external services might be a traveler who needs to rebook a flight during a business trip. The rebooking application could run on the application platform and communicate with the *Global Distribution Services (GDS, Amadeus, Sabre, etc.)* in order to select, confirm and finally book the appropriate flight.

In the future, the integration of web services based on the Universal Description, Discovery and Integration (UDDI) standard will make it significantly easier to extend mobile applications. It will be possible to design business logic components that can be packed into ready-to-use web services which will be able to exchange control information and application data with other applications using automatic, standardized operations.

4.3.3 Mobile device platforms

Stationary desktops and laptops running the Windows operating system and browser technology which enable simple and standardized access to the business logic tier still dominate in today's e-business solutions. In the future, the client environment will

4 Mobile applications and platforms

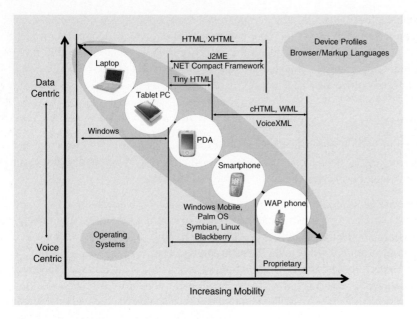

Figure 4.6 Increasing mobile device diversity

change significantly and the use of a variety of mobile devices will increase sharply. This means that enterprises and solution providers alike need to familiarize themselves with a highly heterogeneous client system world as shown in figure 4.6.

It can be assumed that this multifaceted system environment will not get any simpler in the next few years. Innovations and standardizations currently follow one another haphazardly. Product cycles for mobile devices are frequently less than one year.

Today's habitual device classifications in terms of *mobile phones* (WAP), *smartphones, PDAs, webpads, laptops, tablet PCs* etc. will probably not change greatly. However, functional overlaps and the range of variants will increase and other classes of device will probably become of interest, even in the business world (e.g. in-car navigation systems). The range of variants will result from differing display characteristics (size, color), input/output facilities (with/without keyboard, stylus, touch screen), wireless modules (GPRS, UMTS, WLAN, Bluetooth), combinable add-ons (MP3 player, camera, video, GPS, etc.) and, not least, the choice of operating systems (Symbian, Windows Mobile, Palm OS, Blackberry, Linux).

Moreover, the trend towards *intelligent mobile clients* (also called *smart clients*) is unmistakable. Intelligent mobile devices usually require a kind of additional software (middleware) which may consist of browser plug-ins or device profiles and application services.

Intelligent clients offer a series of clear advantages:
- offline applications, databases,
- the ability to load programs over the network,

- support for peer-to-peer protocols,
- asynchronous messaging and electronic wallets,

to name but a few.

However, it should not be forgotten that the task of device administration, which includes the distribution of the software and content, can become exceedingly complex when multiple devices are involved. Browser solutions should therefore always be preferred if the above-mentioned properties or functions are not explicitly required.

In the following, some comments and explanations regarding this increasingly complex software environment are provided.

Operating systems

While Windows will remain the dominant OS for laptops, tablet PCs and webpads, with a market share above 90%, Palm OS, Windows Mobile (Pocket PC and Smartphone), Symbian OS, Blackberry and Linux will continue to fight to establish themselves successfully in the PDA and smartphone market.

Palm OS

is still the OS market leader for PDAs, but is losing market share to Pocket PC in the online enterprise applications sector. *Palm OS* [4.3.2] can claim to provide the widest ranging 3rd party software support and might be able to continue to occupy a leading position in the field of enterprise applications. It also plays a role in online applications where it can provide access to enterprise resources provided that it is equipped with additional security features. With the introduction of Palm OS Cobalt in 2004, PalmSource, Inc. extends its platform in areas such as multimedia and communications and with its Security Framework it tries to expand growth opportunities in the business markets.

Windows Mobile/Pocket PC/Smartphone

are derivates of *Windows CE.NET*. *Windows Mobile* [4.3.3] is the collective term for the *Pocket PC* and *Smartphone* operating systems comprising Pocket PC/Pocket PC Phone Edition and Smartphone. Pocket PC currently has the highest growth rates in the PDA class and will probably be the preferred choice for online enterprise applications in the long term. In contrast, Windows Mobile Smartphone currently claims only a small market share and the long-term outlook is difficult to forecast.

Symbian OS/Series 60 platform

Symbian is a software licensing company owned by Ericsson, Nokia, Panasonic, Psion, Samsung Electronics, Siemens and Sony Ericsson. *Symbian OS* [4.3.4] can be licensed and is an open OS for smartphones that includes wireless computing and telephony. Based on Symbian OS, Nokia has developed the *Series 60 platform* [4.3.5], which is also licensable, runs on Symbian OS and is currently the market leader worldwide in the smartphone device class.

BlackBerry

is a proprietary OS for the *BlackBerry* PDA developed by the Canadian company *RIM (Research in Motion)*, [4.3.6]. The product, which incorporates end-to-end wireless mail and Intranet services, is mainly used in North America, but has now been launched successfully in Europe by a number of network operators.

Linux

is the open source operating system offered by some PDA and smartphone manufacturers since 2003. As open source market penetration will continue to grow, *Linux* can be expected to play an increasingly important role in the mobile device market.

BREW

is a proprietary application platform which is marketed by the US company Qualcomm. Devices running *BREW* are specifically designed for CDMA networks. Such networks are primarily operated in the USA although some are also found in Asia. BREW is therefore of no relevance for the European market.

Proprietary OS

currently mainly provided with WAP phones, these will probably disappear and only survive in the low-cost category.

Browsers

Browsers are frequently provided as a component of the operating system or mobile device. Depending on the device type, a number of different presentation languages are supported:

– WAP phones: *WML*
– i-mode phones: *cHTML* (language defined by NTT DoCoMo, Japan, now also available in Europe)
– PDAs, smartphones: HTML, web clipping (for restricted presentation possibilities). In more recent devices, *XHTML* is also frequently supported. XHTML can be considered as a further development of WML and HTML and will replace the other presentation languages in the long term.

Device profiles

Device profiles constitute a uniform application architecture and platform for intelligent mobile clients running applications locally. These profiles provide application developers with specific definitions of the different devices. Configurations and profiles are defined for different applications. This platform allows applications to be transferred to a range of devices such as mobile telephones, smartphones, TV set-top boxes, embedded devices, and PDAs.

As in the server world, two different platform technologies are also emerging as the leaders here. These can be expected to coexist for the time being. They are the *Java 2*

4.3 Mobile application platforms

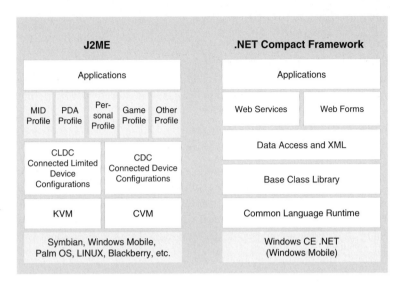

Figure 4.7 Mobile client architecture

Micro Edition (J2ME), specified by SUN and the Java community, and Microsoft's *.NET Compact Framework*, as depicted in figure 4.7.

Java 2 Micro Edition (J2ME)

Java 2 Micro Edition (J2ME) [4.3.7], like Java J2SE (Standard Edition) and J2EE (Enterprise Edition), is part of the Java family of platforms and is tailored to the restricted scope of functions offered by simple devices. It comprises a series of programming interfaces (APIs) and libraries which are familiar to Java developers from the platform family. The Java community is hoping that Java client applications will quickly become widespread as a result. The basic idea behind J2ME is application portability, i.e. applications are executable on all J2ME devices. J2ME implementations are available for the different operating systems, including Microsoft's OS, or may even be provided as part of the OS, as is the case with Symbian OS.

J2ME comes in two different versions. The *Connected Device Configuration (CDC)* technology is based on the classic Java Virtual Machine with full functional scope, whereas the *Connected Limited Device Configuration (CLDC)* technology uses a simplified Virtual Machine that is geared towards the limitations of simple devices (CPU power, memory, display, etc.).

The *Mobile Information Device Profile (MIDP)* is a specific J2ME profile which was defined for smartphone applications. It was the first profile to be developed in the Java Community Process program. Several MIDP versions have since been released. These provide functions and programming interfaces (APIs) for user interfaces, data storage, Internet connections, security functions and application lifecycles.

The MIDP applications based on these programming interfaces are known as *MIDlets*. As long as low-level APIs are not used, MIDlets are portable applications. Another profile, the Personal Profile, the successor to Personal Java, is suitable for a wide range of more intelligent devices, including, for example, Linux-based devices and TV set-top boxes.

The standardization process for PDA profiles was halted in 2003 and attention has now turned to the development of PDA profile options. The J2ME platform will also permit direct access to web services in the network. The new standard, *JSR 172 (J2ME Web Services Specification)*, defines XML processing APIs and RPC-based access to web services.

J2ME is a proven Java-based software framework, provides portability over a wide range of mobile devices with different operating systems, including Microsoft's, and allows the deployment of offline applications as well as a mix of client and server-side programming. As J2ME has been in use for several years, a wide range of applications exists today, mainly in the smartphone sector, thus giving J2ME a lead of about two years over the .NET Compact Framework.

Microsoft .NET Compact Framework

The Microsoft *.NET Compact Framework* [4.3.8] is part of the Microsoft .NET architecture and constitutes a restricted version of the .NET Framework that takes into account the special characteristics of mobile devices. The .NET Compact Framework enables the execution of secure downloadable applications and brings the world of *XML web services* to mobile devices. With the extensions of the *Visual Studio .NET* development environment, developers can reuse existing programming skills and existing code throughout the desktop, mobile device and server environments. By using familiar programming interfaces (APIs) and libraries from the .NET Framework, Microsoft is attempting to use the considerable potential possessed by Visual Basic programmers for the implementation of new client applications.

The .NET Compact Framework delivers the same programming model across a range of devices, thus simplifying the process of developing an application that can run on multiple (.NET) devices. It is based on a virtual machine represented by the Common Language Runtime. It is also designed to be extended with class libraries detailing features that are unique to a family of devices, or even unique to a particular device model.

As well as supporting the common base classes, the .NET Compact Framework also supports connectivity functions for the different wireless networks, XML, functions for data access (ADO.NET, SQL Server CE), and security functions. The built-in security model ensures that malicious code cannot gain access to secure system resources and allows software updates to be delivered over the wireless network.

Through the use of client-side code, the .NET Compact Framework permits the deployment of offline applications and a mix of client-side and server-side programming. The .NET Compact Framework also makes it possible to build and consume web services. XML web services are a useful application model for mobile devices since these need to communicate with a variety of other systems and applications regardless of operating system or programming language.

4.3 Mobile application platforms

Microsoft is known for providing excellent development tools (see next section) and these also include tools supporting the .NET Compact Framework.

In contrast to J2ME, the .NET Compact Framework only runs on Microsoft operating systems.

4.3.4 Examples of forward-looking mobile application platforms

In the early days of the mobile application era, a number of start-up companies offered mobile application platforms and development tools that contained a limited range of valuable features. However, this middleware was often based on non-standard, proprietary software that was not integrated in existing portal server and application server landscapes. The result was that most of these companies were unable to survive.

Since then, all the major platform vendors have adopted tools and features for integrating mobile applications. Microsoft, IBM and SAP now enjoy a secure position in this sector. This is due, on the one hand, to the market penetration of their middleware platforms and applications, and, on the other, to the partially integrated tools and functions that are now provided for the building of mobile applications. Nonetheless, today's implementations are not mature and software versions have short lifecycles. Given that web services will become an important consideration for mobile applications, the three platforms mentioned above are probably the ones that are best placed for the future (For more details, see chapter 5).

Alongside the platforms offered by the major vendors, three examples of specialized mobile business solutions or services are also worthy of mention: Extended Systems' *Mobile Solutions Platform*, the *Managed Mobile Device* service offered by Siemens Business Services and *Mobility Solutions* from Fujitsu Siemens Computers.

Some of the main features of these platforms are briefly described below.

Microsoft Mobile .NET

Microsoft's vision of doing business in any place, with any device, at any time first emerged in 2000 and initial support for mobile devices has been provided in the form of the *Mobile Information Server* and the *Mobile Outlook Manager*, a component of Outlook which runs on the user's PC. Starting from these beginnings, Microsoft's commitment to supporting mobile devices and applications has been impressively demonstrated by the development of Windows Mobile (Pocket PC and Smartphone), the .NET Compact Framework, Outlook Mobile Access and the integration of mobility in .NET servers. Microsoft's Mobile .NET architecture is presented in figure 4.8. It comprises mobile clients, support for wireless networks, enterprise servers and services, web services, user experiences, solutions and tools.

The aspects most deserving of mention are the development tools for mobile applications provided with the *Visual Studio .NET Development Environment* [4.3.9] and its extension, known as *Smart Device Programmability for Visual Studio.NET*, that is used in conjunction with the .Net Compact Framework.

4 Mobile applications and platforms

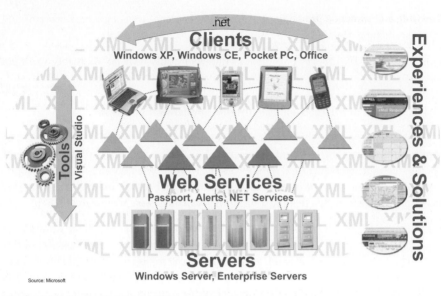

Figure 4.8 Microsoft's Mobile .NET architecture

When designing *ASP.NET mobile web applications*, it is beneficial to separate the definition of the user interface from the business logic and data storage aspects. The key advantage of separating rendering from logic is that code written for a desktop or mobile device application can be reused. Although it is necessary to write one set of *Web Form* pages for the desktop and one set of *Mobile Web Form* pages for mobile devices, they can nevertheless share the same business logic code.

Both the .Net Framework and .NET Compact Framework comprise the concept of *Mobile Controls*. ASP.NET automatically breaks up large *web* pages into smaller units that are appropriate for mobile devices and different containers can be used to render content for ASP.NET Mobile Controls. At runtime, various Mobile Controls for different content types (e.g. textview, textbox, list, link, command, calendar, image, etc.) generate the appropriate code as a function of the device class or even the device type. This means the developer does not need to worry about the rendering specifics of different mobile devices.

Thanks to the concept of Mobile Controls and the reuse of business logic, it is possible to offer users of fixed and mobile devices a more integrated experience. Moreover, development costs can be reduced by using common code while also slashing time-to-market. In terms of usability and productivity, Microsoft's development tools are the best available today.

IBM WebSphere Everyplace family

The *Everyplace* family [4.3.10] consists of a set of components for network connection, enterprise access, transformation, management, development tools and also includes enterprise mobile solutions. The most important are:

4.3 Mobile application platforms

Everyplace Connection Manager

provides secure connections from a mobile device to the enterprise Intranet using a mobile Virtual Private Network via WLAN, GSM/GPRS and other networks. When configured as a WAP proxy it can also provide connectivity for WAP clients. In addition, the Connection Manager supports multiple levels of authentication and encryption and also incorporates WTLS and SSL connectivity. Most important is the dynamic roaming feature that allows mobile users to maintain session persistence when the mobile device changes network, e.g. from WLAN to GPRS.

Everyplace Access

provides the functionality to extend existing or new applications to the wireless world. As shown in figure 4.9, it supports server synchronization of PIM, e-mail functions for Lotus Notes and Microsoft Exchange as well as the synchronization services required to extend enterprise databases and web applications to mobile users.

Everyplace Access additionally provides notification (push) services that proactively notify users of key information or events when triggered by news, e-mail or enterprise applications. Everyplace Access is part of the WebSphere portal and application server infrastructure that combines to constitute a reliable and scalable mobile application platform.

Everyplace WebSphere Studio

provides an integrated development environment for mobile devices, content adaptation and portlet development tools to extend applications to both browser-based and Java-based (J2SE and J2ME) mobile devices.

Because portlets can be used in connected or disconnected browser-based applications, IBM's mobile programming model promotes portals as a mechanism for aggregating information and accessing enterprise services regardless of the device. Consequently, *Everyplace Toolkit* for *WebSphere Studio* also includes portal/portlet tools for creating, testing, debugging and deploying individual mobile portlets and web content and allowing portlet rendering on mobile devices. Templates enable developers to create their own mobile portlets and applications more quickly and easily.

Content adaptation tools, such as markup and annotation editors, allow developers to create new and adapt existing content for multiple markup languages supported by different devices. The Everyplace Toolkit for WebSphere Studio also provides samples and templates for some of the most popular mobile applications.

SAP Mobile Infrastructure

The *SAP Mobile Infrastructure* (SAP MI) is embedded in the *mySAP technology* as well as in *NetWeaver* (details in chapter 5). It consists of the *Mobile Engine (SAP ME)* installed on a mobile device and Mobile Engine server components running on *SAP Web Application Server*. SAP MI includes synchronization and replication features that make it possible to connect the mobile user to the back-end resources in the enterprise

4 Mobile applications and platforms

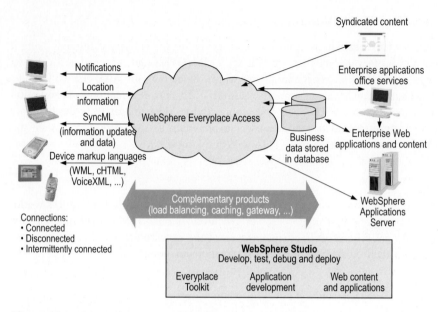

Figure 4.9 WebSphere Everyplace access model (Source: IBM)

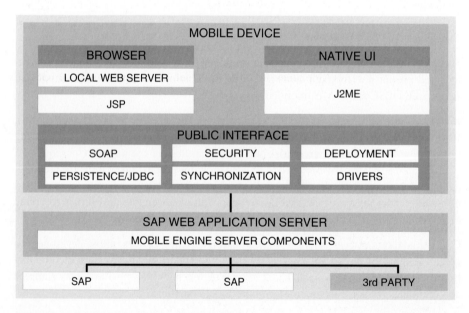

Figure 4.10 SAP Mobile Engine (Source: SAP)

IT landscape. SAP MI uses authentication, role-based authorization and Secure Sockets Layer (SSL) to create a secure, end-to-end connection between the mobile device and the back-end system. It is integrated in the SAP Enterprise Portal and may use central services such as installation, user and application management.

4.3 Mobile application platforms

SAP ME [4.3.11] provides the mobile application platform (see figure 4.10). It is based on J2ME/J2SE as a platform-independent runtime environment for mobile applications and is suitable to run on laptops, PDAs and smartphones. SAP ME supports network connections such as WLAN, GSM/GPRS and Bluetooth.

SAP ME includes its own web server, database and business logic, i.e. it can extend enterprise capabilities to users whether or not they are connected to the enterprise network. It enables multiple users to access the same device, thus ensuring that shift workers are also supported. SAP ME possesses a series of tools which facilitate the development of mobile applications and support the administration and use of these applications. Enterprises and partners can develop their own solutions to work alongside SAP standard mobile application implementations.

Extended Systems Mobile Solutions Platform

The intention behind *Extended Systems Mobile Solutions Platform* [4.3.12], which includes business solutions for sales and field services, is to enable enterprises to optimize their technology investments by making existing applications available to sales representatives and workers in the field, on the road, and in remote office locations within the context of the enterprise network architecture.

The Mobile Solutions Platform provides device access, wireless network support, deployment tools, end-to-end security, synchronization, management/administration and customization features as well as application integration.

The device access capabilities include Palm, Pocket PC, Smartphones, Symbian, browser-based devices (WAP phones, laptops) while network support comprises GSM, GPRS, CDMA, Bluetooth, WLAN, Infrared, Cable/Cradle.

As shown in figure 4.11, the Mobile Solutions Platform provides access to various back-end systems and applications.

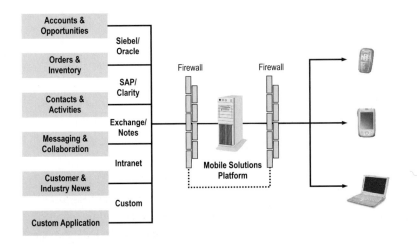

Figure 4.11 Extended Systems Mobile Solution Platform (Source: Extended Systems)

4 Mobile applications and platforms

The platform can provide multiple front- and back-end services and resources in one unified view and is accessible through a single login, thus facilitating workflow management. Pre-built connectors to Siebel CRM, SAP ERP, Microsoft Exchange and Lotus Notes facilitate the integration to enterprises' standard applications. Expanded connectors may integrate custom systems. The platform supports deployment on industry-leading Java application servers on both Windows and Unix operating systems.

The Mobile Solutions Platform is characterized by its system-independence and the wealth of the available device, network and management support.

Managed Mobile Device (MMD)

MMD is a service offered by Siemens Business Services for the management of PDAs and Smartphones with the operating system Windows Mobile. It covers initial installation, the central management of devices, applications and content as well as secure access to enterprise resources.

The initial installation and configuration of the mobile devices is performed by means of a personalized SD/MMC (SD Card/Multimedia Memory Card) which contains all the configuration data, personal data and any customized modules. Once the user has been provided with this card by postal delivery and after plugging in the card and putting in the personal ID, the device will be installed automatically in just a few minutes without any confusing configuration operations and without the need for a cradle.

The main characteristic distinguishing this service from its competitors is that users are able to employ their customized applications productively without any further configurations immediately after card insertion and automatic installation. The central management of the devices together with data and software distribution ensures that appli-

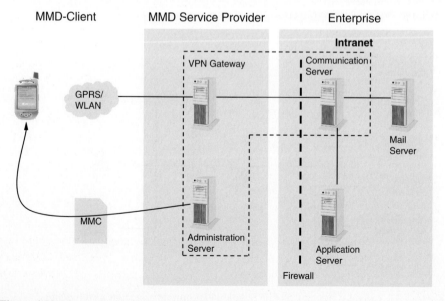

Figure 4.12 Managed Mobile Device (MMD) services

cations and data versions are uniform and up-to-date at only low operating costs. Updates and changes can be performed online via mobile networks (GPRS, WLAN, UMTS) or LAN.

Other advantages of MMD are the high level of security thanks to encryption features, the use of VPN and optional virus protection as well as the high device availability through backup functions and automatic recovery functions in the case of a system fault. With this outstanding properties the MMD is particularly suitable as the basis for mobile business applications with access to the Intranet. The optional e-mail/PIM module makes it possible to use the mail/contact/calendar functions of Microsoft Exchange and Lotus Domino servers.

Mobility Solutions from Fujitsu Siemens Computers

Fujitsu Siemens Computers provides together with partners Mobility and Business Critical Computing solutions [4.3.13] that deliver anywhere, anytime, and any device access to the information services which organizations and consumers require in their business and private lifes.

Fujitsu Siemens Computers' mobility solutions focus around five strategic areas that address particular business mobility needs, namely:

- Security: ensuring end-to-end security to mobility solution infrastructures
- Manageability: ensuring mobility infrastructures remains easy to manage for IT departments
- Messaging: extending messaging and collaboration business infrastructures to the mobile workforce
- Connectivity: ensuring reliable, available, scalable, and secure wireless access to corporate infrastructures and applications
- Business Information Access: extending and providing access to business information and application infrastructures for extending business processes and functions, typically involving critical applications such as Enterprise Resource Planning (ERP), Customer Relationship Management (CRM) and Sales Force Automation (SFA).

Fujitsu Siemens Computers offers a comprehensive range of mobile products which includes Pocket LOOX PDA, LIFEBOOK professional notebooks, STYLISTIC Tablet PCs, CELSIUS Mobile workstations and FUTRO thin clients.

4.4 Example applications

The first wave of *mobile enterprise applications* is over. Some of the early technology and mobile (proprietary) platform providers have disappeared, while mobile business projects have often failed to meet expectations or have not proved to be of real value to companies.

Studies by analysts show that the level of usability and the features provided by mobile devices are considered to be sufficient (with the exception of battery power), but that wireless support, application integration and services still need to be improved. Security is the only truly critical issue and may prevent the deployment and broader acceptance of mobile applications.

It is interesting that CEOs, business unit executives and CIOs provide a quite different assessment of the problems encumbering mobile business solutions. While CEOs mainly point to the high costs of introduction and operation, business executives cite only the introduction cost combined with features that are still required in order to add value to mobile solutions. CIOs refer to inadequate security as the main reason preventing introduction.

Nevertheless, recent years have shown that enterprises can expect mobile applications to provide real value in the following areas:
- Sales force automation
- Field service
- Supply chain optimization
- Tracking and logistics
- Process monitoring

B2E applications such as sales force automation and field service are discussed in the following section. A simple look at the main characteristics of the other application fields is taken below.

Supply chain optimization

The efficiency of a supply chain depends on the optimal coordination of the various stages that are involved in the creation of a product, for example on an assembly line or in the delivery of a service. This coordination can be optimized by a control center which knows the location of the individual objects and can actively control the movement and coordination of these objects in accordance with predefined process models. Cross-enterprise solutions are the most popular ones.

The location of these moving objects at any given time can be achieved by deploying wireless technologies, such as RFID (Radio Frequency Identification), GSM/GPRS, and GPS, either automatically (e.g. by means of embedded RFID chips) or by individuals (e.g. an assembly line manager) who transmit the location data via GPRS or WLAN to the control center.

Some of the benefits are increased speed of production, fewer bottlenecks, efficient use of stocks and flexible exception handling.

Tracking and logistics

The human errors and uncontrolled shipment activities that may occur during logistical and shipment operations frequently create problems for providers and result in customer dissatisfaction. Through the deployment of wireless technologies, items for shipment can be traced precisely irrespectively of their location, while different activities such as the choice of transport vehicle, route coordination, partner coordination, and cost-related measures can be efficiently organized. As mentioned in connection with supply chain solutions, different wireless technologies may be combined and deployed.

The benefits are enhanced precision, reduced response times, cost savings, customer and partner satisfaction.

Process monitoring

Many enterprise operations can be viewed as a series of connected transactions extending throughout the value chain. Enterprise applications support various processes such as human resource processes, customer profiling, order processing, shipping, billing, inspections, quality assurance, repairs, etc. The monitoring of such processes in order to uncover bottlenecks or errors and identify performance criteria is essential if continuous improvement is to be achieved. It makes sense not to limit these monitoring tasks to wireline networks.

The way such processes are supported by mobile technologies depends very much on the kind of process itself. Just to give one example: It could be much more efficient to locate spare parts for IT equipment in a set of on-the-road vehicles instead of storing them in a conventional warehouse. The vehicles' locations and routes can be checked in real time, and optimally modified as a function of the reported events. This could considerably shorten downtimes and improve service levels.

4.4.1 B2E applications

Analysts predict that *B2E applications* will become important components of successful mobile business solutions. The example in figure 4.13 provides an illustration of such applications.

Studies suggest that, depending on the branch of industry in question, between 20% and 80% of an enterprise's employees can be considered to be mobile workers or traveling employees and executives, using the criterion that more than 20% of their working time is spent out of their office or they urgently need mobile support during their trips. On average, about 40% of such personnel are employed as sales staff, while nearly 30%, the second largest group, work in the field service, followed by traveling employees at 20% and executives/managers at 10%.

PIM (Personal Information Management, i.e. e-mail, calendar, contacts, and notes), interfaced with Microsoft Exchange or Lotus Notes, is vital to all these groups and is therefore considered to be a top-priority, horizontal mobile application. *Travel assistance services (flight information, reservations, booking, route finding, location finding, etc.)* constitute another horizontal application which could be provided alongside PIM either by enterprises themselves or by network operators (e.g. location-based services) or service providers (e.g. global distribution services, such as offered by Sabre or Amadeus).

4 Mobile applications and platforms

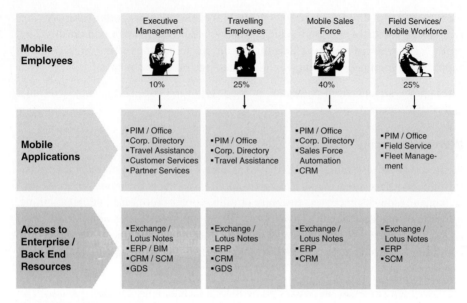

Figure 4.13 B2E applications

The other example applications shown in the diagram either need to be integrated in enterprises' specific data resources or applications (e.g. directory services, databases, data warehouses) or belong to the category of vertical applications because they are dedicated to specific tasks and have to be connected to enterprise applications (e.g. CRM, ERP, SCM). For the most part, such applications will be provided by enterprises themselves or by specialized outsourcing service providers which operate applications, services and processes on behalf of their customers (enterprises).

The scenarios of travel assistance services, sales force automation and an example field service solution are illustrated below in order to increase readers' awareness of mobile solutions and demonstrate the viability and benefits of such approaches.

Seamless mobile travel services

Seamless mobile travel services which support travelers before, during, and after the trip, as depicted in figure 4.14, provide an excellent example of a valuable mobile service:

Travelers usually use their own computer to make travel arrangements, e.g. to set up the itinerary, book flights or train tickets, rent cars, or reserve hotel rooms in accordance with the company's travel management rules. During this process, the traveler can check his/her mileage account or upgrade flights if desired. The travel portal offers additional services which can be booked in advance, such as evening or weekend events at the final destination.

On the way to the airport, the traveler is automatically alerted about possible traffic jams and diverted to an alternative route if necessary. Even before entering the airport, the traveler uses push technology on the phone to check into her or his flight, obtain a parking space, gate and seat number and find out the scheduled departure time.

78

4.4 Example applications

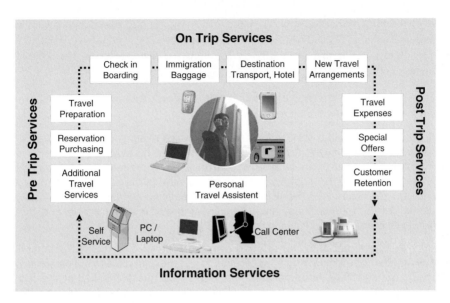

Figure 4.14 Seamless travel management

Before meeting the customer, the traveler might check in at the hotel and access company resources in order to obtain the latest sales figures or update a presentation. The portal authenticates the user, who will be logging in from either a laptop or PDA, and routes him/her through to the appropriate applications.

There is no need for a secretary to make the travel arrangements, especially when it is necessary to change flights or hotel reservations or cope with any other unforeseen events that occur during a trip.

The personal travel assistant, implemented as a portal software component, helps the traveler, who may be in New York, to rearrange and rebook the trip immediately while his or her secretary is still asleep in Munich. The travel portal also knows the traveler's location and is informed of his or her booking preferences as well as the company's travel rules and regulations. Moreover, the personal assistant provides weather information, traffic information, airport and check-in data, and schedule changes. Optional local guides, maps, and transportation support, coupled with entertainment and shopping services, will help travelers make the most of their leisure time.

As the travel portal is even able to trace rebooking activities, it can generate a travel expense report by the end of the trip. Business intelligence software integrated in the portal can analyze the traveler's trips and help the company obtain better booking conditions and cut costs by optimizing travel expense processes and improving the productivity of traveling employees.

Mobile sales force automation

Sales professionals are by nature highly mobile individuals and can achieve significant improvements in productivity by using wireless technologies to communicate more effectively. *Mobile sales force automation* can eliminate the information gaps that most sales people are familiar with, such as those relating to customer purchasing behavior, new product configurations, and order status. Moreover, mobile solutions can enable the seamless exchange of customer data between sales and service employees who may often be working simultaneously at different locations at a customer's site. This kind of coordination improves responsiveness and customer satisfaction.

The following scenario, which is typical of a sales professional's working day, shows how wireless technologies can increase productivity:

Robert, a sales professional working for a company which offers IT services and products, starts his working day by connecting his laptop from his home via DSL and VPN to the corporate employees' portal, answering any mails he has received, looking up his scheduled appointments (Outlook/Exchange), and reviewing the status of customer's orders (CRM) and shipment dates (ERP). Robert is identified and authenticated easily and automatically by means of a smartcard which is inserted in his laptop slot and contains his digital certificates and passwords.

To visit the first customer of the day, Robert uses his Pocket PC with GPRS and GPS capability and the Tom Tom Navigator application to find the best route to the customer's location. On his way there, he remembers that a technical question asked by the customer has not yet been answered. Using his GPRS mobile phone, he accesses a WAP application to obtain the telephone number of a technical expert from the corporate directory. He calls the expert and clarifies the question.

At the car park at the customer's site, Robert connects his Pocket PC via GPRS and VPN to the corporate network to access the CRM application that allows him to check the latest field service reports concerning his customer. He notices that a serious problem has occurred with an update installation of a mySAP application earlier in the morning. With a few stylus taps on his Pocket PC, he asks to be notified automatically by the CRM application when this failure has been eliminated.

Robert then presents a new service level concept at the customer's office using an offline application running on his laptop and explains the technical details of the open question. The customer asks to be informed of some critical shipment dates for ordered products. Robert again uses his always-on PDA and connects to the ERP application to get the required information. He is relieved to learn that the products have already been shipped the day before and will easily arrive before the deadline. During his final discussion with the customer, his PDA beeps and Robert is notified that the service team has solved the update problem and normal operation has resumed. The customer expresses his satisfaction and signs a new service level agreement.

Robert's next visit is to a coffee shop. After presenting a voucher and obtaining a new PIN, Robert is able to use the shop's WLAN hotspot to connect his laptop via the VPN to the corporate network. He transmits the data of the new service level agreement to the CRM system in order to provide the latest information for the monthly report which has to be finished the same evening. At the same time, following the success of the recent customer meeting, Robert requests the CRM system to send out offers and proposals to present the new service level concept to five more customers. The CRM system provides multichannel services and, because it is informed of the customers' communication capabilities and preferences, it knows whether it is best to send them faxes or mails or to contact them by phone. In real time, Robert is informed by the CRM system that one of the selected customers should be contacted by phone. Robert looks up the customer's activities history in the CRM system and phones immediately to set up a meeting.

Robert stays in the coffee shop while the corporate central administration system actively updates corporate data based on Robert's working profile and downloads it to his always-on PDA. Robert is notified that some new product configurations have been released and the prices are added to the downloaded Excel price tables. Because this is relevant to his next customer visit, he downloads the new data sheets to his laptop, connects the laptop and PDA via Bluetooth and adds the data sheets and price tables as appendices to the draft contract which he is to discuss during his following meeting.

At the next customer's site, he finds a printer and prints out the updated contract and appendices via a wireless Bluetooth connection. This means that he is able to discuss the contract with the printed document on the table as most customers prefer.

Before Robert leaves the customer's car park on his way to the airport in the late afternoon, he accesses a WAP application from his mobile phone and orders a bouquet of flowers to be delivered to his wife as a birthday surprise the following day. Then he requests a parking slot in the airport's parking area by sending an SMS, specifying the required time to the parking service operator. A few seconds later, he receives the response SMS containing the slot identification and sends another SMS to confirm the booking. Both the flowers and the car park fee will be paid for via the network operator's phone bill.

Once at the airport, Robert has an hour to wait and is again able to connect his laptop to the corporate network via the airport WLAN hotspot. He goes through the list of e-mails and downloads a PowerPoint file, updated by a colleague, which he needs for the next day's presentation. Next he starts the enterprise's e-learning program in order to complete his knowledge about US GAAP balance sheet methods. The central e-learning web application has monitored the state of Robert's knowledge and registered which modules have been stored locally on his laptop. Robert completes the test for the last lesson and downloads the modules that make up the next lesson in order to be able to continue learning offline.

In the evening, at the hotel where he will be staying, Robert uses his mobile equipment for his leisure activities such as sending MMS, listening to MP3 music and finding a restaurant.

Mobile field service

The following example, *m-butler*, is a mobile application offered by Siemens Business Services that can be customized to fit in with various field service scenarios. The overview in figure 4.15 shows the field service provider, a mobile field engineer and the customer location.

The field service provider offers maintenance and repair services for complex medical systems, such as computer tomography, angiography, x-ray systems, etc. The service provider operates a call center, with the CRM and ERP components being provided by the SAP/R3 system, in order to provide customer care, respond to requests and support maintenance and repair operations. Furthermore, a communication center interfaces with the R3 system and controls the workforce operations of some one hundred field engineers. This also includes a dispatching service that manages communications by sending e-mails, SMS and faxes and receiving messages.

The mobile field engineers are usually on the road and communicate with their control center via PDA and GSM/GPRS networks.

4 Mobile applications and platforms

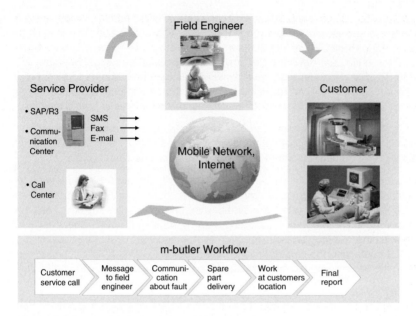

Figure 4.15 Mobile field service: m-butler

A typical customer request process concerning a defective machine begins with a customer call to the Call Center. If the Call Center agent cannot help to rectify the described fault, the fault process is initiated in the ERP system and assigned to an appropriate service engineer depending on availability, qualifications and distance from the customer site. These field engineer parameters are constantly monitored and the repair order is automatically assigned to the selected field engineer.

The CRM system knows the customer's history and machine configurations and the Call Center agent can type in some characteristic fault symptoms in an appropriate fault category mask. By comparing these against a fault history database, the ERP system can retrieve repair instructions and, if necessary, can check the spare parts inventory and order the delivery of spare parts in advance to the customer's or field engineer's location.

The service engineer communicates online with the Communication Center and the R3 system using his PDA to exchange the relevant information, such as the customer's location and history, machine configuration, fault specifics, repair instructions, spare parts delivery, etc. He confirms the order and specifies the expected time of arrival. The service engineer is then guided to the customer's location by his PDA navigation system.

The service engineer collects the material delivered in advance from a drop-off point and scans in the part IDs using his PDA's scanning application.

When the service engineer arrives at the customer's premises, he sends an on-site repair message. Once the work has been successfully completed, the service report is prepared in an R3 mask, presented on the PDA and submitted to the R3 system. The report consists of information about working hours, customer data, material consumption, expense data, fault-related and quality assurance statements, as well as spare part returns in cases where expensive parts need to be returned to a repair center. The cen-

4.4 Example applications

tral R3 system processes the report data automatically and carries out the appropriate follow-up processes such as billing, updating the customer history and the fault databases, and spare parts tracking.

This example application again shows how enterprises that offer this kind of field service can optimize processes in a way that brings benefits to both their customers and themselves. The benefits to the customer – fast, competent, convenient repair processes, reduced machine downtimes and loss of revenue – result in customer satisfaction and retention. The benefits to the enterprise help improve its competitiveness. These result in significant cost savings and enhance many areas of enterprise operation such as the deployment and motivation of field engineers, cost transparency, simplified administration of customer service calls and control of field engineers, improved material and quality assurance processes, etc.

4.4.2 Other mobile applications

Mobile applications will influence virtually every human activity. Therefore not only network operators, but many other service providers such as financial institutions, insurance companies, the trading, retail and wholesale sectors, agencies, content providers, governments and others will participate in the mobile business world.

Mobile payment and mobile ticketing are interesting, lucrative areas of development and dozens of different mobile solutions are already available today. The next step that needs to be taken in these areas is to consolidate and standardize the solutions in order to generate greater momentum.

Mobile advertising, shopping, auction and trading portals and solutions also constitute current examples illustrating the scope of mobile applications. Even government agen-

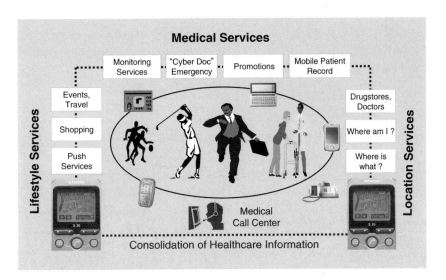

Figure 4.16 Mobile Healthcare Life Portal

4 Mobile applications and platforms

cies now use wireless technologies, for example for monitoring crime-related events and criminals.

Although it is not the ambition of this book to describe all these inspiring applications, the example of the *mobile Healthcare Life Portal* in figure 4.16 may help demonstrate how most individuals' lifestyles will be affected by new mobile solutions in the future.

This portal provides consolidated healthcare information to its subscribers and comprises lifestyle services, medical services and location services that can be accessed via a variety of mobile devices. It could be offered by a private healthcare insurance company whose core business is the insurance of special medical services. By offering additional services, the company is able to differentiate itself from its competitors.

The range of personalized, consolidated healthcare information such as patient records, coupled with monitoring services (e.g. diabetes) and medical consulting, not to mention the coverage of health-related leisure activities (lifestyle services) such as sports, gymnastics, wellness, healthy eating, shopping and travel information, etc. and additional location services (where is the nearest pharmacy?) could prove to be very attractive to most of the portal's users.

For an example of a real portal of this type, see [4.4.1].

4.4.3 Prospects involving UMTS

Despite the arrival of UMTS in Europe in 2003/2004, GSM/GPRS networks and applications will remain in use at least through 2010. It is therefore important to stress that mobile business is already offering the types of valuable applications that have been described above. Nonetheless, the new features and services offered by UMTS will enhance existing applications, while new business opportunities will open up new market segments.

Quality of service (QoS) levels will be a key success factor, while the bandwidth capability of UMTS will be crucial for the provision of improved services and the creation of new business opportunities.

Download times for typical applications Examples

Application	ISDN	GSM	GPRS	UMTS
E-mail file 10 Kbytes	1 sec	8 sec	0,7 sec	0,04 sec
Web page 20 Kbytes	2 sec	20 sec	1,6 sec	0,1 sec
PowerPoint file 2 Mbytes	4 min	28 min	2 min	7 sec
Video clip 4 Mbytes	8 min	48 min	4 min	14 sec

QoS requirements for application classes Examples

Application	Data Rate	Delay Time	Reliability FER
Conversational voice	< 25 Kbit/s	< 150 ms	< 3%
Videophone	< 384 Kbit/s	< 150 ms	< 1%
Voice messaging	< 13 Kbit/s	< 1 sec	< 3%
Web browsing	< 50 Kbit/s	< 4 sec/p	< 3%
E-commerce	< 50 Kbit/s	< 4 sec	0%
Streaming video	< 384 Kbit/s	< 10 sec	< 1%
Telemetry (Monitoring)	< 25 Kbit/s	< 10 sec	0%

Source: UMTS Forum

Figure 4.17 UMTS – service quality

As shown in figure 4.17, typical download times will be reduced significantly in UMTS networks. Application classes such as videophone, streaming video or multimedia messaging require the greater bandwidth capability provided by UMTS networks in order to offer improved quality. Today's GSM networks already meet other QoS requirements, such as low delay time. For example, browsing the web does not make sense with a GSM mobile device. While a GPRS device might be an acceptable way of performing this task, a UMTS device offers users a completely new experience. Common experiences of fixed-line networks provide a good analogy with performance varying from low-speed modem to ISDN and on up to DSL.

The UMTS Forum has defined six basic *3G/UMTS service classes* which might drive the 3G market:

- mobile Intranet/Extranet access (business)
- location-based services (consumer and business)
- rich voice (consumer and business)
- multimedia messaging services (consumer)
- mobile Internet access (consumer)
- customized infotainment (consumer).

Given the focus on enterprise applications, the first three of these service classes are the most significant and will be examined in more detail below.

Mobile Intranet/Extranet access is already a widespread phenomenon today. However, UMTS will represent a new departure in terms of user experience and bandwidth which will make new practical applications possible. Browsing with transmission rates of 144 kbit/s or more is a quite inspiring experience that makes it a simple task to download PowerPoint files or other bulk data. The ability to transfer usable quality video clips will clear the way for new applications, such as downloading instruction videos to assist maintenance engineers in the repair of complex machines.

Location-based services are also offered by most network operators today. With the exception of the improved location sensing methods, there is no essential difference between the service quality of UMTS and GPRS-based applications. In order to ensure that these services are available worldwide, it is important that network operators are able to expand their roaming agreements. Furthermore, the success of location-based services primarily depends on it being a profitable proposition for a variety of different partners to participate in the total value chain. These partners may be network operators (owners of the location's geo-coordinates, billing), content providers and content aggregators, as well as solution providers, service providers, enterprises and consumers.

The *3G rich voice service* is a real-time, two-way service for businesses and consumers that provides advanced-voice capabilities such as concurrent voice and data services using VoIP, voice-activated net access and web-initiated voice calls, while still offering traditional mobile voice features. Voice is an essential component in many data-oriented services and will quickly evolve into a packet-based, IP-oriented service to enable new applications such as speech recognition and voice-activated Intranet access.

Mobile videophony is a natural evolution of today's voice services and rich multimedia services may very well become valuable applications for enterprises in the long term.

4.5 Summary and recommendations

Business outlook

The outlook for mobile business solutions seems very promising. According to a study by the Boston Consulting Group, the expected gain in productivity to enterprises in 2006 due to mobile business solutions is expected to amount to $520 billion worldwide. An average increase in productivity of 6% is predicted. Enterprises will spend $340 billion on establishing and operating mobile business solutions. This means that $180 billion of added value will be created. The main factors for successful deployment will be cost efficiency, improved processes and asset management, increased employee effectiveness, customer retention and new business opportunities.

According to Gartner, the global IT economy will have rebounded strongly by 2006. Most enterprises will soon change their strategic focus from cutting costs and protecting profits to driving growth aggressively.

One of the driving factors that will be particularly influential in the field of mobile business will be the changing significance of *work and leisure*. With the introduction of flexible working hours, traditional fixed time work is evolving into *anytime work*. The emergence of distributed teams means that traditional fixed place work is changing into *anywhere work*. Finally, in a *connected society*, work will ultimately be performed in virtual collaborative environments created and mediated by IT systems. Gartner believes the always-on or connected society will rapidly emerge during the next decade. In Gartner's view, by 2007, over 75% of EU and US citizens will have the option of immediate access to e-services for over 80% of their nonworking time.

Architecture

Mobile solutions should be based on proven, standards-oriented infrastructures and easily integrable, modular building blocks and multitier architectures which enable step-by-step implementations that cater for the requirements of users while also responding to the needs and capabilities of both business units and IT organizations.

Reusable web services integrated in enterprises' portal architectures are recommended as the best way to meet economic targets while also achieving the agility and flexibility which are needed to stay competitive.

While the portal architecture will dominate enterprise business architectures, direct access from the client to web services in the network (e.g. for travel reservations) together with the offline processing of the results (e.g. entry of relevant data in the business traveler's appointments diary and itinerary) will significantly expand the spectrum of possible applications in the medium term. However, this does not mean that intelligent clients are compulsory for modern mobile business solutions. Centralized applications with browser clients are much easier to manage and often the most promising solution.

Strategy

Enterprises need to build mobile support into their application architecture. Although this should not prevent the necessary experimentation, these initial projects should be seen as part of a larger strategic plan and provide short-term return on investment. Therefore 'low-hanging fruits' and 'quick wins' should be the first application areas. The recommendation is to keep first implementations simple, but to consider the long-term infrastructural, architectural and strategic implications carefully from the very outset.

In particular, mobile applications and solutions must be framed within a comprehensive enterprise security and web services infrastructure strategy. Moreover, service-oriented architectures, business process management and cross-enterprise processes must be taken into consideration when designing mobile solutions (For more details, see chapter 5). Enterprises that ignore the impact of mobility on their infrastructures and architectures are not only neglecting an increasingly important part of their business but will inevitably see their software maintenance costs soar.

Smart enterprises should be looking critically, but also imaginatively, at the potential offered by mobile solutions and gauging that potential against the technological, organizational and process implications of wireless implementations. In most cases, they will discover compelling business cases for moving forward with mobile solutions sooner rather than later.

5 Web services

As mentioned in chapter 3, the pressures on IT executives have strongly increased during the past years. They have to cut costs while at the same time to innovate IT-infrastructure. Moreover they need to improve customer services, to be more competitive and to respond quickly to the business's strategic priorities.

Two fundamental reasons are behind all of this hassle: The heterogeneous system and application landscape and the rapidly changing market requirements.

Most enterprises cannot take a single-vendor approach to IT, because available application suites are not sufficient and flexible enough, which potentially leads to higher costs. Embracing heterogeneity therefore often is the better practice, because a best-of-breed approach can be more affordable and efficient. Interoperability obviously is the only way to overcome these inconsistencies and may even drive new IT investment.

Increasing market changes are the second issue. Business must adapt rapidly in today's dynamic competitive environment, and the IT infrastructure must follow. Change is an ever-present issue in the IT world for several reasons:

Broad economic forces including globalization and e-business are accelerating the pace of change. Global competition leads to shortening product cycles, as companies try to gain advantage over their competition. Customer needs and requirements change more quickly in response to this cycle of competitive improvements in products and services. Finally improvements in technology continue to accelerate, feeding the increased pace of changing customer requirements.

Executives need to find ways to solve today's problems, such as:

– Challenge to address the changing needs of customers in a cost-effective way
– Costly, inflexible integration technologies that cause unacceptable risks to the enterprise
– Increasing complexity of IT environment
– Monolithic business applications that require expensive customization and maintenance
– Getting locked into vendors' products
– Complex automation of business processes that involve partners and customers with inadequate security
– Lack of visibility and control into automated business processes for line-of-business management

- Limited ability to participate in value networks because of complexity and insufficient security

Business is calling upon IT more than ever to respond quickly and efficiently to these multiple and serious challenges.

In this tough environment enterprises highly welcome an evolutionary, standards-based architectural approach, which addresses all of the issues mentioned above.

This approach is a web services based architecture known as *Service-Oriented Architecture (SOA)*.

5.1 Web services paradigm – SOA

The *Web Services Paradigm* refers to the *Service-Oriented Architecture (SOA)*, an architecture that constitutes a distributed computing environment in which applications call functionality from other applications either locally or remotely over an internal network or an IP-network in a loosely-coupled way.

Web services are self-contained, self-describing modular and autonomous applications. They may be deployed intra-enterprise as an easier way of distributed computing or published, located and invoked across the Internet. Web services published on the web (software as a service) can be used by any application at any time. The web services components will remain consistently regardless of various deployments.

The goal of web services is to enable *application-to-application communication*. This is achieved by a document-oriented way of distributed computing.

The following aspects describe what makes up web services:

- The service is represented by software that is first of all capable to process an XML document it has received from an invoking application via any internal interface or IP-network. The internal structure of this software as well as the realization of the requested functionality does not play any role. Whether it is based on object-oriented techniques or it operates as a stand-alone process or is a thin layered front-end of an existing enterprise application, is not of any importance. This software only needs to be capable of processing well-defined XML documents and performing the functionality requested in these documents.
- The *XML document* is the keystone of a web service, as it contains all the application-specific information. This document is described using an XML scheme, and the two applications that are engaged in the conversation need to have knowledge of the same description in order to interprete and validate the document correctly. For these descriptions the *Web Services Description Language (WSDL)* is used.
- The *Address* defines where the service can be found, i.e. a transport protocol (e.g. TCP, HTTP, etc.) combined with a network address.
- The *Envelope* encapsulates the XML document and some system information the two communicating applications may want to exchange in the message. This system

information allows, for example, routing and security information to be added to the message without the need to modify the XML document. The message protocol that is used for almost all web services is SOAP (Simple Object Access Protocol). The SOAP message consists of two possible elements: a soap-header, in which all the system information is kept, and a soap-body, which contains the XML document that is to be processed by the web service.

Service-oriented architectures

SOA describes a distributed application construction that has been in principle in use for many years. *CORBA (Common Object Request Broker Architecture)*, in use since the late eighties, promoted by the *Object Management Group* and mainly deployed in telecommunication applications is one example. The *DCOM (Distributed Component Object Model)* of Microsoft is another. Both concepts provide interface definition languages (IDL, MIDL) and tightly coupled distribution mechanisms that allow local or remote invocations.

In principle, SOA allows designing applications that provide services to other applications through published and discoverable interfaces. In this sense SOA might be defined as an application architecture in which all functions are implemented as independent services with well-defined invokable interfaces, which can be called in sequences to form business processes.

However in contrast to CORBA and DCOM, SOA based on web services constitutes a loosely coupled model, as depicted in figure 5.1, provides platform independency (regarding the two camps, Java and Microsoft), as well as language, transport and message format independency.

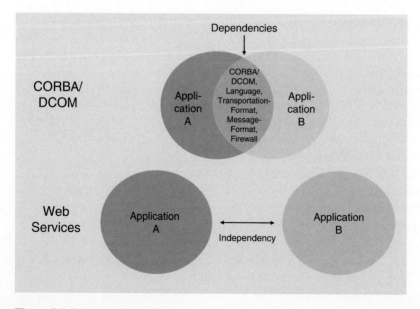

Figure 5.1 Independency of platforms

5.1 Web services paradigm – SOA

Moreover the passing through firewalls using HTTP is enabled, *WSDL (Web Services Description Language)* is bound to the service it describes and the service is accessed electronically at a location, which may not be known to the requester but can automatically be discovered.

The SOA based on web services is characterized by the ability of *publishing* a service on an IP-network in a registry. The network is either public (Internet) or private (enterprise). The registry is standardized, called *UDDI (Universal Description, Discovery and Integration)* and may be either public or private, too.

UDDI consists of an XML schema that defines four data structures: business definition, service definition, binding specification and programmatic interface as well as a set of APIs that operate on those structures.

The web services are described by the standardized WSDL. The WSDL listing is comprised of three elements: the white pages, which contain basic information about the providing company and its services, the yellow pages, which organize services by industry, service type and geography, finally the green pages, which include the technical mechanisms, i.e. how to find (e.g. URL) and execute a web service.

The SOA provides in addition to the *publishing* two other significant capabilities, that are taken advantage of at runtime of an application that invoke a web service: the *discovery*, the ability to find a required functionality (service) and the *binding*, the ability to connect automatically to this functionality.

Figure 5.2 shows the three corresponding roles: the web service provider, the web service requester and the web service broker (UDDI).

After a web service is built by a web service provider and posted to a company's or a broker's UDDI registry (P in the diagram) any invocation via the network can occur.

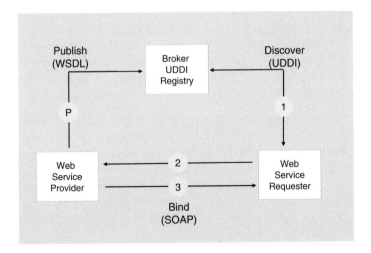

Figure 5.2 Web services based service-oriented architecture

A typical transaction flow comprises 3 steps. The web service requester searches the UDDI registry and finds a description of the desired service (1). The web service requester then connects to the web service provider via the *SOAP (Simple Object Access Protocol)* to obtain and activate the web service (2). After executing the web service the deliverables are sent back again via SOAP to the web service requester (3), where they are processed in the requester's application.

Benefits and limitations of SOA

Benificial aspects

The most important new aspect about web services and SOA is its ubiquitous support by all major vendors. Most likely this is not at least due to some convincing advantages such as:

– Flexibility in new software design
– Reuse of business components in networks
– Interoperability and integration capability
– Ease of assembling new business processes

Several recent developments in the software industry have helped to bring SOA forward. With personalized, web-based, portal-style user interfaces over multiple channels an increasing number of solutions require the reuse of application components. Different users such as customers, employees, managers using many devices (laptops, PDAs, smartphones) in different situations (home, office, and hotel) all may request access to the same set of business applications. The loosely coupled SOA provides the natural basis for reuse of applications to multiple categories of clients. Thus, the transition to multi-client and multi-channel applications pushes forward the web services based software design.

No doubt, SOA will imply more competition and innovation of application development. Best-of-breed business components can be encapsulated as autonomous web services and be published to UDDI registries as reusable services with the accessibility of the whole world. This will not only become an excellent business opportunity for smart software start-ups, but also established vendors will tend to modularize their application packages and offer components as web services via the Internet to more customers.

Another fundamental need is the better interoperabilty of application platforms of different vendors such as IBM, Microsoft and SAP as well as the integration of enterprise applications from different vendors or with home-grown applications. Many projects have created programmatic interfaces to wrap legacy and other existing external functionality for assembly into heterogeneous composite transactions. Composition and integration of existing and new real-time transaction patterns are a natural fit of SOA.

SOA evolution of IT applications

Probably the most desired value of SOA on the foundation of web services is its capability to assemble easily ad hoc processes and its representation of an enabling technol-

5.1 Web services paradigm – SOA

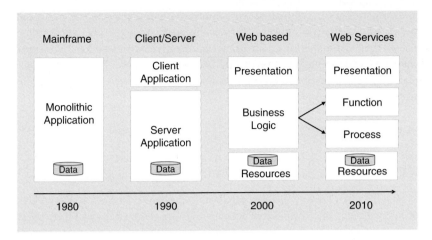

Figure 5.3 Evolution of IT application architectures

ogy for process integration. As shown in figure 5.3 this will lead to another architectural split of business application layers.

The old monolithic application paradigm, characterized by unstructured and inflexible applications, designed with 3rd and 4th generation program languages, running on mainframe systems, supporting thumb, text oriented terminals has been replaced by a 2-tier client/server application paradigm in the late eighties.

As mentioned in chapter 2, ten years later another paradigm has emerged as the result of significant technology developments and business-related requirements: The web-based e-business. The evolution of the Internet technology surely has become the main driver to shift the IT architectures to today's state-of-the-art multi-tier architectures. This architecture comprises the presentation tier, providing mainly browser clients, the business logic tier, which represents the centralized, functional and procedural application and the resource tier containing databases, web content, legacy systems and other corporate services like directory services.

The Service-Oriented Architecture (SOA) on the foundation of web services now enables a new paradigm for the design and operation of business applications: The separation into functions and processes.

In this paradigm, business processes and activities can be supported efficiently by the composition of coordinated web services, which may represent distinguished business functionalities. The loosely coupled mechanisms of SOA in combination with a new business process execution language (BPEL, details later) and workflow engines, which control the defined process flows provide the ability to set up rapidly ad hoc processes by leveraging components of existing applications and integrate them with new web services.

However this paradigm, which can be described as a two level programming model (function distinguished from process), will have significant impacts on the design as well as on the operation of applications. In the design phase the composition of web services means new challenges concerning the solution architecture, the coordination of services, and the handling and coordination of multi-services transactions. The operation of web services-based applications and processes also imply challenging issues, such as quality of services, service level agreements, as well as web services and process management.

Limits and open issues

SOA is neither a universal remedy for the multiple existing shortcomings in today's mix and match IT-architectures nor is it the solution for all upcoming challenges.

Though SOA relays to a loosely coupled model it is probably not the best practice in the case of long-running asynchronous processes. SOA's natural strenghts rather lay in real-time request-response exchanges (synchronous and asynchronous) than in more event-driven processes.

SOA requires an environmental framework, i.e. a state-of-the-art application platform, such as Microsoft .NET, SAP NetWeaver, IBM WebSphere or BEA WebLogic. Unfortunately a full platform independency has not yet been achieved.

Applications, whose business logic components are used in a closed application domain or will be neither reused nor changed do not benefit from SOA because of the additional design and development effort.

The most critical aspects of SOA and web services are still some pending security issues. A more or less extensive framework of security-standards has been worked out, not yet finished, and applicable products are available on the market now. But for mission critical processes embedding external web services via the Internet the existing security measures are not sufficient for the most cases. More details are covered in chapter 6.

Furthermore SOA and web services deployment are still critical where an application requires the transactional handling of sequential request-response exchanges. In many cases existing applications cannot be wrapped as web services that match the high level of *ACID (Atomicy, Consistency, Isolation, Durability)* transactional processing. Extended transactions therefore will become very important in the design phase. They define how non-ACID transactions should be managed acceptably, if any events cause that a transaction cannot be finished successfully. As an example, long-running activities can be structured as many independent, *short-duration transactions* to form a logical *long-running transaction*.

Another critical aspect to be considered if deploying web services is the coordinated collaboration of web services with old applications as well as the provisioning of complex functionality achieved by the aggregation of various web services. Business processes usually comprise various coordinated activities, where contexts, dependencies and events have to be regarded. This requires a coordination framework with appropriate coordination protocols to address those issues. Today there is little experience how these challenges can be responded successfully.

Finally there are some issues concerning the deployment of published web services in mission critical enterprise application, such as trust, guaranteed availability and quality levels, and the ability to negotiate contracts with sufficient flexibility.

Summary

In the long term the values of SOA are evidently.

SOA
- leverages open standards to represent virtually all software assets as services including legacy applications, packaged applications, J2EE components and web services
- effects that individual software assets become building blocks that can be reused in developing other applications
- provides developers with a standard way of representing and interacting with software assets without having to spend time working with unique interfaces and low-level APIs
- helps reducing the complexity, cost, and risk of integration by providing a single, simple architectural framework based on web services in which to build, deploy, and manage application functionality.

SOA is useful in many aspects and should be part of the most forward-looking software projects. Over time, the lack of SOA experience will become a competitive disadvantage for many enterprises. They must understand the essence of SOA and web services as well as their strenghts and limitations in order to be able to identify their roles in modern application architectures and business solutions.

5.2 Web services standardization

The *web services standards* and standard proposals can be structured as illustrated in figure 5.4. The standards and protocols may be distinguished in three blocks: the description/discovery block, the infrastructure and deployment block that contains standards and protocols for deploying web services, and the web services implementation framework. For better understanding the various standard purposes, the infrastructure and deployment block is separated in the transport, messaging, quality of services and processes/composition layer.

Standards that serve as a basis for creating and using web services have been deployed since several years. These include SOAP, the extensible XML-based protocol for exchanging information in distributed, heterogeneous system environments, WSDL for describing call interfaces and UDDI for registering and locating web services as well as the underlying transport protocols such as HTTP, TCP/IP, and others.

A series of *extended standards* is necessary in order to realize the vision of a business web, where web services can be used as application components and combined dynamically in order to represent new business processes. What is needed are enabling ser-

5 Web services

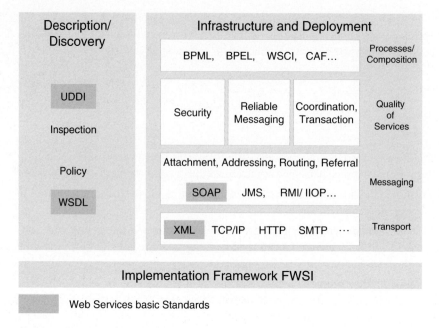

Figure 5.4 Web services standards and standard proposals

vices, protocols and languages, which guarantee quality levels for reliable message transport, for security and transaction processing, for monitoring and accounting, for collaboration and orchestration. These *extended services* are essential for ensuring the secure, permanent, reliable and coordinated use of web services.

Extended services are primarily defined, specified and prototyped by well known vendors such as IBM, Microsoft, SAP, BEA, and Sun. Bodies like *OASIS (Organization for the Advancement of Structured Information Standards)* and the standardization organization *W3C (World Wide Web Consortium)* are continuing to drive these technologies until a standard is concluded.

Global XML Web Services Architecture

An important step of the web services standardization development was Microsoft's publication of a specification called *Global XML Web Services Architecture (GXA)* at the end of 2001 [5.2.1]. This specification was then extended with the assistance of other vendors during the course of the last years with concrete standards and protocols being added.

According to Microsoft, GXA is based on four design principles:
– Modular
  GXA uses the extensibility of the SOAP specification to deliver a set of composable modules that can be combined as needed to deliver end-to-end capabilities. As new capabilities are required, new modular elements can be created.

- General Purpose
  GXA is designed for a wide range of XML web services scenarios, ranging from B2B and EAI solutions to peer-to-peer applications and B2C services.
- Federated
  GXA is fully distributed and designed to support XML web services that cross organizational and trust boundaries and do not require centralized servers or administrative functions.
- Standards-based
  As with previous XML web services specifications, GXA protocols will be submitted to appropriate standard bodies and Microsoft will work with interested parties to complete their standardization.

Web Services Interoperability Organization (WS-I)

IBM and Microsoft formed the *web services Interoperability Organization (WS-I)* in 2002 in a bid to ensure the interoperability of web services implementations from different vendors. The aim of the WS-I organization [5.2.2] is to link various web services approaches with each other. WS-I provides guidelines, best-practice examples, tools and test environments for ensuring that web services can communicate with each other across platform and vendor boundaries. Furthermore, WS-I provides a so-called basic profile, which contains implementation guidelines and recommendations as to how interoperable web services can be created on the basis of the core technologies and protocols (SOAP, WSDL, UDDI, XML and XML Scheme Definition, XSD).

Currently defined standards and discussed proposals

The web services standardization is an ongoing process. Actual information about web services standards is available on the web [5.2.3].

Some of the important web services standards and proposed specifications, which are shown in figure 5.4 are described briefly as follows:

WS-Inspection

The WS-Inspection specification provides an XML format for assisting in the inspection of a site for available services and a collection of rules for how inspection related information should be made available for consumption. A WS-Inspection document provides a means for aggregating references to pre-existing service description documents which have been authored in any number of formats. These inspection documents are then made available at the point-of-offering of the service as well as through references which may be placed within a content medium such as HTML.

WS-PolicyFramework

The WS-PolicyFramework defines a general purpose model and corresponding syntax to describe and communicate web services policies so that service consumers can discover the necessary information to get access to services from a service provider.

5 Web services

WS-Attachments

This specification defines an abstract model for SOAP attachments and based on this model defines a mechanism for encapsulating a SOAP message and attachments in a DIME message (Direct Internet Message Encapsulation). It makes no sense in some application scenarios to transfer pure XML-coded data to a web service: For example, if a picture or a graphic is to be included as an attachment, or in the case of nested SOAP messages. DIME specifies how such attachments can be packaged and WS-Attachments define how DIME-coded attachments should be handled in the SOAP protocol.

WS-Addressing

WS-Adressing provides transport-neutral mechanisms to address web services and messages. Particularly, this specification defines XML elements to identify web service endpoints and to secure end-to-end endpoint identification in messages. This specification enables messaging systems to support message transmission through networks that include processing nodes such as endpoint managers, firewalls, and gateways in a transport-neutral manner.

WS-Routing

WS-Routing is required for transporting messages via a dynamically configured network path. An alternative return path and any intermediate stations can be specified for the messages along the network path. The model for intermediaries may support direct identification or a description of the type of service that a selected intermediary can perform.

WS-Referral

WS-Referral extends the WS-Routing concept. WS-Referral is required for the routing and administration of routing directories stored on the intermediate nodes. The reason for this is that web services communication (exchange of requests and responses) only takes place directly between two neighboring computer nodes in exceptional cases. In most cases the communication path will extend over a number of intermediate nodes, depending on the network topology and the defined fallback routes.

WS-Security

WS-Security describes SOAP extensions for guaranteeing the integrity, confidentiality and authentication of SOAP messages. Furthermore, the handling of security tokens is also defined. More detail about WS-Security and other security standards in this context are explained in chapter 6.

WS-ReliableMessaging

This specification describes a protocol that allows messages to be delivered reliably between distributed applications in the presence of software component, system, or network failures. The protocol is described in this specification in an independent manner allowing it to be implemented using different network transport technologies. To support interoperable web services, a SOAP binding is defined within this specification.

WS-Coordination

This specification describes a framework for providing protocols that coordinate the actions of distributed applications. Such coordination protocols are used to support a number of applications, including those that need to reach consistent agreement on the outcome of distributed transactions. The framework enables an application service to create a context needed to propagate an activity to other services and to register for coordination protocols. The framework enables existing transaction processing, workflow, and other systems for coordination to hide their proprietary protocols and to operate in a heterogeneous environment. Additionally, this specification describes a definition of the structure of context and the requirements for propagating context between cooperating services.

WS-Transaction

WS-Transaction was defined in conjunction with WS-Coordination. WS-Transaction guarantees a consistent status across all participating processes and data at any point in time. WS-Transaction distinguishes between two different coordination instances: Atomic Transaction and Business Activity. An 'Atomic Transaction' involves communication by processes with very short runtimes within a closed application domain. A 'Business Activity' involves cross-company business process procedures that are processed asynchronously over a longer period (long-living transactions).

Business Processes

The tough struggle for vendors in accomplishing their web services technologies is demonstrated using the example of specifications for cross-company business process communication. There are a number of contending proposals in relation to this topic, each with a somewhat different focus and specification depth.

The *Business Process Modeling Language (BPML)* was published 2002 by the Business Process Management Initiative. This initiative covered more than a dozen well-known vendors, such as BEA, CSC, HP, IBM, SAP, and Sun. BPML allows a company's business processes to be modeled across all levels. Every individual action of a process can be defined, even in the case of complex, cross-company business processes. Business processes are depicted as graphical objects that can be changed via a simple user interface.

BEA, SAP, and Sun developed an XML-based specification, the *Web Services Choreography Interface (WSCI)*, which describes dynamic interfaces for web services, via which data can be exchanged using static business rules.

Microsoft developed its proprietory business process language XLANG used with its BizTalk integration and orchestration server and IBM developed the web services Flow Language (WSFL).

Finally IBM and Microsoft have used their developments (WSFL and XLANG) as a basis for developing three complementary specifications together with BEA, i.e. WS-Coordination, WS-Transaction and the *Business Process Execution Language for Web services (BPEL4WS or short BPEL)* in order to regulate the workflow between service-based business processes. Cascadable web services may be created, which for example allow flights, rental cars and hotel rooms to be booked within one consistent process. If the flight is cancelled, the hotel reservation and the rental car are cancelled automatically with the assistance of a compensation transaction and the user will be informed accordingly.

In the meantime more or less all major software vendors will support BPEL and Microsoft has announced a migration path from XLANG to BPEL. Therefore BPEL probably has the best chance to become the cross-enterprise business process language standard.

WS-CAF

The purpose of this recently initiated OASIS *WS-CAF (Web services Composite Application Framework)* Technical Committee [5.2.4] is to define a royalty-free, generic and open framework for supporting applications that contain multiple web services used in combination (composite applications).

Framework for web services implementation

OASIS members have formed a new *Framework for Web Services Implementation (FWSI)* Technical Committee [5.2.5] to produce guidelines that assist system integrators and software vendors in implementing web services solutions. The purpose is to facilitate implementation of robust web services by defining a practical and extensible methodology. It will comprise implementation processes and common functional elements that enterprises can adopt to create high quality web services systems without re-inventing them for each implementation. It attempts to solve the problem of the slow adoption of web services due to lack of methodologies to implement web services, and lack of understanding of whether solutions proposed by vendors have the necessary components to implement reliably an application based on web services.

Standardization outlook

The major software vendors and standardization organizations have shown a strong interest to cooperate in developing web services standards because they all recognized that web services can only gain broad acceptance with adequate mechanisms to guarantee interoperability.

However the standardization is an ongoing process with frequently extended versions and additional discovered new fields where standardization is needed. Examples are web services security, policy, provisioning, long-running transaction, federation, composition, orchestration and management.

Some of the mentioned standard proposals are vendor proposals but not yet taken up by standardization organizations (e.g. federation). Unfortunately involved players have different business interests that cause overlapping or disagreement of standard proposals preventing unified deployment and interoperability.

5.3 Web services impacts

Web services have the potential to drive the next evolutionary step in the development of the Internet, the business web. They will offer the greatest benefits for communication between enterprises (B2B) for enabling the implementation of complex, dynamic, cross-enterprise business process operations. They will help to automate the processing of order, delivery and payment transactions. Thanks to simple implementation and the use of widely known standards, web services should also allow small and medium-sized companies to participate in e-business. Unless security, web services do not require a sophisticated new IT-infrastructure and networking, they rather may be embedded in existing environments as shown in figure 5.5.

Two partner enterprises A and B are shown that access different external web services (payment processing, dispatch logistics). These may be chargeable services offered by a web service provider. In addition both enterprises access an external authentication web service in order to be able to authenticate to the web service provider and to each

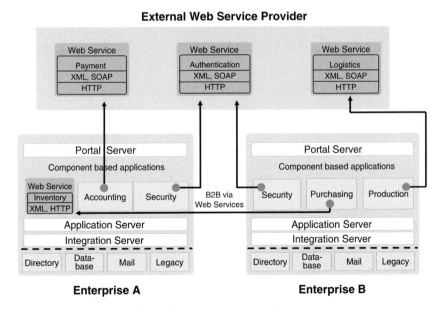

Figure 5.5 Web services embedded in existing IT infrastructure

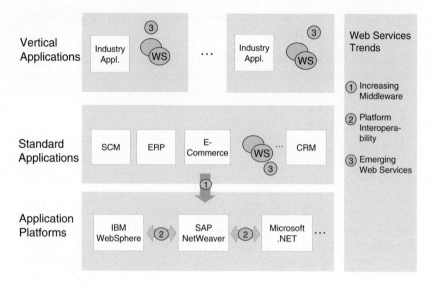

Figure 5.6 Web services impacts (1)

other. Moreover, enterprise A provides a web service that allows enterprise B to query the current inventory from the purchasing application. Both enterprises use appropriate application servers with a component application model. These application servers are capable based on web services standards to invoke and run web services in combination with component applications, such as purchasing, accounting, security, etc.

Though web services may be embedded in existing IT-infrastructure there will be significant impacts on the one hand on the shaping of middleware as well as on the total architecture of business applications on the other hand. This is mainly due to the facts that web services technology will create more competition, more standardized autonomous business functions as well as enable more flexibility to react to changing market requirements.

The Internet, SOA and web services will become the foundation for B2B, B2C and B2E e-business.

As depicted in figures 5.6 and 5.7 five trends are of significant importance and will change the architecture of e-business solutions:

Increasing middleware on application platforms (trend 1)

Today's appropriate application server support the basic web services standards, i.e. provide web services container that are able to run web services and offer tools to develop web services or to wrap existing applications to be deployed as web services.

Standard applications such as SCM, ERP, CRM are farreaching isolated from each other but do perform some common horizontal functions, e.g. security, personalization, user management, identity management and others. Some of these functions may be soon provided by application platforms in the form of web services, which can be invoked by the standard applications whenever they need to perform these functions. Obviously this will help to increase productivity of enterprises and will free development resources of standard software vendors so that they are able to focus more on innovative functions to improve their software packages.

Platform interoperability (trend 2)

As mentioned at the beginning of this chapter, IT executives are under pressure to improve the interoperability of different vendors' platforms and applications. Interoperability should be achieved on all three server levels, the portal, the application and the integration server.

An enterprise may provide access for multiple user groups via different portals but the groups may use equally applications, services or enterprise resources. Web services constitute an adequate technology to achieve this interoperability in future sytems. With the *WSRP (Web Services for Remote Portals)* standard, content from other sources or applications running on other platforms can be integrated as remote portlets. As WSRP include presentation, service providers determine how their content and applications are visualized for end-users. Therefore the integration is easily done and portal designers are not required to make any manual content- or application-specific adaptation.

Common portal services such as authentication, location based services and billing services will be implemented as web services, platform independently and therefore deployable from different enterprise portals. Enterprise resources, e.g. web content or database information will be made available to the multiple user groups by standardized web services that response to the user's queries.

State-of-the-art application server support the basic web services standards and provide tools to develop web services as well as they are equipped with containers to run web services. Interoperability between platforms of different vendors by deploying common web services and by web services based interaction between applications will become mainstream. Another standard will improve the interoperability among J2EE platforms. The *web service for J2EE (JSR109)* architecture is a service architecture which leverages the J2EE component architecture to provide a decoupled client server programming model which is portable across J2EE application servers.

Emerging web services (trend 3)

The web services paradigm will push the e-business by implying more competition and innovation of application development. Best-of-breed business components can be encapsulated as autonomous web services and published to UDDI registries as reusable services with the accessibility of the whole world. As shown in figure 5.7 this means an enrichment of automated business functions as well as the capability to integrate those functions in well defined business processes.

Publishing web services will become a new chance for smart software start-ups to offer best-of-breed business functions. Even more important, the established business stand-

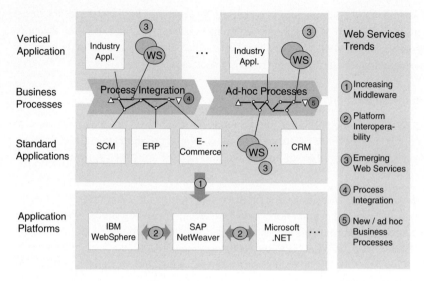

Figure 5.7 Web services impacts (2)

ard application vendors, such as SAP, Peoplesoft or Siebel will modularize their application packages and offer components as web services via the Internet.

Moreover proprietary industry specific applications will be supplemented or replaced by vertical web services, which may be offered by software vendors or by companies of the manufacturing, chemical, transportation, or any other industry that are interested to publish such an industry specific web service, e.g. for better collaboration with their business partners.

Business process integration – the real-time enterprise (trend 4)

To be successful in today's rapidly changing market, enterprises require solutions that allow integrating business processes across different vertical markets and various application platforms. Effective business integration enables disparate business resources to work together, both inside and outside an enterprise, to support a company's business strategy.

To meet these crucial challenges enterprises must be able to optimize processes by combining and correlating functions from today's distinguished applications such as ERP, SCM, e-commerce and vertical applications. The integration and exploitation of isolated applications enable cross-functional processes to obtain real-time results. Business process integration in this sense is the way to become a real-time enterprise.

Ad hoc business processes (trend 5)

Enterprises face a number of challenges in order to address the continual changes taking place in the market today. They need to adapt new business rules, financial models and industry position to find new ways to acquire and keep customers. They should

5.3 Web services impacts

develop new business, enter new markets, create new sales models and build new and efficient electronic purchasing channels while integrating existing ones.

The dynamics of e-business today demand business agility to adapt rapidly to new market forces and opportunities. Enterprises must be able to seize market opportunities and provide appropriate service level management to exceed customer expectations. They have to offer continually value-added differential to their customers, on price, service or any other value that meets customers' needs.

This means companies must be able to set up ad hoc processes very quickly in order to adapt to new market requirements, e.g., the exploitation of existing CRM functionality and industry-specific applications in combination with web services orchestrated in a shortly arranged workflow may increase the level of agility substantially.

Business integration with web services

According to the trends depicted, enterprises will be forced to focus increasingly on business integration and business process management deploying web services technology.

As shown in figure 5.8, business integration comprises four integration levels:
– User integration (including customers, business partners and employees)
– Integration of internal and external applications
– Integration of information, including content- and knowledge-management
– Process integration: integration of internal and external processes

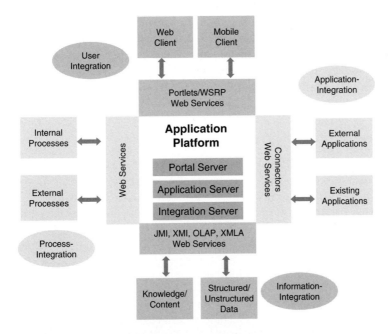

Figure 5.8 Business integration with web services

User integration increasingly takes account of personal requirements as well as of the context of each user and the enhanced needs in terms of mobility and security. At the same time, it permits more efficient collaboration, with the result that time-critical processes can be significantly improved. Integration is achieved by portlets which simply can be adapted to portal frameworks and by the emerging *WSRP* standard. Services such as user management, roles, personalization may be increasingly provided as portal related web services.

In the case of application integration, the time-consuming concept of point-to-point integration is replaced by high-performance integration servers with a wide range of connectors, component and message brokers and, in the long term, by web services.

The integration of information may be achieved on the metadata level by standards that include the *Java Metadata Interface (JMI)* and *XML Metadata Interchange (XMI)* and in addition by support of *OLAP (Online Analytical Processing)*, which allows generic access to a wide variety of applications as well as *XML for analysis (XMLA)*, which defines a similar API based on SOAP and XML. Beyond pure messaging functionality a centralized integration knowledge- and content-management is useful. Beside a more efficient management the benefit of centralizing is the ability to deliver built-in content, such as business scenarios, business process definitions, and mappings.

The integration of internal and external business processes, as well as the realization of ad hoc processes, which have to be implemented quickly (in a few days) in response to changing requirements, will play an important role in the future. In this field, web services will establish themselves as the underlying technology, provided that the security mechanisms for cross-enterprise communications, some of which are currently only partially implemented, can be extended sufficiently to find widespread acceptance.

In the past, individual business processes were supported by separate applications. This has frequently resulted in the creation of isolated solutions which, although internally optimized, contribute insufficiently to overall requirements. The integration technologies that are now available permit a more efficient and simultaneously more flexible integration of the entire existing and future application landscape both within and between companies.

Business process management

Business Process Management (BPM) is a methodology, as well as a collection of tools that enable enterprises to specify step-by-step business processes. Proper analysis and design of BPM flows require a strong understanding of the single business steps that must be performed to complete a business process. As BPM executes a business process, these steps will often correspond to well-known business activities, such as checking credit ratings, updating customer accounts and checking inventory status. Effectively, the BPM process flow is often just a sequence of well-known services, executed in a coordinated way.

An efficient method to design business solutions more flexibly is to separate business process flows from business logic implementation by deploying the SOA (loosely coupled web services) in combination with a process execution language, e.g. BPEL.

BPEL exclusively uses web service interfaces when exporting and importing messages. Separating business process flows from business application logic provides process independence. It defines what needs to be done, when and how, by whom or by which application. This separation-concept enables the integration of business processes, by combining functions from distinguished applications, e.g. representing an optimized workflow of order processing. This separation-concept enables the flexibility to create ad hoc new processes which may increase enterprise's agility farreaching independently from underlying organizational and IT resources that support these processes.

The predecessor of *BPM,* the classic document workflow, focused on humans performing the services. Enabled by the advanced integration of applications, BPM can combine both human and automated agents doing the work to deliver the services but now focussing on the automation part. SOA is an architectural approach that thrives on turning enterprise computing assets into well-defined services. It is a natural fit with BPM because of this reliance on services. SOA exposes services, and BPM, which demands process flow completion, consumes services. If done properly, SOA opens a vast inventory of services for BPM to glue together into a comprehensive flow.

Agility is obvious, flow and service exist independently, and each brings its own flexibility. A flow can be changed and can incorporate new services. New services can be created and then composed via BPM into new composite applications.

Effective BPM solutions return control of business processes back to business people from information technology people. This means that line-of-business managers can change business processes and quickly adapt them to changing market conditions. BPM also provides decision makers with up-to-date business information, allowing them to make better business decisions immediately.

As depicted in chapter 3, forward-looking integration servers offer such BPM modeling and simulation tools as well as workflow engines, which are able to execute business processes.

Web services management

The business oriented management of web services is aimed at supporting critical applications that require enterprises or IT service providers to manage the service platform, the deployment of services, applications, and processes. Web services management products must provide the critical infrastructure necessary for companies to take their fine-grained, atomic web services and other data sources and compose them into coarse-grained business services that make up a service-oriented architecture.

Once web services technology consolidates and an increasing number of web services becomes available the attention of the management issues will be obvious. Enterprises will soon require tools that support and automate their web services management efforts. So far neither the scope nor the standardization in this area has been well defined and developed. However the interest in this area is demonstrated by recent standardization proposals. OASIS therefore has formed the Technical Committee *Web services Distributed Management (WSDM)* [5.3.1] to bring forward the management issue.

Web services management is essential for enterprises, which operate their applications and processes by themselves. But it is even more important for IT and BPO service providers and there are functional extensions needed.

The scope of web services management may comprise:
- Infrastructure and application management
- Monitoring and metrics
- Security and certification services
- Service level agreements, billing and financial services, contract management.

Infrastructure and application-level management are extensions to traditional management functions due to the fact that web services constitute an additional layer on top of state-of-the-art middleware.

Monitoring service execution means monitoring business interactions with partners and customers. Enterprises are under increasing pressure to measure the value of their IT investments and from a business perspective need to gain visibility into IT operations. The holistic view of service interactions is of particular benefit and metrics will help to evaluate and improve web services based business processes.

With an increasing number of published web services from sources that are more or less unknown, security, availability, and trust will become top issues for enterprises. The certification of those services as well as guaranteeing the quality of services may become interesting management subjects for IT and outsourcing service providers. Moreover appropriate service level agreements, billing and financial services, and the management of contracts concerning web services based solutions are challenging new business opportunities for such service providers.

5.4 Forward-looking SOA based application platforms

The major application platform vendors already have adopted the web services technology and currently evolve their platforms to SOA. Examples are shown in the following section.

5.4.1 SAP NetWeaver

SAP's *NetWeaver* platform [5.4.1] is an example of a forward-looking application platform demonstrating the coexistence of both the traditional application world (SAP R/3, mySAP) and the new SOA/web services paradigm.

In the 1990s, SAP captured the leading position in the world market for business software, primarily with its ERP software SAP R/3. By the end of the 90s, this position was threatened by a number of quickly growing software providers with internet-based, enterprise-wide solutions which were initially received very positively by the market (e.g. Ariba, Commerce One, i2, Siebel). SAP responded to this by developing its mySAP technology and then successively extended its offering with CRM, SCM and further components. Today, SAP is recognized as a market leader in these fields of application, too.

The latest challenge now is to implement a service-oriented architecture (SOA) in the future solutions landscape, using web services as the basic technology. SAP has responded to this development firstly by supporting web services in mySAP components and, in autumn 2002, with the announcement of its *xApps* technology. xApps enables cross-functional processes to be generated, based on existing and also on non-SAP systems, which link information and functions of different applications with each other so as to obtain efficiently the required results and workflows.

Enterprise Services Architecture (ESA) and the NetWeaver platform

Following the announcement of its technology platform NetWeaver in 2003, SAP now has enforced end-to-end SOA support and at the same time has undergone a significant shift in its business strategy. On the one hand, SAP has moved into the world of technology and platform providers to be at least partly in direct competition with Microsoft, IBM, BEA, and Sun. On the other hand, SAP is abandoning its old approach of exclusively backing an end-to-end SAP solution world for its customers. SAP is shifting its emphasis much more toward standards (Java, XML, web services) while focusing on the interoperability and integration of NetWeaver platforms and applications with middleware products from strategically important partners, such as Microsoft and IBM.

NetWeaver provides the IT basis for a service-oriented architecture. This is designated by SAP as an *Enterprise Services Architecture (ESA)*. ESA is intended to provide the basis for flexible and extensible business solutions in heterogeneous IT landscapes, but can also be taken as a basic concept for complete business integration. SAP envisages that ESA will extend the web services paradigm to enterprise-class business architecture. In this sense ESA is a blueprint for comprehensive, service-based business applications.

SAP defines ESA as follows:
- ESA empowers all people participating in a business process, both inside and outside the enterprise,
- ESA encompasses all information relevant to the process,
- ESA integrates all systems important to the process – independent of being internal or external, SAP or non-SAP.

ESA enables the design of a complete solution for a process. It provides the architectural framework for process modeling and for the application of web services by integrating them into existing solution landscapes. This should put businesses in a position in which they can adapt business processes quickly and efficiently to change and react flexibly to new market requirements.

In future, all SAP solutions such as SAP R/3 enterprise, all mySAP solutions and all xApps will be developed in line with the ESA concept.

NetWeaver provides SAP with the technological basis it needs to implement the ESA vision. Two aspects of the NetWeaver/ESA concept must be differentiated, in order to understand it as a whole. These aspects are reflected in the combined functionalities of the NetWeaver platform, that is to say, in their variants
- as a runtime and integration platform for existing and new SAP applications,
- as an open interoperability and integration platform with a special focus on interoperability with IBM's WebSphere and Microsoft's .NET technologies.

Runtime and integration platform for SAP solutions

As a platform for all current and future SAP solutions, NetWeaver offers a number of new functions and integration functions that are used in full or in part by the various SAP solutions. This impacts both the further development of SAP R/3 Enterprise versions as well as the mySAP and xApps solutions as shown in figure 5.9.

The *SAP R/3 enterprise* solution will use the new NetWeaver functions (e.g. the portal) via so-called extensions. Solutions based on *mySAP technology*, which are available as isolated solutions (e.g. *mySAP ERP*) or as bundled solutions (e.g. *mySAP Business Suite, mySAP Smart Business Solutions*), will also gradually be able to use the NetWeaver functionality. SAP is expected to define and implement the migration of its solutions to the NetWeaver platform in separate stages in its product and release strategy.

Some of NetWeaver's key functions are also offered as individual components. These key functions include, in addition to the Web Application Server (WAS), the Enterprise Portal Server and the Exchange Infrastructure (XI), additional components used by many SAP applications.

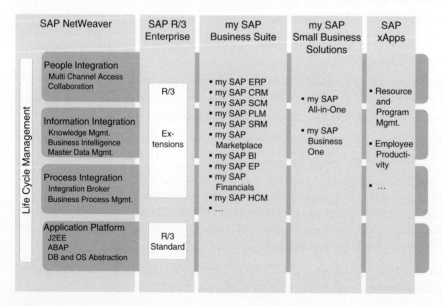

Figure 5.9 SAP NetWeaver

Here is a short description of these key elements:

- Portal infrastructure
  is available as the component *mySAP Enterprise Portal* and enables a unified, personalized and role-based access of users, partners as well as employees to the connected heterogeneous IT-environment.
- Collaboration
  provides the dynamic real-time communication among teams or flexibly established communities. It comprises features such as common access to e-mails, calendar, chat-rooms and storage of commonly used documents.
- Multichannel access
  is part of the component *mySAP Mobile Business* and comprises the connection to the enterprise applications and resources via fixed or wireless networks. It includes voice and data services.
- Knowledge management
  provides user-oriented services, which enable access to the content management system of SAP or third parties. Integrated tools support search, taxonomy, classification and information publishing as well as correlated workflows.
- Business intelligence
  The *mySAP Business Intelligence* component allows the analysis, distribution and integration of relevant information in real-time. It offers a tool set, which relieves the design of interactice, individual reports and applications.
- Master data management
  enables the integrity of data comprising the whole heteregeneous IT infrastructure of an enterprise. It allows the harmonization of the core data over the heterogenous system landscape.
- Exchange infrastructure
  The component *SAP Exchange-Infrastruktur* comprises the *Integration Server* and the *Business Process Management* and provides the necessary integration methods and tools for the integration of SAP applications as well as 3rd party applications. (More details later in this section)
- Application platform
  The component *SAP Web Application Server* is the runtime environment of all SAP applications. It supports SAP's key technologies *ABAP (SAP's object-oriented programming language)* and J2EE. This enables to protect effected investments and in addition provides the openness for future applications based on open standards. An integrated web services framework supports platform-independent web services. The security framework provides features such as single sign-on, role-based authorization, centralized user management, secure and encrypted data exchange and finally support of digital signatures and public key infrastructures.
- Lifecycle management
  This component supports the software-cycles, including design, implementation, test, versioning, maintenance. SAP has decided to take the open-source-framework *Eclipse* as the basis for their Java development environment.

5 Web services

Open interoperability and integration platform

Medium-sized companies and in particular large companies are increasingly opting to use SAP, IBM and Microsoft as their main providers for their technological infrastructure and business solutions. A crucial factor in determining the overall costs is how well middleware and applications of the various manufacturers work together. This is why there has been increased pressure on these three software manufacturers to improve interoperability.

SAP has come up with an effective response to this challenge with its open interoperability and integration platform, NetWeaver. NetWeaver supports important standards promoted by international organizations, such as *W3C*, the *Web Services Interoperability Organization (WS-I)*, the *Java Community Process (JCP)* and *OASIS*.

Furthermore, SAP has negotiated agreements for close cooperation with IBM and Microsoft, to improve the interoperability of their middleware products and technologies. As a result, interoperability components, interfaces, and to a certain extent integration projects will continue to be produced and extended.

As depicted in figure 5.10 the interoperability efforts with *IBM WebSphere* and *Microsoft .NET* encompass joint support of important interoperability standards as well as interoperability on different levels:

– Application and development platform
  Like the corresponding platforms available from IBM and Microsoft, SAP Web Application Server (WAS) supports a series of open standards (XML, SOAP, WSDL, UDDI etc.). Bidirectional communication to J2EE applications is supported by means of the SAP Java Connector (JCo) and to .NET via the SAP .NET connec-

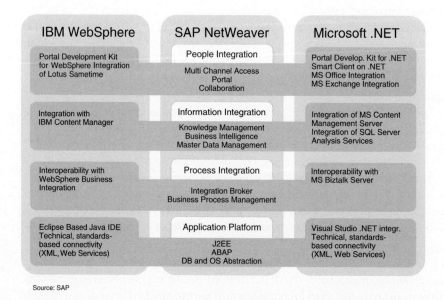

Figure 5.10 NetWeaver – Interoperability with IBM WebSphere and Microsoft .NET

tor. Customers who use WebSphere or .NET can therefore access existing business objects and integrate these in SAP applications. In their Java development environments, SAP and IBM both base their solutions on the Eclipse Open Source framework, thus resulting in greater interoperability with WebSphere Studio Application Developer. The SAP .NET connector also provides support for the Visual Basic development environment.

- Portal level
  SAP will support the recently introduced *WSRP (Web Services for Remote Portlets)* standard and ensure compatibility with the *Java Portlet Standard JSR 168*. In this way, the portal can accept transparent portlets created in other development environments. SAP is developing Portal Developer Kits for IBM WebSphere and Microsoft .NET. This will enable developers to develop portal services in a WebSphere or .NET environment and embed these in the SAP portal. At the same time, SAP has made available XML schemes for some hundreds of BAPIs (proprietary SAP interfaces). This means that the corresponding SAP applications can be easily embedded in WebSphere or .NET environments using Web services.

- Collaboration
  IBM and SAP cooperate on integrating Lotus Sametime (instant messaging, web conferences, and virtual teamrooms). Interaction with data from Microsoft Exchange and Office as well as with Lotus Domino is available already.

- Data, analysis and information tiers
  Microsoft's SQL Server Analysis Services can be used as multidimensional datastores in *SAP Business Warehouse (BW)*. Corresponding management tools are integrated in the two systems. At the metadata level, SAP provides data integration based on *JMI (Java Messaging Interface)* and *XMI (XML Metadata Interchange)*. OLE-DB for OLAP and *XMLA (XML for analysis)* for analytical purposes are also supported.

  SAP KM (Knowledge Management) supports standards for accessing, interacting and preparing unstructured information and provides open APIs that permit connections with other repositories. Integration scenarios involving the SAP KM repository framework and IBM's and Microsoft's content management systems currently are examined.

Exchange Infrastructure

Nevertheless SAP's Exchange Infrastructure constitutes the centerpiece of the NetWeaver interoperability features and particularly comprises the business process management.

The *Exchange Infrastructure (XI)* is SAP's integration server. It forms part of most SAP solutions but can also be obtained as a separate unit in the form of the SAP Exchange Infrastructure.

The Exchange Infrastructure provides a number of adapters for interoperability purposes. These include a JMS adapter for interoperability with *WebSphere Business Integration* (MQSeries), or partner adapters to *Microsoft Message Queuing* (MSMQ) and *BizTalk*. As of 2004 it provides an adapter framework based on the *Java Connector*

5 Web services

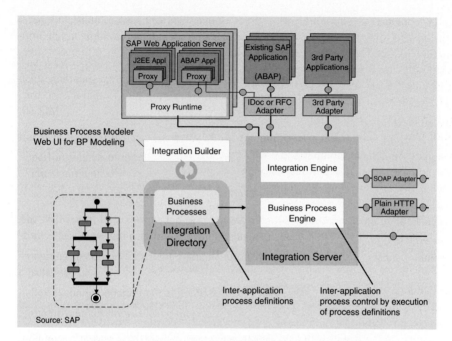

Figure 5.11 SAP Exchange Infrastructure – Business process management

Architecture (JCA). It will be possible to integrate third-party JCA adapters into this framework, for example those supplied by IBM which already offers a number of them. However, SAP does not intend to develop these adapters.

As shown in figure 5.11 the Exchange Infrastructure consists of the integration server runtime system and the associated integration knowledge that is stored in the Integration Directory and Integration Repository. The integration server conducts XML/SOAP-based communication between application components from various SAP sources or sources from other suppliers.

The integration directory contains information that is required at runtime, for example interfaces such as *BAPIs, IDocs, (i.e. SAP proprietary interfaces), RFCs (Remote Function Calls)*, mappings, routing rules, addresses and workflows. Integration scenarios and business processes are stored in the integration repository during development. The repository already contains a range of scenarios and processes for the integration of SAP applications. Partners and customers may add others as required, including third-party applications.

The Exchange Infrastructure runs only on SAP's Web Application Server but is increasingly being positioned as an open integration platform, e.g. through support for the industry standard *RosettaNet, Chemical Industry Data Exchange (CIDX)* or *Petroleum Industry Data Exchange (PIDX)*. Moreover it supports an open adapter framework based on JCA, and may include partner profiles in the integration directory and offers a connection tool for SMBs (Small and Medium Business).

The major functional extension of the latest release consists of the advanced business process management. It now permits the combination of applications to form so-called adaptive processes which can comprise an entire value-added chain.

The BPM consists of the following components: Integration Builder, Integration Repository, Integration Directory, and Business Process Engine.

The Integration Builder is SAP's process modeling tool, supports BPEL, permits the import and export of process definitions and enables the integration of business scenarios and business processes. As already mentioned scenarios and processes are stored in the Integration Repository. The Business Process Engine forms part of the XI Integration Server and controls the process steps in accordance with the flows defined in the Integration Directory.

An open issue is how secure cross-enterprise processes can be implemented.

xAPPS

xApps are a new breed of applications, embedded in the NetWeaver platform, that are designed to enable both business improvement and innovation. With abilities to combine existing heterogeneous systems into cross-functional, end-to-end processes, xApps may align people, information, and business processes for increased competitive agility. It means greater agility for adapting to changing business realities spanning corporate units and business partners. It also means to get the most out of what already exists: employees, knowledge, products, business relationships, IT solutions and other assets.

Developed by SAP but also by selected partners, xApps will target cross-functional business processes. xApps families will include e.g. enterprise change management, product portfolio management, employee relationship management, and employee services automation, to name only a few, and the families are expected to grow rapidly. Furthermore xApps are becoming a promising way to implement best-of-breed applications.

The design targets of the xApps paradigm have been
- to snap in existing infrastructure with different back-end systems
- to take full advantage of the evolving NetWeaver platform
- to guarantee consistency across user experience as well as across objects and services that are stored underneath
- to support semi-structured or ad hoc processes.

The architectural approach of xApps comprises
- a model-driven approach. Everything is modeled in one single repository and then the code is generated out: the UI, the integration proxies, the content of all other repositories that are able to be integrated. In that way new platform features can easily be adopted.

- the service-oriented architecture, which enables xApps to use existing business objects, application logic, persistence services, processes, workflows and user interfaces.
- a pattern based approach for interface design. Familiar patterns increase consistency, improve the user experience and ease the application design.
- a standardized object access including lifecycle services and services like search, classify, etc. From a programming point of view this provides a high level of productivity.

As a summary, at design time xApps developers can use the existing NetWeaver tools, such as UI modeler, process and workflow modeler, business object modeler, service modeler, while at run time they can take advantage of the NetWeaver features and services such as knowledge management or business process management.

Assessment

With its NetWeaver platform, SAP has chosen a course of action that will take the open nature of SOA into account while ensuring the long-term uniform implementation of this architecture in all SAP applications.

SAP is on its way to become completely independent of middleware from other manufacturers (e.g. BEA WebLogic, IBM WebSphere), with its NetWeaver technology platform. This independence on the one hand ties up development resources, since SAP will have to develop competitive middleware components itself. On the other hand, all SAP solutions will only be based on one platform in the future, no matter whether it will be J2EE or ABAP; this will save development and test resources and be strategically of importance.

In an upcoming modularized application world based on SOA and web services SAP can even be expected to market its NetWeaver technology platform as an open platform independently of SAP applications. Deploying NetWeaver's platform services, such as the application, portal and XI server, enables enterprises to integrate whatever offered web services to support their business processes as flexibly as possible.

SOA undoubtedly will set in motion the market for innovative solutions and services and offer new opportunities to niche players with very specialized or innovative services. This means increasing competition for SAP in terms of solutions, but on the other hand gives SAP the opportunity to offer its own web services as standard network services that can be used regardless of the platform deployed. SAP should be in a good position to do this, considering its existing application and process expertises.

5.4.2 Other vendor's platforms

Technologies and architectures such as XML, web services, SOA and BPM have changed significantly application platforms of all major software vendors in the past years. Besides SAP particularly Microsoft and IBM offer comprehensive middleware platforms suitable for forward-looking e-business solutions with properties and features described in this chapter.

5.4 Forward-looking SOA based application platforms

In the following just a few highlights are mentioned.

Microsoft

As depicted previously Microsoft [5.4.2] has been one of the two outstanding promoters (IBM is the other) of web services technology and standards from the beginning. Therefore the .NET framework has incorporated XML and web services technology from the design. Furthermore Microsoft has defined service-oriented application architecture for .NET, which comprises:

- UI components
  UI (User Interface) components form the interface to the end user. This can be a web application or a Windows application. User interfaces are created using ASP.NET WinForms and/or WebForms, with functions for server-side controls, plausibility checks, rendering and data formatting.
- UI process components
  In many cases, user interaction with the system follows a defined process sequence. As an example users first enter their order information (product selection, quantity) then define the payment method (bank details, account number) and finally provide delivery information (required delivery date, shipping address). UI Process Components can be used to synchronize and orchestrate these logically harmonized sub-steps. Process flow and state management are then no longer hardwired into the user interface.
- Service interfaces
  To make business logic available in the form of a service, a service interface is provided. The service interface describes issues such as format, protocol, security and exception handling and can be used by a number of other service users.
- Business workflows
  Many business processes comprise a number of steps which have to be carried out in the correct sequence. Business workflows define and coordinate long-running, multi-step business processes and can be implemented using business process management tools such as BizTalk Server Orchestration.
- Business components
  Business components can be used to map business rules or to carry out specific business-related tasks. Business components implement and represent the business logic of the application.
- Business entities
  In many applications, data must be transported from one layer to another. The data represent real-world business entities, such as products or orders. The business entities used internally in the application generally employ data structures such as ADO.NET DataSets, DataReaders or XML Streams.
- Data access components
  In most applications, data sources (databases) must be accessed. For reasons of improved scalability, configurability and ease of maintenance, data access functions should always be implemented in a separate layer.

– Service agents
   If a business component requires information from an external service, the communication interface must be supplied with data correctly. Service agents hide the often rather complicated communication interface in an external service and can take over data format mapping if the user's application is using other data formats than the external service.

Microsoft has consolidated its .NET Enterprise Servers under the brand name *Windows Server System 2003*. The Application Infrastructure contains *SQL Server, Content Management Server, Commerce Server, BizTalk Server* and *Host Integration Server*. The Information Worker Infrastructure comprises *Project Server, Exchange Server* and *SharePoint Portal Server*. The IT Infrastructure contains: Internet Security & Acceleration Server, Systems Management Server, Application Center and Operations Manager.

An example of the seamless integration of systems and services, being disjointed until now, is the access to *Amazon.com* from *Microsoft Office System*. While working with Office, users can get access to Amazon's products directly without opening a web browser. The integration is achieved through Amazon's web services so that users can access Amazon from the Research Task Pane, available in the Microsoft Office 2003 Edition. Users will be able to access information at Amazon and buy items without launching a browser or closing the Office document, e-mail message or presentation application they are using at the same time. The applications will also allow users to add footnotes, bibliography entries or book cover art from Amazon into Microsoft documents without having to do so manually.

The Research Task Pane uses XML to allow retrieval and navigation of web-based information from within Office programs. It is a feature of the desktop applications Word and Excel; Outlook messaging and collaboration software; PowerPoint; Access; OneNote, which enables note taking; and Publisher and Visio drawing and diagramming software.

IBM

IBM is today the market leader for J2EE application server with its *WebSphere product family*. As a pure middleware vendor IBM focuses on mission-critical middleware such as portal server, application server, integration server including BPM, on interoperability with other platforms based on standards, as well as on cross-company business transactions including security aspects and cross-company business processes. IBM's focus on technology and standardization has been web services and business integration for the recent years.

The WebSphere application server provides the J2EE technology-based platform integrated with tools that support web services standards, such as SOAP, UDDI, and WSDL [5.4.3]. The incorporation of web services enables to build WebSphere software applications that dynamically interact with web services using SOAP, UDDI, WSDL, and XML. Web services made available by other vendors can also be incorporated. Furthermore the WebSphere Application Server administrator manages the security and lifecycle attributes of these services. WebSphere as well enables the transformation of existing applications into web services.

As the WebSphere family comprises portal, application and integration server it constitutes a rich application platform based on SOA and web services technology, including BPM. IBM WebSphere Application Server is a high-performance and scalable transaction engine for dynamic e-business applications. The Open Services Infrastructure allows companies to deploy a core operating environment that works as a reliable foundation capable of handling high volumes of secure transactions and web services.

5.5 Summary and recommendations

For the first time in IT history, a new architecture (SOA) is being jointly promoted by different technology proponents (Microsoft on the one hand, Sun/IBM on the other) as well as by application vendors (SAP, Siebel, etc.). It is worth noting that the market leaders (IBM, Microsoft, and SAP) are obviously closing ranks very tightly. IBM, Microsoft and SAP are expected to deliver the interoperability services they have announced, both in their own interests and in the context of their customer requirements. This will strengthen the positions of the three market leaders and create a new triumvirate of power that will place other competitors in a difficult situation.

However enterprises' focus will shift from the platform and middleware to business process integration and to industry-specific applications. In these areas more competition in general and particularly between SAP, IBM and Microsoft can be expected for the next years.

Web services will become mainstream for application deployment and particularly for business process integration. Therefore it is important that enterprises move to understand this technology. Application integration today often managed by point-to-point 'spaghetti' connections will successively be replaced by integration technologies deploying web services.

Enterprises should immediately begin strategic planning for future service-oriented architectures on the foundation of web services including every area of the enterprise infrastructure. Strategic planning will enable them to determine web services classes that are most appropriate for their needs. It is important to point out, that enterprises must make security an integral part of the web services strategy and planning efforts.

In addition enterprises should increase education and development efforts to get familiar with web services standards and technologies and improve their expertise.

For first implementations 'keep it simple' will be the best strategy. Companies are recommended to approach this new technology conservatively by maintaining independence from mission-critical applications.

According to recently published analysis of Meta Group three deployment phases of web services in business solutions are ongoing and expected:

Phase 1 (2003/2004)

Enterprises evaluate the advantages/disadvantages of web services and SOA and assess their existing EAI products and infrastructure. They deploy web services in internal integration projects and implement some non-critical applications based on web services. They start to develop roadmaps and projects to transform existing architecture into SOA.

Phase 2 (2005/2006)

IT budgets will grow again. The majority of enterprises will deploy web services. Web services will not only be applied to basic and static services but will increasingly create a dynamic environment. External partners will be involved and cross-enterprise processes will be supported by web services technology.

Phase 3 (2007/2008)

The paradigm *software as services* will become reality. Web services are capable of composing dynamically adjusted, running applications used by business partners and customers mainly without human intervention. SOA and integrated infrastructure are becoming norm within large enterprises. Late followers will adapt web services, too.

Considering Professional IT Service Provider

It may be assumed that SOA and the web services technology will enforce the outsourcing trend. Moreover the combined capabilities of business process design, business integration and outsourcing might turn out as a key success factor of modern business solutions. Therefore enterprises are recommended to consider taking advantage of professional services of competent IT and outsourcing service providers.

Enterprises should prefer such service providers, which in general have the technological SOA/web services expertise (development, deployment) but in particular also have extensive experiences in the strategic competence areas: process design, business integration, and web services management (infrastructure, applications, monitoring, metrics, security, certification, contracts, SLAs, etc.). Service providers' platform neutrality and interoperability expertises should be of advantage. In addition the service provider should be able to offer demanded outsourcing services.

6 Security focus areas

2005 some 80 percent of all companies will be using the Internet either wired or wireless as an integral part of their business processes. Consequently, many companies will be confronted with the problems of information security that are inexorably linked with the use of the Internet.

As shown in figure 6.1 hackers and system administrators alike were busier than ever in 2003, a year that brought a 68% increase in computer security incidents and vulnerabilities, according to statistics published in February 2004. According to the *Computer Emergency Response Team (CERT)*, the computer security clearinghouse at Pittsburgh's Carnegie Mellon University, 137529 incidents, including web site attacks, malicious viruses and network intrusions, were reported in 2003. The numbers are up from 82094 the previous year, CERT indicates. To put the figures into perspective, incidents reported 2003 accounted for 42% of all attacks reported since 1988, the first year CERT began keeping records [6.1].

There is still a lack of information on how seriously security incidents actually affect business in the short-term and long-term. The estimation of the worldwide economic loss caused by viruses only is in the magnitude of billions of dollars.

It goes without saying that enterprises and credit card organizations and financial service providers in particular have no interest in publishing their real losses caused by security incidents. They certainly would not like to risk their reputations. Experts agree that most security breaches go unreported.

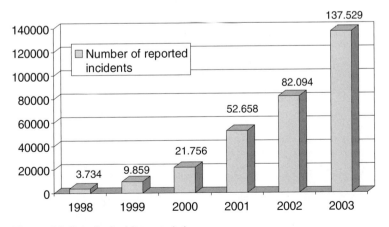

Figure 6.1 Security incidents statistics

6 Security focus areas

6.1 Dangers and vulnerabilities

Cross-company business processes frequently involve enabling access to enterprise networks and resources for customers, business partners and suppliers. Information values that were kept carefully under lock with traditional business solutions are now made accessible.

As depicted in figure 6.2 this obviously involves security risks, since a wide-reaching and open network has a number of potential attack points. The challenges involved with wireless Internet access and the increasing integration of mobile employees, business partners and customers have led to a situation in which deficiencies and security vulnerabilities are rising exponentially. In the world of the service-oriented achitecture and web services technology, characterized by cross-enterprise transactions and independent web service providers, a new dimension of business risks will arise and extended high level security measures will become indispensable.

The more corporate B2C, B2B and B2E business processes rely on open networks, the greater the chance that someone with malicious intent will hack in and damage the systems that run the business. Furthermore, there is no such thing as a typical corporate enemy.

Disgruntled employees and hackers are the most likely sources of attacks, but competitors and even foreign governments may try to breach systems and steal or manipulate crucial information. Espionage of business and technology assets and secrets is the most underestimated threat in the world today.

Most common attacks

Some of the most common attacks are shown in the following representation.

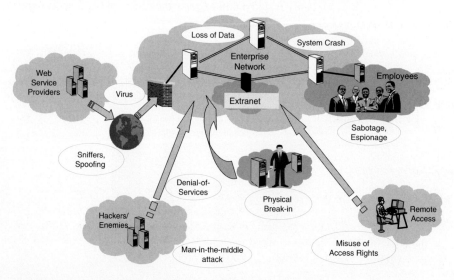

Figure 6.2 Dangers and vulnerabilities in e-business scenarios

6.1 Dangers and vulnerabilities

Viruses

are the most common form of security breach. A virus is a program or piece of code that is loaded onto an organization's computers without its knowledge and that runs against its wishes. Viruses attach themselves to programs or files. Most are self-replicating, quickly using up all available computer memory, and many of them can transmit themselves across networks.

Packet sniffers

A packet sniffer is a software application that uses a network adapter card to capture all packets that are sent across the network. Sniffers are used legitimately in networks today to aid in troubleshooting and traffic analysis. Because several network applications send data in clear text (telnet, FTP, SMTP, POP3, etc.), a packet sniffer can also provide sensitive information such as usernames and passwords.

IP spoofing

An IP spoofing attack occurs when a hacker pretends to be a trusted computer. A hacker can do this in one of two ways: the hacker either uses an IP address that is within the range of trusted IP addresses for a network or an authorized external IP address that is trusted and has access to specified resources on a network. IP spoofing attacks are often a launch point for other attacks. The classic scenario is launching a denial-of-service (DoS) attack using spoofed source addresses to hide the hacker's identity.

Password attacks

Hackers can launch password attacks using several different methods, including brute-force attacks, Trojan horse programs, IP spoofing, and packet sniffers. Although packet sniffers and IP spoofing can yield user accounts and passwords, password attacks usually refer to repeated attempts to identify a user account and/or password. These repeated attempts are called brute-force attacks.

A brute-force attack is often launched using a program that runs across the network and attempts to log in to a shared resource, such as a server. When hackers successfully gain access to resources they have the same rights as the users whose accounts have been compromised. If the compromised accounts have sufficient privileges, the hackers can create back doors for future access without needing to worry about any status or password changes to the compromised user accounts.

Denial-of-services

In a Denial-of-Services (DoS) attack, a hacker gains access to several computers connected to the Internet and installs code on these systems. At the hacker's signal, the systems start to send data to targeted web sites. The sudden burst of network traffic overloads the web servers and the networks they are connected to, slowing performance and eventually crashing the site.

Man-in-the-middle attacks

A man-in-the-middle attack requires that the hacker has access to network packets that come across a network. An example of such a configuration could be someone who is working for an ISP (Interner Service Provider), who has access to all network packets transferred between his employer's network and any other network. Such attacks are often implemented using network packet sniffers and routing and transport protocols. The possible applications of such attacks are theft of information, hijacking of an ongoing session to gain access to private network resources, analysis of traffic to obtain information about a network and its users, denial of service, corruption of transmitted data, and introduction of new information into network sessions.

Physical break-ins

In this attack intruders actually gain access to a data center or steal equipment. Data center security must go beyond a simple lock and key. Data centers may represent the most valuable assets of a company. Stolen laptops and PDAs are a common and costly problem, not only because they are expensive to replace but also because of the proprietary information that may be stored on them.

6.2 Security embedded in e-business solutions

Security and the according methods, measures, techniques and components cannot clearly be distinguished from well defined hardware and software components that are deployed in e-business solutions. Whether considering hardware, software or networks, security is a ubiquitous embedded piece of hardware or software of any mainframes, servers, desktops, laptops, mobile devices, routers, switches, access components, operating systems, middleware, standard applications, vertical applications, web services and business processes. Nonetheless this does not imply that there are in addition some discrete security components such as crypto-boxes or firewalls which have been designed for special purposes as security-appliances.

It is important to point out, that every of the above mentioned components needs to be equiped with proper security features in order to achieve end-to-end security, which is the ultimate requirement for reliable e-business solutions.

6.2.1 The house of e-business security

Enterprises are recommended to build a kind of *house of e-business security* as a prerequisite to achieve end-to-end security with their business processes. Figure 6.3 shows the construction of that house. The *policy* as the foundation defines how to use the business assets and *trust* as the roof of the house, which creates and establishes the confidence among all partners. In the middle of the house are the *goals*, which are intended to reach. Various security *techniques* are used to build that house, but figure 6.3 shows rather the essential techniques than a comprehensive security world.

6.2 Security embedded in e-business solutions

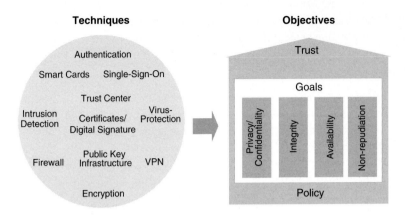

Figure 6.3 The house of e-business security

Security goals

Security in e-business solutions has many different facets, but the main goal is protecting the confidentiality and privacy, integrity, and availability of the information an organization owns or has custody over. A violation of any of these components can quickly put an organization at risk, from a liability perspective as well as in terms of its reputation. In addition non-repudiation is an essential property in the context of e-business transactional applications.

The above qualities are defined as follows:

Confidentiality and privacy

means the prevention of disclosure of sensitive information to unauthorized recipients. Confidential information will be kept secret, with access limited to appropriate persons. Confidentiality reduces or eliminates the risk of financial loss, public embarrassment, or legal liability from unauthorized disclosure of sensitive, critical or personal information.

Integrity

means the completeness and soundness of information. Information will not be accidentally or maliciously altered or destroyed. Integrity ensures that information is authentic and changed only in a specified and authorized manner and by an authorized individual. It reduces or eliminates the risk to the business that critical information can be accidentally or intentionally manipulated.

Availability

refers to the accessibility of systems and information to authorized users. Information and communication services will be ready for use when expected. Availability ensures that systems operate promptly and services are not denied. When systems are available close to 100% of the time, missed opportunities or interruption of operations due to the inaccessibility of information are significantly reduced.

Non-repudiation

means that business partners can trust each other and that business transactions are verifiable. This is a method by which the sender of data is provided with proof of delivery and the recipient is assured of the sender's identity, so that neither can later deny having processed the data.

The importance of policy and trust

Security policy

The security policy is the foundation for secure e-business and m-business transactions. Effective security begins with the articulation of the policies for access to enterprise assets. This articulation defines the proper business use of all asset types (data, applications, etc.) by different categories of enterprise users (sales force, engineers, controllers, marketers, etc.).

Enterprise access policies are even more important in mobile business because of the sheer scale of the challenges. Mobile devices obviously increase the number of devices per user. This means that the number of discrete assets and users to be managed increases exponentially and also that threats to the enterprise increase accordingly.

Comprehensive policy definition and management recognize that employees will have multiple devices and may use multiple network service providers for access to corporate data.

Trust

In today's uncertain economic climate trust is the one thing above all that is needed for business to compete successfully. Confidence is a great enabler, letting exploit new opportunities with e-business – reaching more customers, working more closely with suppliers, empowering employees and driving new revenue streams. But confidence only comes when every participant is convinced that every business related interaction is handled totally secure.

Most common security techniques

Security techniques comprise a wide field of technologies. The *Computer Security Handbook* [6.2.1] is recommended for readers who want to experience a comprehensive view of security techniques, basic technologies as well as a wide field of security related issues.

Over the last decade an evolutionary process has brought out some mature security techniques which are suited to achieve the aforementioned security goals. Among these techniques, the following are the most commonly used with today's business solutions.

6.2 Security embedded in e-business solutions

Authentication

provides a means for identifying an object – a user, a system, an application and so on. After being authenticated, the object can be granted access to the services it requires, and its activities can be monitored. Authentication mechanisms range from the familiar username and password to authentication certificates to sophisticated biometrics systems which authenticate users through physical characteristics such as fingerprints.

Authentication is a foundation of any security implementation, and is often a key part of other security solutions.

Anti-virus software

There are several types of anti-virus software – from solutions that protect individual user devices to those that protect file and messaging servers – and all are necessary in the fight against viruses. An effective anti-virus strategy also includes regular software updates to protect against the latest threats, as well as ongoing education to ensure that users are aware of the dangers and how to avoid them. Most important, the anti-virus strategy must specify standards for desktop configurations and usage. Restricting which software employees are permitted to load on their devices can help prevent viruses from being introduced and can solve breaches more quickly if they occur.

Virtual private networks

Virtual Private Nerworks (VPN) allow remote employees to access the corporate network using the Internet as the transmission medium. Encryption technology and secure tunneling protocols make the network private, even though communication takes place over public phone lines or radio networks. In effect, the VPN makes possible the secure exchange of information across a public network which is indispensable when deploying mobile devices in radio networks.

Firewalls

A firewall examines data as it enters the corporate network and blocks traffic that does not meet specified criteria. There are several types of firewalls, and all can be used in combination. A proxy server intercepts all messages entering and leaving the corporate network and hides the true network address. A packet filter examines data packets entering or leaving the corporate network and accepts or rejects them on the basis of specified criteria. An application gateway secures specific applications. A circuit-level gateway applies security mechanisms when a connection is established; after that, network traffic flows without further checking.

Intrusion detection systems

Applications that actively monitor operating systems and network traffic for attacks and breaches are called *Intrusion Detection Systems (IDS)*. The goal of IDS is to provide a near-real-time view of what is happening on the corporate network. There are two approaches to intrusion detection: network-based and host-based. Network-based systems sniff the wire, comparing live traffic patterns to a list of known attacks. Host-based systems use software agents that are installed on all servers and report activity to a central console. A complete solution involves both types. Both require a regularly updated list of known attacks, just like anti-virus software.

Transport encryption

Transport encryption is implemented in standard transport protocols such as the *Transport Layer Security (TLS)* and the Secure Socket Layer (SSL) protocols used for communication via Internet as well as for the Wireless Transport Layer Security (WTLS) protocol designed for WAP applications in wireless networks. These protocols allow the transmission of messages preventing eavesdropping, tampering or message forgery.

The protocol takes the messages to be transmitted, fragments the data into manageable blocks, optionally compresses the data, applies a hashed message authentication code and then encrypts and transmits the result. The received data is decrypted, verified, decompressed, reassembled and then delivered to higher level protocols.

Data encryption

Data encryption is applied to protect any content (text, data, graphic, voice, video) stored on any device, server or other storage medium and to assure that only authorized people who possess the secret (key) needed for decryption can access and manipulate the content.

Single sign-on

The purpose of Single *Sign-On (SSO)* is that a user can securely access all those – and only those – resources for which he or she is authorized as determined by the security policies, with a single logon regardless of what systems, applications and resources he or she is accessing during a session or a predefined timeframe.

Certificates/digital signature

A trustworthy institution, i.e. a *Trust Center (TC)* or a *Certification Authority (CA)* carries out the assignment of the pair of keys to a particular person, generates the appropriate certificates and distributes them (see public key infrastructure).

Digital certificates are used to generate digital signatures and digital signatures are applied to guarantee data/content integrity. Digital signatures are electronic signatures linked to the signed data in such a way that tampering does not pass unnoticed and the sender can be unequivocally identified. Digital signatures are also used for user authentication. Other forms of electronic signatures, such as PINs, do not protect data integrity. In order to create a digital signature, the signing person uses a private key exclusively owned by him or herself. The private key has a matching public key that can be used to verify the signature.

Public key infrastructure

The *Public Key Infrastructure (PKI)* is an infrastructure used for both authentication and encryption. It combines software, encryption technologies and services to protect network communications and e-business transactions. PKI involves a system of digital certificates – an attachment to an electronic message that can encrypt data and verify that the sender is who he or she claims to be – as well as certificate authorities, a third party that issues the digital certificate. PKI protects information assets by authenticating identity using a digital certificate, verifying integrity by ensuring that messages have not been altered or data corrupted and ensuring privacy by protecting information from interception during transit.

Smartcards

Secrets like private keys are best stored in tamper-resistant moduls. Smartcards are based on such tamper-resistant chip technology that implies hardware and software protection measures and represents a very high security level. Smartcards or processor based chipcards (ICC, Integrated Circuit Card) have been standardized for more than 10 years (ISO 7816). In general the smartcard is a multifunctional tool which makes the smartcard an ideal tool for realizing applications like employee or citizen identity cards that comprise a multitude of applications like admission control for buildings and rooms, cashless staff restaurant payment, user authentication for applications and networks and digital signatures as proof of origin for electronic documents.

6.2.2 The holistic security solution

Most existing information security concepts are primarily tailored to the aspect of IT security. However, technical security solutions are no longer sufficient on their own to deal with future requirements. Technical, personal and operational security measures must be combined in order to implement a truly comprehensive information security policy. This means that all the different perspectives of information security in a company must be taken into account.

Enterprise view

The enterprise view is the perspective of the Chief Executive Officer (CEO). This perspective involves the company as a whole and deals with obligations to employees, shareholders and the public, as well as responsibility for legal compliance. Information security must comply with the higher-level and strategic objectives of the company. One of the important tasks of the CEO includes defining master agreements for dealing with disasters (disaster recovery and business continuity).

Business process owner view

Business process managers are responsible for the efficient and smooth operation of their business processes. To do this, they must recognize the information security risks that could endanger the execution of their business processes. They have to initiate suitable technical, organizational and personal measures to limit these risks.

IT view

The role of the Chief Information Officer (CIO) involves providing IT infrastructures and the associated security measures and services for supporting the business processes and corporate goals of the enterprise. The provision of these infrastructures and services must comply with profitability principles. An efficient solution can be best achieved by avoiding specific isolated solutions. Suitable security architectures and services are needed and a standard security portfolio must be defined. This portfolio must be heavily derived from the company's strategy and the company's business processes in order to comply with present and future information and communication variants.

Information security management system

A holistic approach for information security takes all these different views into account and consists of the following components that can be combined to form a suitable project approach. The objective of an information security management system is to establish corporate assurance on information security and transparency on its current status for senior management.

An *Information Security Management System (ISMS)* consists of a documentation set defining and supporting the business and various information security procedures and processes in different categories (e.g. access control, personal security) which provide guidance to staff and information to senior management on the ongoing effectiveness of the ISMS. To be effective the ISMS must have a manageable size and its boundaries should be clearly defined. Large corporations invariably need to establish many separate ISMSs, each under local management control and direction that are then aggregated on higher levels.

The process of operating a management system with a security focus is very similar to operating a management system with, for example, a quality assurance or environmental focus. Many organizations have an active quality management system which is regularly audited against standards such as ISO 9001. ISO 17799 has enabled this principle to be extended to information security. It is not necessary to achieve formal certification to benefit greatly from implementing the ISMS within an organization. However, unless the implementation of the ISMS is approached in a methodical manner, so that formal certification could be feasible at a later date, the full business benefits are unlikely to be realized.

An information security management system is implemented by identifying the current gaps according to the categories given by the ISO 17799 and defining appropriate actions to achieve the described objectives. A corporate policy that gives direction on the objectives of information security within the company is issued and appropriate bodies are installed (with participation of senior management) to support the ISMS objectives throughout the enterprise.

A holistic security concept considers the different perspectives mentioned above and comprises a portfolio of standardized security architectures, components, services and

6.2 Security embedded in e-business solutions

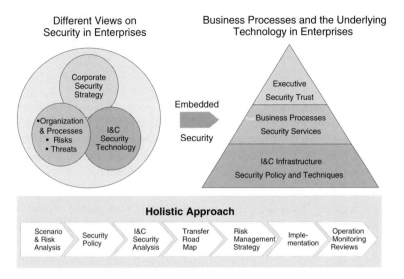

Figure 6.4 The holistic security solution

policies. Based on these concepts, reliable business processes can be implemented along the consult, design, build, operate and manage value-added chain.

Figure 6.4 shows the comprehensive enterprise views, the corresponding, embedded security of the I&C-infrastructure, the business processes and the enterprises executive level as well as the successive steps to accomplish a holistic security solution.

Holistic security solutions should be based on a standard security portfolio and implemented in a business oriented way considering both business scenarios and threat scenarios.

There are various business scenarios of relevance to the present situation such as mobilizing employees, evolving new customer channels, integrating supply chain partners, establishing new offices, incorporate web services and many others.

Threat scenarios consider all types of dangers such as sabotage, espionage, oversight, impairment which could damage enterprise assets, employees or business processes.

Security solutions should be evaluated systematically walking through step by step along the total value chain (consult, design, build, operate and maintain) to establish solutions to safeguard the future.

Typically this may include the following steps and key questions:
- Risk analysis of business processes: What are the values of the business process to be protected? What risks must be guarded against? What are the priorities? What are the principles to follow?
- Security policy for business processes: How should people handle security? Who is responsible for what? What are the auditing, reporting and monitoring measures?

6 Security focus areas

- Security analysis of the existing I&C infrastructure and applications: What is the current security status? What are the weaknesses and threats for which meaningful measures are required? What supplementary measures are needed as a result of the previous evaluations?
- Transfer plan and security roadmap: How does the security strategy influence the transfer plan? What elements should the future security portfolio consist of? How should the appropriate security architecture look like? Which security techniques are preferable? What are the priorities for different scenarios? What benefits and costs can be expected for the individual measures? How should the measures be paid for? Who can implement the measures and when? What are the impacts on the business processes?
- Risk management strategy: What is the procedure for damages not guarded against? How can unforeseeable incidents be handled? What is the escalation procedure?
- Implementation: What is the development process and should it be integrated in the application development process? How far are migration and integration evolved in the ongoing operation?
- Operation, monitoring, reviews, audits, and certifications: How can be assured that the security level is documented accurately and maintained once it has been achieved? How can be assured that proactive and appropriate security requirements will be considered for new scenarios or changing business processes?

The security policy, security roadmap and the risk management are the cornerstones of this process where the top management needs to be involved and where it should clearly define its strategy and prevailing conditions. This will aid in a consistent enterprise-wide understanding which is the basis for deriving appropriate targets and scorecards.

Risk management

Business processes are increasingly dependent on information technology. This trend means that an IT failure can result in high losses or even dramatic consequences for a company.

In the aftermath of September 11th 2001, direct insurers and reinsurers realized that the corporate reliance on international networks opened the way for claims running into the billions. Reinsurers therefore canceled contracts involving insurance against loss of production due to IT crashes. Responsibility for this insurance risk was then shifted to the direct insurers, many of whom likewise considered the stakes to be too high and therefore also canceled their contracts.

The consequences of this development mean that enterprises now carry more responsibility for taking their own precautionary measures and security must be considered in a new light. The IT infrastructure is an essential criterion for the stability and availability of most business processes. Yet increased availability also entails higher IT investment and operation costs. As depicted in figure 6.5, the aim is to achieve cost effective protection, i.e. to find the right balance between under and over protection.

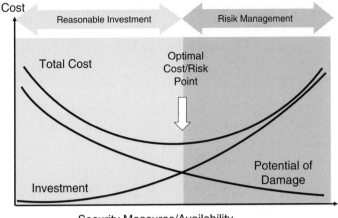

Figure 6.5 The optimal cost/risk point

In this context *desaster recovery* and *business continuity* planning is an essential task for enterprises, which have recognized the importance of risk management.

In general business continuity planning is a three step process:
- Conduct an analysis that defines critical processes, identifies and prioritizes risks to those processes and establishes policies to avoid or mitigate those risks.
- Devise a disaster recovery plan for critical systems and resources. This includes establishing recovery teams, setting up notification procedures, determining meeting sites, tracking inventories of hardware and software, having readily accessible contact information on vendors, and clearly defined back up and recovery techniques.
- Set up intervals of training and testing for the disaster recovery team and the business continuity plan as a way to make revisions and stay confident the plan is battle tested.

Disaster recovery planning is a complex task. However it is important to keep the plan simple and manageable for those that carry it out in cases of emergency.

Dependent on the *security strategy* and *risk assessments*, enterprises must find out the optimal cost/risk point, i.e. how much investment in security measures is reasonable and how to manage the remaining risks. Whereby risk means the evaluation and the weighing up of possible threats and vulnerabilities, to which corporate assets are exposed to.

The diagram in figure 6.6 shows a systematic approach how enterprises can handle and manage risks.

It makes sense to distinguish identified and accepted risks and to assume that there are some risks still not identified. Even if making provisions by appropriate precautions (e.g. reserves), enterprises must be aware that there are the remaining risks: accepted and not identified risks. On the other hand very risky business activities should rather

6 Security focus areas

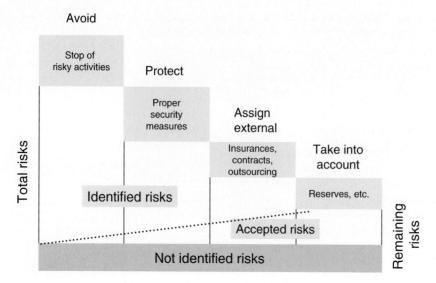

Figure 6.6 The management of risks

be avoided in order to prevent that a company will be threatened in its core business. Very often the major share of the identified risks can be protected by adequate security measures, which include organizational, personal and technical aspects. And finally some of the risks may be recognized to be best covered or managed by insurances or external companies, such as service providers, which offer managed security services or take over the outsourcing of whole business processes.

Managed security services

As *end-to-end-security* with e-business processes is a very complex issue but nonetheless more or less indispensible, the trend to take advantage of *Managed Security Services* has become apparent in recent years. Obviously service providers with special security expertise can do a more competent and reliable security job than enterprises, which core business is e.g. manufacturing or trading.

Experienced security service providers, which offer *Managed Security Services*, can often avoid significant damages by proactively preventing escalating security incidents and thereby save enterprises a lot of money and reputation.

The Slammer Worm is a perfect example. It caused an Internet breach that should have been prevented, because the vulnerability was announced more than six months ago.

In the early morning hours (USA) of January 25th, 2003, network administrators first detected the Slammer Worm. Within minutes, the worm had propagated itself around the world, doubling the number of infected hosts every 8.5 seconds. Within ten minutes of its outbreak, Slammer had infected more than 90 percent of vulnerable hosts. Slammer exploited a six-months-old vulnerability in the Microsoft SQL Server, affecting Windows NT, 2000, and XP systems running unpatched Microsoft SQL Server 2000 and Microsoft Desktop Engine (MSDE) 2000 applications.

The Slammer Worm slowed the Internet to a crawl by generating massive levels of network traffic as it scanned IP addresses. The result was approximately $1 billion in damage due to extensive web and financial network troubles, including ATM networks and credit card validation systems.

By taking advantage of Managed Security Services enterprises in such cases can avoid a lot of hassle.

Offered by a competent service provider Managed Security Services may provide for protecting critical assets dedicated expertises, such as:

- Joint preparation of information security (IS) policies, IS management requirements and IS roadmap, all tailored to the enterprises requirements
- Remotely managed and monitored firewall and VPN solutions to help detect and respond to malicious hacker attacks. Experts may help to establish and maintain adequate configurations to ensure the availability, integrity, and confidentiality of networks and data.
- Real-time security monitoring and expert analysis of alerts. Management may include remote configuration, signature updates system, software support and system upgrades.
- Evaluation and scanning of Internet-exposed systems such as firewalls, web servers, and mail servers to detect viruses, unauthorized access and to prevent tampering or theft.
- Assessment of security configurations against stated policies, helping to eliminate exploitable vulnerabilities that pose a threat to e-business initiatives.

Example: security portfolio of a security service provider

Coming back to the proposed holistic security solution, enterprises should walk through step by step along the total value chain (consult, design, build, operate and maintain) to establish end-to-end security solutions.

Hereby enterprises should consider carefully their different acting options. The first option may consist in providing the total security services by an own organisation, which is fully responsible. Another option could take advantage of Managed Security Services, i.e. the outtasking or outsourcing of defined security services with service level agreements. The next option is the business process outsourcing, which means that a service provider takes over the full responsibility for e.g. human resource processes or other support processes including end-to-end security. In this case an enterprise can better focus on its core business processes. A further option finally is the strategic outsourcing, which means that the service provider takes over the total I&C activities including any assets, contracts and employees. Furthermore any combinations of these options are conceivable.

Corresponding to these options various security service providers offer their different services to the market. The ones primarily offer security products and related services such as e.g. Entrust or Symantec, the others provide business process solutions with embedded security and related services such as e.g. IBM Global Services or Siemens Business Services.

6 Security focus areas

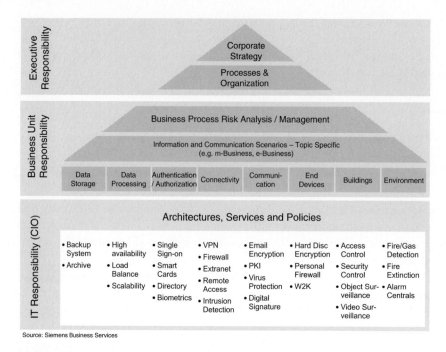

Figure 6.7 Security portfolio

The latter persues the idea of a holistic security solution and offers services along the total value chain, consult, design, build, operate and maintain. As an example the security portfolio of Siemens Business Services [6.2.2] is shown in figure 6.7.

This portfolio addresses the three levels of different responsibility of enterprises: IT responsibility (CIO), Business Unit responsibility and Executive responsibility.

The CIO level portfolio comprises the I&C security architectures, services, policies and products spanning from back up systems via smartcards, VPNs, digital signatures, PKI, intrusion detection, single sign-on, etc. to the surveillance of buildings and fire/gas detection. Security technology and product partners of Siemens Business Services cooperate with these security offerings.

The portfolio for the Business Unit level takes into account the various business scenarios as well as the specific communication, access, device, processing, environmental, etc. needs and provides enterprises with methods and services for risk analysis and management.

Finally the offerings for the Executive level include the development of a security strategy that is aligned with the strategy of the company as a whole and deals with obligations to employees, shareholders and the public, as well as with the responsibility for legal compliance. Furthermore it includes the definition of master security processes and organizational responsibilities.

An example of a security services provider with an interdisciplinary portfolio is the Institute for Secure Telecooperation (SIT[6.2.2]) of the Fraunhofer Gesellschaft in Ger-

6.2 Security embedded in e-business solutions

many. SIT combines its own competence of IT and telecommunication technologies with the social, economical, organizational and jurisprudential competence of partners from research, industry and government to produce solutions which are legally and socially compatible, and thus widely acceptable.

6.2.3 Relevant focus areas

As carried out in the previous section e-business security is an issue with various facets and many subjects of importance that companies need to understand and to make decisions about. Examples such as the implementation of a PKI or a cross-enterprise identity management including customers, partners and employees may illustrate the wide scope. The three security topics depicted in figure 6.8 belong to the focus areas of most enterprises today.

Mobile security

Although wireless Internet applications are taking off more gradually than early marketing might have forecast, the trend towards more ubiquitous access to corporate data via the Internet will grow as wireless device technologies, bandwidth, and particularly security improve. However, wireless access raises security challenges beyond those normally encountered with wireline business on the Internet.

The individual security and reliability of any single piece of equipment, subsystem or process remain mandatory. What matters ultimately is end-to-end trust, reliability and confidentiality of the transaction that employees, customers, partners or suppliers have access to. The requirement for end-to-end security measures and integrated risk assess-

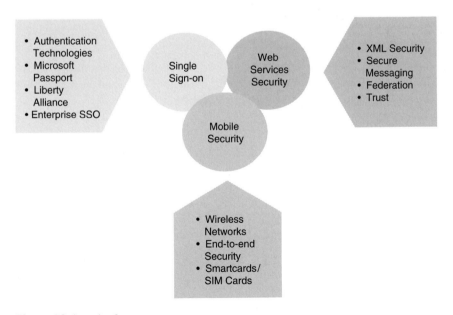

Figure 6.8 Security focus areas

ment is therefore obvious. The complexity and interdependence of e-business transactions have become so critical that transactions must be managed and secured as a whole.

Mobile business processes pose new challenges for enterprises. Securing data and transactions from the wireless device, through the air, through carrier links, over the Internet, and onto the protected server involves bringing together security issues at multiple levels. Smartcards and SIM cards might be valuable components to meet such challenges. Details are covered in section 6.3.

Single sign-on

IDC estimates that the number of Internet users worldwide will double between 2001 and 2006, increasing from 500 millions to 1 billion. However the reality shows that there is a growing gap between business openness, the increasing needs of access that companies face with their customers and partners, and the existing firewall IT-infrastructure, which is not capable to manage these future security requirements.

Customers, supply chain partners and employees need to communicate and share information on an immediate basis no matter what time of the day and where in the world offices or workers are located. But it is important that this has to be carried out in a confident, secure and highly available manner.

For the various user groups with very different business-profiles authentication and authorization must provide appropriate protection to resources in a cost-effective and manageable manner. Web based single sign-on authentication systems reduce management costs significantly and moreover enhance the user's experience by avoiding the omnipresent passport hassle.

The strength of authentication that is required depends on the risks associated with the business process, service, application or system to which authenticated access is requested as well as the costs of mitigating those risks.

Two classes of web based single sign-on platforms can be distinguished: Internet SSO-services such as Microsoft Passport or the Liberty Alliance Project and enterprise SSO-services, which are embedded in the enterprises' application platforms.

The details are covered in section 6.4

Web services security

The benefit of having a loosely-coupled, language-neutral, platform-independent way of linking applications within organizations, across enterprises, and across the Internet deploying web services are becoming more and more evident. However in the past, security concerns were the main inhibitor of the widespread deployment of web services.

A framework of security standards for web services has been worked out recently, not yet finished, but applicable products based on XML-security have been available on the market in the meantime.

Web services security provides a general-purpose mechanism for associating security tokens with SOAP messages in order to guarantee reliable messages.

Trust will play a central role with web services as associated partners may not know each other. Trust covers the model for establishing both direct and brokered trust relationships including third parties. Trust policy and how to construct federated trust scenarios are the top challenges. Details are covered in section 6.5.

6.3 Mobile end-to-end security

Modern e-business architectures will migrate toward integrated e-business and mobile-business architectures by supporting devices via both traditional wired and wireless networks. For the foreseeable future, mainstream m-business enterprise solutions will consist of integrating m-business into existing e-business architectures.

The front-end platform (web server/mobile access/portal server) supports both wireline and wireless devices as shown in figure 6.9. This platform can be described as a unified platform as it enables wireline and wireless access and it hosts a portal which is common to both wired and wireless channels of communications. The front-end platform provides interfaces to back-end systems, application servers, databases and other enterprise resources such as legacy systems and directory services. In addition, further interfaces to external services such as a banking payment system may be implemented. For example, the unified platform might connect a user to a banking payment system regardless of whether he or she is sitting at the computer or using a smartphone to shop on the go.

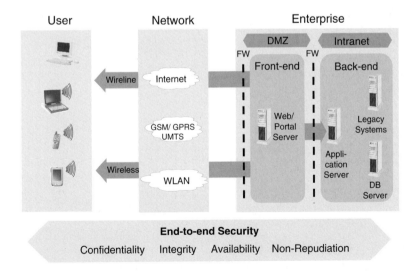

Figure 6.9 E- and m-business security architecture

6 Security focus areas

Front-end servers are usually located in the so-called *Demilitarized Zone (DMZ)* with a firewall to protect against unauthorized access through the open networks. Further firewalls may protect back-end systems, the Intranet or special enterprise network segments depending on the chosen security topology.

6.3.1 Network channels

Risks are inherent in any wireless technology. Some of these risks are similar to those of wired networks, some are exacerbated by wireless connectivity. The obvious source of risks in wireless networks is that the technology's underlying communications medium, the airwave, is somehow open to intruders.

The loss of confidentiality and integrity and the threat of denial of service (DoS) attacks are risks typically associated with wireless communications. Unauthorized users may gain access to enterprise systems and resources, corrupt the data, consume network bandwidth, degrade network performance or launch attacks that prevent authorized users from accessing the network.

Typical threats and vulnerabilities to wireless networks include the following:

– Unauthorized access to an enterprise's network through wireless connections, bypassing any firewall protections
– Sensitive information that is not encrypted (or that is encrypted with poor cryptographic techniques) and that is transmitted between two wireless devices may be intercepted and disclosed
– DoS attacks directed at wireless connections or devices
– Steal of the identity of legitimate users and masquerade as them on internal or external corporate networks

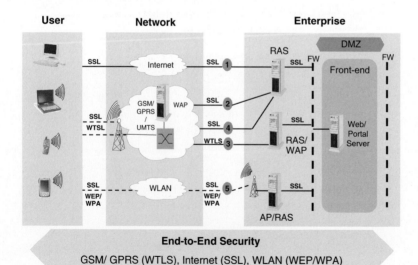

Figure 6.10 Secure network channels

- Sensitive data being corrupted during improper synchronization
- Malicious entities violate the privacy of legitimate users and track their movements
- Misuse of third-party, untrusted wireless network services to gain access to enterprises' network resources
- Internal attacks via ad hoc transmissions

Concerning the wireline and wireless transmission protocols five different network channels to access a front-end can be distinguished as shown in figure 6.10. In any case the enterprise dial-in is controlled by a *Remote Access Server (RAS)*.

Wireline Access via SSL/TLS (Channel 1)

Security transport services for wireline devices such as PCs and laptops are provided by the standard Internet protocol *SSL/TLS (Secure Socket Layer/Transport Layer Security)*. HTTPS (HTTP secure) connections use this protocol regardless of the mediating Internet service provider. However in order to guarantee a high level secure connection during the dial-in procedure and for others than web applications, a VPN (usually based on the IPSEC standard) must be established between the client and the target front-end. VPN includes client/server authentication and secure tunneling via encryption of the transmitted messages.

Access via GSM, GPRS, UMTS with WAP devices (Channel 2)

Global networks such as GSM, GPRS and UMTS operate with different standards, protocols and qualities of service and differ in their security characteristics.

GSM networks, for example, have embedded security architecture but use short voice encryption keys (64-bit), a weak encryption algorithm, and do not support encryption of SMS messages. Moreover there are no integrity checks and user authentication cannot prevent man-in-the-middle attacks. Therefore additional security measures are required for a secure transmission over the air to the Internet.

WAP (Wireless Application Protocol) phones or mobile devices with a WAP browser are switched to the front-end of an enterprise via the WAP gateway, usually located at the network operator's site.

The client is connected by securing the transmission path from the client to the WAP gateway via the wireless network as well as from the WAP gateway to the front-end via the Internet.

WTLS (Wireless Transport Layer Security) is the standard security protocol for managing secure WAP connections via the wireless network (See later in this section for more information). WTLS provides features such as data encryption, data integrity, and client/server authentication.

The *WAP standard* [6.3.1] has defined three security classes for mobile device communication with a WAP gateway:

- Class 1: Data encryption (*WAP 1.1*)
- Class 2: Server (gateway) authentication (*WAP 1.1*)

– Class 3: Client (mobile device) authentication (*WAP 1.2*)

Appropriate features and services for the second transmission path are provided by the standard Internet protocol SSL/TLS.

Because WTLS has been optimized for use over narrow-band communication channels, it is not compatible with SSL/TLS, i.e. it provides different encryption algorithms.

This incompatibility means that the data is exposed briefly during the process of converting the WTLS protocol into TLS/SSL and vice versa in the WAP gateway, thus leaving open the possibility of a security breach, especially for staff physically operating the WAP gateway system. Even if both the wireless network and the Internet each have high-performance security mechanisms, additional measures such as service level agreements with a network operator are required for end-to-end security.

Access via enterprise WAP gateway (Channel 3)

The security risks outlined above have prompted some enterprises (i.e. banks) to operate their own WAP gateway in a trusted environment which they can control themselves. In this case the network operator's mobile switching center can switch the device directly to the enterprise's WAP gateway. Security services are also provided by WTLS and SSL/TLS protocols.

Access via GSM, GPRS, UMTS with IP devices (Channel 4)

There is an increasing range of GSM/GPRS/UMTS-capable wireless IP devices with HTML browsers (i.e. laptops, PDAs, smartphones). The WTLS protocol is usually not applied to these devices. End-to-end security on the transport level is instead achieved by the SSL/TLS protocol and/or a VPN.

Access via WLAN (Channel 5)

Mobile devices with a WLAN network access (802.11x, Wi-Fi) are connected to the target front-end via the wireless access point (WLAN AP) located somewhere in a hotspot area such as an airport or in a wireless area of an enterprise. These devices partly obey the *Wired Equivalent Privacy (WEP)* standard, an encryption mechanism between the device and the access point. However the standard contains some major security weaknesses to do with static keys, short key lengths, handling of larger configurations and changing of access points during user's movements. That is why additional VPNs are essential for these network configurations.

More recently shipped WLAN components apply the *WPA (Wi-Fi Protected Access)* standard [6.3.2], which has been defined by an industry-consortium and address all known weaknesses of WEP. WPA must be seen as an interim standard. It improves security and includes some work which already has been done by the *IEEE 802.11i* Task Group. It currently defines a standard called *RSN (Robust Security Network)* intended for a (real) secure future WLAN. However components, that will apply 802.11i are expected to be available not before late 2004 or 2005.

6.3 Mobile end-to-end security

Compared to WEP, WPA Version 1 will include improvements, such as dynamic keys, improved message integrity checks, automated key management services, cypher and authentication negotiation services. WPA Version 2, available 2004, will replace the currently used RC4 encryption engine with *AES (Advanced Encryption Standard)* and will also support pre-authentication and roaming.

Using WPA on enterprise WLANs will reduce the need for additional protection mechanisms such as VPNs, at least for some business scenarios, though these will still be necessary when using a public network.

On the transport layer WLAN HTTPS connections are secured like wireline configurations by applying the SSL/TSL protocol on both the server and the client side.

Other network channels

Mobile networks such as DECT and Home RF are not covered in this book as these technologies are usually not applied in sensitive business data applications.

Bluetooth on the other hand has the potential to become the standard for ad hoc networks which will play an important role in business scenarios. The Bluetooth security is not just a simple issue and the standard includes five different security profiles: the device discovery application profile, the headset profile, the dial-up networking profile, the LAN access profile and the synchronization profile. Therefore the details are not covered here, but may be looked up in the Bluetooth Security White Paper [6.3.3].

Though the standard already defines security features for authentication and encryption that are adequate for many business applications, Bluetooth networks cannot be recommended to be deployed in highly sensitive business solutions or for access to protected Intranet resources, because there are still some security weaknesses. While encryption is robust, the challenge is in the initial authentication of a device, where there is a reliance on a possibly insecure exchange of secret keys.

Hopefully this may change within the next years if Bluetooth will become an official IEEE standard. The Working Group 802.15.1 is currently evaluating how to improve the Bluetooth security, e.g. by supporting digital certificates and PKI.

6.3.2 End-to-end secure application platform

As mentioned previously, particular attention must be paid to ensure that *end-to-end security* is fully embedded in modern application architectures and platforms as shown in figure 6.11. This includes wired and wireless devices, Internet/Intranet and mobile networks, gateways, web, portal and application servers as well as legacy systems, database servers and other enterprise resources.

The achievement of end-to-end security requires the implementation of several security techniques in any of the platform elements. The range covers from authentication to PKI as depicted in figure 6.11. In the following the security requirements for the different platform elements are described.

6 Security focus areas

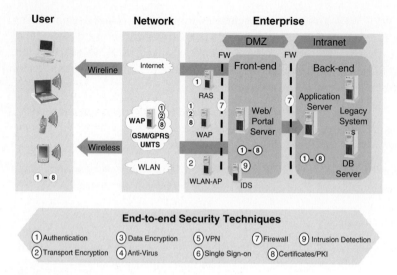

Figure 6.11 End-to-end secure application platform

Mobile devices

Enterprises and consumers will seek a variety of devices depending on price, functionality, and specific features optimized for data and voice applications.

Over a period of time, competing platform technologies such as Palm OS, Microsoft's Mobile Windows (and Pocket PC, Smartphone), Symbian and even Linux will flood the marketplace. New technologies such as Sun's J2ME (Java 2 Micro Edition) and Microsoft's .NET Compact Framework probably have the potential to change existing application paradigms. In particular the download capability of objects and applets as well as interfaces for invoking XML web services directly might provide new application potentials but also raise additional security issues.

In general there are some additional security concerns with mobile devices:

– The small size and mobile use make them more likely to be stolen or lost.
– Employees often purchase and use mobile devices without notifying the CIO organization.
– Wireless handheld devices are often used for both personal and business data. Users that purchase these devices on their own often do not consider the security implications of their use in the work environment.
– Many users have limited security awareness or training with the use of handheld devices and are not familiar with the potential security risks introduced by these devices.
– Mobile device users can download a number of programs, games, and utilities, including freeware and shareware program from untrusted sources. These downloads may contain Trojan horses or other malicious code that can affect the user's mobile device, the user's PC through synchronization, or the enterprise network resources.

6.3 Mobile end-to-end security

Technically a distinction can be made between WAP devices (mobile phones, PDAs) and TCP/IP devices (PDAs, laptops). Security techniques and features differ for these categories as demonstrated in the following.

WAP devices

The WAP Forum has defined standards that take account of the restricted technology of WAP devices. Published specifications include *WAP 1.1* (1999), *WAP 1.2.1* (2000), *WAP 2.0* (2002).

Included in the WAP standard are security specifications for *WTLS*, *WMLScript Crypto Library* and *WIM/WPKI*, which cover authentication, transport encryption, certificates, digital signature and PKI support.

WTLS Class 1 defines mechanisms for key exchange and data confidentiality and integrity.

In addition to class 1 mechanisms, *WTLS Class 2* also defines mechanisms for certificate based server (WAP gateway) authentication.

In addition to class 2 mechanisms, *WTLS Class 3* also defines mechanisms for certificate based client (WAP device) authentication.

WMLScript Crypto Library specifies the library interface to provide persistent authentication for transactions that may occur during a WTLS connection. This is required in many applications, for example e-commerce, where constant proof is needed that someone has authorized a transaction. The way to provide such proof called *signText* in the standard is to associate a digital signature with the data generated as the result of a transaction, such as a purchase order.

The server must have access to a user's certificate in order to verify the digital signature. The server can do this in several ways:

– The certificate is appended to the signature.
– The public key hash is appended to the signature. The server is able to fetch the corresponding certificate from a certificate service.
– A URL of the certificate is appended to the signature. The server is able to fetch the certificate using the Internet.
– The server knows the user certificate based on a previous data exchange.

The *WIM (Wireless Identity Module)* is used in performing WTLS and application level security functions, and especially to store and process information needed for user identification and authentication. The functionality is based on the requirement that sensitive data, especially keys, can be stored in the WIM, and all operations where these keys are involved can be performed in the WIM.

A basic requirement for WIM implementation is that it is tamper-resistant. This means that certain physical hardware protection is used which makes it impossible to extract or modify information in the module. The technology used in smartcards is an example of this kind of protection. Regular mobile phones and PDAs cannot be considered tamper-resistant. Extracting information from the module with these devices may be difficult but still possible with proper equipment.

The WIM usually is implemented on a smartcard. The WIM is defined as an independent smartcard application, which makes it possible to implement it as a WIM-only card or as a part of multi-application card containing other card applications, such as the SIM.

For WTLS, the WIM is used for the following purposes:
- performing cryptographic operations during the handshake, especially those used for client authentication
- securing long-term WTLS secure sessions

The WIM is used to protect permanent, typically certified, private keys. The WIM stores these keys and performs operations using these keys. The operations are:
- signing operation for client authentication when needed for the selected handshake scheme
- key exchange operation using a fixed client key
- the private keys never leave the WIM.

Application level security operations that use the WIM include signing and unwrapping of a key. Both these operations use a private key that also never leaves the WIM. These operations are meant to be generic in order to serve any applications defined in WAP (e.g. using WMLScript) or outside WAP.

A key must be unwrapped when an application receives a message key enciphered with a public key that corresponds to a private key in the WIM.

Digital signatures may be used for authentication or non-repudiation purposes (e.g. to sign a document or confirm a transaction = signText operation). A separate key is usually used for non-repudiation purposes and the user is requested to enter authentication information (PIN) for every signature made.

As well as WTLS and WAP application layer security, the WIM may also be used to secure non-WAP applications that require a tamper-resistant device to perform the following functionalities:
- Signing for authentication purposes (e.g. SSL, TLS)
- Signing for non-repudiation purposes (e.g. S/MIME)
- Private key decryption (e.g. S/MIME)
- Storage of user certificates (e.g. SSL, TLS, S/MIME)
- Storage of trusted CA (Certification Authority) certificates (e.g. SSL, TLS, S/MIME, Java security)

The deployment of WIM and certificates requires a public key infrastructure which is specified in the WPKI standard.

As well as these security features defined by standards, additional features may also be implemented depending on the range of *SDKs (Software Development Kit)* offered by the device vendors. This means that data encryption, VPN or single sign-on might be implemented if the device is capable of such functions and this security feature is required by the IT-organisation.

TCP/IP devices

This device category is currently represented by laptops and PDAs. More and more mobile phones with the standard WAP 2.0 implementation will be part of this category also.

The main operating systems in this category are Windows XP for Laptops as well as Palm OS and Windows CE.NET (with its derivations: Pocket PC and Smartphone) for PDAs. Symbian may be dominating in the smartphone class and Linux may increase its marketshare in this category in the long term.

The integrated security features of these operating systems have improved generally in the recent years but often are not sufficient to allow access to an enterprise's Intranet resources.

Because of the different OS types and versions and the still short product lifecycles, it does not make sense to take a closer look here to the respective security features. The details may be captured from vendor's actual product information or from security white paper, such as *Security on the Pocket PC* [6.3.4] and *Handheld security for the mobile enterprise, Palm OS* [6.3.5].

Instead table 6.1 shows the required security functions, needed for business applications, distinguishing two different protection levels and considering Windows Mobile and Palm OS. However this should be taken only as a proposal that will help to give orientation for IT organizations. In a real security project enterprises must weigh up carefully risks against measures and may come out with different results.

Table 6.1 Required security features of PDAs

Security Level/ Security Features	Secure Access	Confidential Access	Remarks
Local authentication Pin, Password Biometrics	√ Nice to have	√ Nice to have	7 or more characters Fingerprint, signature
Remote authentication web site Remote Access Server PKI based	√ √ Nice to have	√ √ √	Access to Intranet SSL authentication e.g. CHAP, Radius e.g. digital signature
File encryption	Nice to have	√	128 bit keys
VPN client	√	√	IPsec
Anti-Virus	√	√	Automatically updated
Personal Firewall	√	√	Required if Internet access is allowed
PKI Support	Nice to have	√	End-to-end support
Digital Signature	Nice to have	√	X 509 standard
Smartcard Support	Nice to have	√	Smartcards hold private keys, certificates

The level 'secure access' is defined as access to intranet resources, which is not considered at a confidential level and is deployed as interactions in non mission-critical applications. The level 'confidential access' means access to confidential information applying for example in mission critical applications.

As operating systems may not have included all of the required security features, 3rd party software can help to complete the features. Here are some examples of proven components for PDAs:

- *Certicom movianCrypt* (authentication, file encryption, for Windows Mobile and Palm OS)
- *Glück & Kanja Technology AG, CryptoEx Volume* (encryption)
- *Certicom movianVPN* (VPN for Windows Mobile and Palm OS)
- *Certicom Trustpoint Client* (PKI for Palm OS)
- *Entrust VPN client* (VPN portal solution for Windows Mobile)
- *Checkpoint VPN-1Secure Client* (VPN and Personal Firewall for Windows Mobile)
- *F-Secure* (Anti-Virus for Windows Mobile and Palm OS)
- *Trend Micro PC-cillin* (Anti-Virus for Palm OS)
- *Trend Micro Office Scan* (Anti-Virus for Windows Mobile)

Enterprise front-end and back-end

Remote access server, authentication server

Whenever a mobile user wants to access the enterprise Intranet she or he has to dial-in the *Remote Access Server (RAS)* first. The RAS and a connected authentication server may provide different authentication mechanisms such as password, Secure-ID card or certificate based, e.g. with a smartcard, and may establish the VPN connection. A pure password authentication is not adequate for allowing access to an Intranet. Instead a strong authentication method is necessary, i.e. something you know, like a password, and something you have, like a Secure-ID card or a secret key, must be used in combination. PKI based authentication methods deploying digital signatures can be assumed as very acceptable. Methods with a higher security level like retinal scan or fingerprint scans (representing something you are) are usually not applicable in traditional business applications and deployed for specific solutions only.

RAS are offered by Cisco, 3Com, Nokia and others and should be located in a company's trusted environment to prevent authentication manipulation.

Besides the dial-in authentication various other authentication procedures are necessary with e- and m-business solutions, such as WAP gateway authentication, web/portal/application server authentication and authentication dedicated to applications as well as single sign-on. These procedures do not run on the RAS, they rather are integrated in the aforementioned servers and applications. Details are covered in section 6.4.

6.3 Mobile end-to-end security

WAP gateways

The *WAP gateway* is operated either by network carriers or by enterprises.

Today's application platform families for enterprises such as IBM WebSphere, BEA WebLogic, SUN ONE, Oracle Application Server, SAP NetWeaver and Microsoft Exchange Server have all integrated WAP gateway functions including authentication, integrity, confidentiality features with PKI support, compliant to the WAP standards V. 1.2.1 and V. 2.0.

Enterprises therefore do not need to install separate WAP gateways if they utilize one of these application platforms. However they must ensure a trusted environment for the WAP gateway software because of the exposed data during the process of converting the WTLS protocol into TLS/SSL and vice versa.

Web server, portal server, application server

E-business and m-business solutions are based on application platforms. *Web server, portal server, firewalls* and *application server* typically may be configured as had been shown in figure 6.11. However, dependent on the overall security architecture, the portal server e.g. could be located behind the second firewall. In principle all of these servers are required to provide the following security features:

– Authentication
– Role based authorization
– Transport encryption (SSL/TLS)
– Data encryption
– VPN support
– Single sign-on (web applications)
– Digital certificates, digital signatures
– PKI support

The previously mentioned application platforms (Microsoft, IBM, SAP, BEA, SUN, Oracle) provide such features more or less based on reliable and modern technologies (e.g. XML security).

To guarantee end-to-end security these security features in addition are required on integration servers and back-end systems. Especially legacy systems often only provide proprietary protocols and features, which in some cases may cause severe interoperability concerns with modern application platforms.

It is important to point out that even if these mentioned security features are available and proper implemented in the different systems and servers, security breaches cannot be excluded. Especially web servers (mainly Microsoft's IIS) are target of thousands of hackers, who try to attack enterprise networks daily. Again and again they find vulnerabilities (e.g. buffer overflow) and IT-organizations therefore must carefully obey CERT instructions.

6 Security focus areas

Virtual private networks

In effect, the VPN makes possible the secure exchange of information across a public network regardless of where the user is geographically and whether she or he is in a hotel, in an office or on the road. The deployment of VPN technology is a must if employees, customers or partners want to have access to corporate resources in the Intranet.

An appropriate enterprise VPN solution should include all mobile devices connectable via LAN/WLAN/GPRS and regard different connection channels to the enterprise. As an example the CORINA (Corporate Remote Intranet Access) solution, offered by Siemens Business Services, provides these different channels as shown in figure 6.12.

CORINA is a client/server application consisting of the client parts running on laptops, tablet PCs and PDAs and the server part running on a Windows or Unix based remote access server.

The CORINA family provides 4 distinct access channels, which support different network scenarios:

VPN dial-in

The dial-in channel provides remote access to the corporate access server via PoP (Public access Points) lists worldwide. Besides conventional wired access using analog and digital phone connections, mobile radio networks work on the basis of GSM/HSCSD. In the latter case a mobile phone is usually connected via infrared to the laptop. It provides the access to the remote access server via the mobile network.

VPN Internet

CORINA PIN (Remote access via Public Internet) affords the user mobility by using public Internet connections, e.g. from cafes, hotels or airports. In cases where public

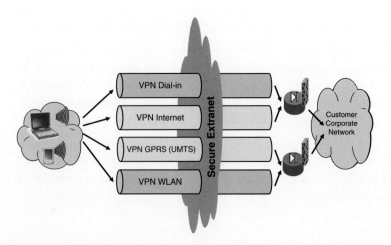

Figure 6.12 VPN solution

resources are used for data communications, security will be shifted from the network to the applications. Connection is possible via modem, high speed x-DSL or direct LAN access to the Internet.

VPN GPRS

This solution offers the user remote access to corporate resources using the GPRS network in two different ways. The laptop user can get secure access to corporate resources via a GPRS mobile phone connected to the laptop. Alternatively only the phone is used to get WAP access to appropriate corporate data via a WAP gateway.

VPN WLAN

As part of the CORINA solution the wireless access points operated by Siemens Business Services are configured in a secure wireless Extranet and tied into corporate Intranets via secure defined gateways. The WLAN inherent security protocol WEP is not used in the conceptual CORINA design because of its unsuitability for large-scale application scenarios. Instead the wireless access point is viewed as a dial-in PoP (without the actual dial-in) and is used to create a secure wireless Extranet. A dynamic *DHCP (Dynamic Host Configuration Protocol)* safeguards transport to the targeted remote access server of the corporate network.

6.3.3 Summary and recommendations

The mainstream of mobile business solutions will be the integration into existing e-business architectures. As end-to-end security mainly means platform embedded security it is crucial to implement mobile applications on forward-looking, standard based, reliable and secure platforms.

Technical, personal and operational security measures must be combined in order to implement a truly comprehensive information security policy. This means that all the different perspectives of information security in a company must be taken into account with regard to the additional mobility aspects. The security policy, security roadmap and the risk management are the cornerstones of a continuing security process.

The Business Unit level should take into account the various mobile business scenarios as well as the specific communication, access, device, processing, environmental, etc. needs in order to enable the IT organization to set up the right policy and to implement appropriate security measures.

Finally the Executive level should be aware of the opportunities and risks of mobile business and should align the security strategy with the business strategy of the company as a whole.

Enterprises should carefully consider involving experienced security service providers. Competently managed security services can often avoid significant damages by proactively preventing escalating security incidents and thereby save enterprises a lot of money and reputation.

6.4 Authentication, single sign-on

The challenge

About ten percent of the world's population log onto the Internet at least once a month. They will use 1 billion different devices, from PCs to mobile phones, to connect from their homes, work, schools, libraries, cafés and airports.

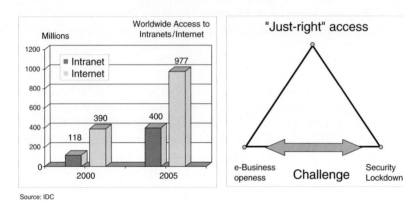

Source: IDC

Figure 6.13 Internet/Intranet access

Looking ahead, International Data Corp. [6.4.1] estimates that the number of Internet users worldwide will double between 2001 and 2006, increasing from 500 millions to 1 billion (figure 6.13).

The wireless Internet/Intranet access and the greater integration of mobile employees, partners and customers mean another new challenge with average annual growthrate of about 28% to 400 million users in 2005.

The challenge enterprises face is to find the right balance between optimizing accessibility to corporate resources while maintaining sufficient levels of security so as not to endanger the business. This is a delicate balance that can only be accurately determined by examining the business context and evaluating the business risk.

6.4.1 Definitions

Identity

Identity is the digital synonym of a user or an object. The identity should be unambiguous and may be a name, a mail address, a passport, a social number, etc. A certificate is a secure *electronic identity*, a *digital passport*, conforming to the *X.509 standard*. Certificates typically contain a user's name and public key.

Network identity refers to the global set of attributes that are contained in an individual's various accounts with different service providers. These attributes include such information as name, phone numbers, social security numbers, addresses, credit records and payment information. For individuals, network identity is the sum of their financial, medical and personal data, which must be carefully protected. For businesses, network identity represents their ability to know their customers and constituents and reach them in ways that bring value to both parties.

Identity management

means the control and automation of the process that controls who has access to which objects, based on their digital identity information. There is a strong emphasis on the management aspect of enterprise identity management in that many of its facilities are administratively focused. It provides a single point of administration for provisioning and deprovisioning accounts, as well as managing the lifecycle of accounts and their appropriate digital identities.

Authentication

is the act of proving the identity. To be able to access a web site or resource, a user must provide authentication via a password or other authentication means like tokens, smartcards or biometrics.

Authentication is based on 3 factors: something only you know (e.g. password, PIN), something only you have (e.g. token, private key) and something only you are (e.g. fingerprint, retina scan). A *one-factor authentication* often is called *simple authentication* while the *strong authentication* only can be achieved by deploying the *two- or three-factor authentication*.

Single Sign-on (SSO)

enables a user to access multiple systems and resources after being authenticated just one time.

Typically, a user logs in just once, then is transparently granted access to a variety of permitted services and applications with no further login being required until after the user logs out. SSO has the advantages of being user friendly and enabling an organization to manage authentication consistently, but has the disadvantage of requiring all systems to trust the same authentication service. Web based SSO-systems use browsers to provide access to web applications, but access to other enterprise resources and even legacy systems can be enabled by customizing and deploying special interfaces.

Federated SSO enables users to sign on with one member of an affiliate group and subsequently use other sites within the group without having to sign-on again.

Authorization

is the act of granting approval. Authorization to databases or applications is the permission to get access to these resources by means of e.g. access control lists or certificates or other simple or complex access control methods.

6 Security focus areas

Access control

comprises of a combination of tasks to guarantee that only authorized users are allowed to get access to network or enterprise resources. These tasks may include access policy, authentication, identity management, authorization segregated according to the user's roles, auditing, monitoring and supervising.

6.4.2 Authentication techniques and building blocks

Internet as well as enterprise applications which should be protected against unauthorized access are supported by authentication techniques and services, which can be structured in building blocks as shown in figure 6.14.

This diagram depicts a quite comprehensive overview in a structured manner. It demonstrates the complexity of authentication consisting of these various building blocks and the challenge to fit them together suitably in order to achieve end-to-end authentication or even SSO.

The different layers are described in the following sections.

Authentication methods

As depicted in figure 6.15 enterprises can choose among different *authentication methods*. Usually a combination of some of these methods turns out as the appropriate solution.

Alternatives for authentication methods include variations on one of the three authentication factors – *something only you know, something only you have, or something only you are*. These roughly correspond to alphanumeric passwords, access tokens or

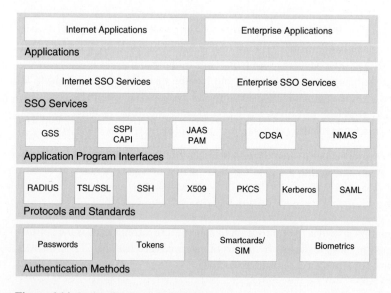

Figure 6.14 Authentication building blocks

6.4 Authentication, single sign-on

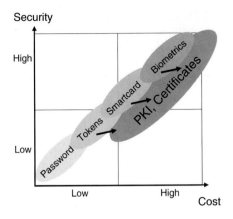

Figure 6.15 Authentication methods

devices, smartcards and biometric devices. Nevertheless, while various technical mechanisms for authentication each have an inherent strength, the way that organizations deploy or use them appropriately to the policy is just as important as to provide real security.

Passwords

remain the dominant identification and authentication method in the Internet. Passwords require a user or application to enter a character string, which is submitted over the network and matched against a password database or file maintained by an authenticating program. Unfortunately, passwords and PINs provide only weak authentication because there are many points of attack. Only some points of attack can be closed off by encrypting password information when it is sent over the network.

The weakest link in password/PIN security is the human element. People use short passwords, some of which are easily guessed or easily fall to dictionary attacks where a program compares a hashed password value against a dictionary of words, or word combinations. PINs or short numeric strings are inherently weak. Only strong passwords such as 225.xA6$zo can stand up to dictionary attack.

Enterprises should use only strong passwords and set up strict policies. These include educating users not to write their passwords down and locking accounts after a small number of invalid logon attempts. Frequent password expiry is another strong and often used password policy. In general, strict password policies tend to increase end-user training and support costs. Such policies may also decrease usability. There is a trend towards self-service password management, which leverages a directory to control one's own profile. That profile is then reused on many systems through password synchronization, password reset, or login redirection.

Tokens

Access tokens or devices represent the *something you have* authentication factor. They can be provided through hardware tokens, software tokens, or other types of systems. For each type of access token, organizations must consider not only the ability of the

155

token itself to protect the secret algorithms on which authentication depends, but also its ability to create a trusted verification path between the user, the client device and the authentication server.

Typically, access token solutions create the trusted verification path by protecting private keys in hardware and/or encrypting shared secret keys over the network. Organizations should also put time and effort into designing the policies for identifying the user and issuing tokens to users.

Typical hardware tokens are devices such as RSA Security's SecurID that display number sequences. These sequences change on a fixed one-minute interval to create one-time passwords with PINs, or *challenge/response* devices such as ActivCard, that have a display plus a numeric keypad.

In the challenge/response scenario, a user starts a logon session by typing in a user ID. If the user ID is validated, a number is returned to the screen, which represents the challenge. The user then enters this number into the hand-held device and the device returns another – the response. The user types this response into the logon session and if it is accepted, the system logs the user in.

Software tokens operate similarly to hardware tokens, except that a software program installed on a user's device provides the token generator, or the challenge/response system.

Smartcards/SIM cards

In general the smartcard is a special type of token as it is a multifunctional tool and can be used in a whole range of enterprise security applications.

Smartcards or known as processor based chipcards, *ICC (Integrated Circuit Card)*, have been standardized for more than 10 years (ISO 7816) and deployed in many different application scenarios: Admission control for buildings and rooms, cashless staff restaurant payment, user authentication for applications and networks and digital signatures as proof of origin for electronic documents are some of the possibilities that have been applied so far. This makes the smartcard an ideal tool for realizing applications such as employee identity cards that comprise a multitude of different applications.

One example is the Siemens Corporate Card which is deployed as an employee identity card worldwide, which is used for admission control and for severel security applications based on private keys stored on the smartcard and on a corporate wide PKI.

Secrets such as private keys are best stored in tamper-resistant modules. Smartcards are based on such tamper-resistant chip technology that implies hardware and software protection measures and represents a very high security level. Moreover these media are state of the art, portable, standardized and exchangeable among different devices, which means that users carry their private keys with them like a credit card and can use them with various devices.

SIM cards used in mobile phones are based on the same processor based ICC technology and *ISO standard 7816* but are now mainly used only as a token to authenticate subscribers to their network. However this will soon change since mobile devices compliant with the WAP standard 1.2 or 2.0 are now available on the mass market. Part of this standard is the Wireless Identification Module. As depicted previously WIM provides a dedicated specification for security token for users, which includes private keys and user certificates as well as cryptographic functions.

Biometric devices

Biometric authentication matches some physical characteristics (representing something you are) of a user against a database record. Common methods include retinal, palm, or fingerprint scans as well as voice recognition. After years of development, these systems have become more reliable, yielding fewer false positives and false negatives. Prices are also falling, making biometrics increasingly practical, though still far more expensive than the free password.

Technically, biometric authentication is the strongest form of authentication because a person cannot change easily such a basic personal attribute as the retinal blood-vessel pattern, fingerprint, or vocal-tract configuration. However, organizations must ensure that the biometric system, like any physical access device, provides a trusted verification path between the user and the authentication service.

Some promising hybride approaches combine portable smartcard devices with biometric data: private key, password, and user verification process are all protected through local encryption and PIN access.

Digital certificates/PKI

PKI is an infrastructure used for both authentication and encryption. It combines software, encryption technologies and services to protect network communications and e-business transactions. PKI involves a system of digital certificates – an attachment to an electronic message that can encrypt data and verify that the sender is who he or she claims to be – as well as certificate authorities, a third party that issues the digital certificate. PKI protects information assets by authenticating identity using a digital certificate, verifying integrity by ensuring that messages have not been manipulated or data corrupted and ensuring privacy by protecting information from interception during transit.

Authentication protocols and standards

As depicted in figure 6.14 several authentication protocols are intended for general-purpose use by multiple applications. Standards authentication protocols include the Transport Layer Security (TLS)/Secure Sockets Layer (SSL), Remote Access Dial-in User Services (RADIUS), Kerberos V5, Security Assertion Markup Language (SAML), XML Signatures (XML-Sig) and others. In addition, public-key and other cryptographic frameworks provide security mechanisms and data formats to the protocols. These include X.509 certificate formats, Public Key Cryptography Standards (PKCS), as well as other mechanisms, e.g. for hashing such as Digest-MD5, Secure Hash Algorithm (SHA-1) and the emerging Advanced Encryption System (AES) standard.

6 Security focus areas

Remote Access Dial-in User Services (RADIUS)

RADIUS [6.4.2] is a today widely used protocol for authenticating dial-in or Internet access based on a central security server model. RADIUS encrypts user ID/password information or challenge/response token information over the network.

While initially created to support remote or network access servers, RADIUS has evolved to provide a standard mechanism for Internet service providers (ISPs) to relay authentication requests back to corporate customers. Particularly popular on the Virtual Private Network (VPN) environment, product lines from Check Point, Cisco, RSA SecurID, and many others implement RADIUS as a front-end authentication mechanism to corporate authentication services.

Transport Layer Security/Secure Sockets Layer (TLS/SSL)

TLS/SSL [6.4.3] deploys a handshaking procedure to authenticate the server and the client through X.509 certificates, to negotiate the algorithms for the session, and to exchange session keys for encryption and message digests. The client authentication (optionally) requires that the client has the server's public key or certificate. TLS/SSL is used for web client authentication; the certificates in TLS are actually issued to the client's device and its software, not to any person or application using the device.

Secure Shell (SSH)

SSH [6.4.4] is a secure protocol and set of tools for secure, remote user authentication and access to servers. SSH can be used to secure any network-based traffic by binding it to a certain port at both ends. SSH runs on most UNIX systems, NT, and client platforms, and there are open source SSH solutions for these environments. The SSH protocol consists of three major components: The TLS provides server authentication, confidentiality, and integrity, the User Authentication Protocol authenticates the client to the server, and the Connection Protocol multiplexes the encrypted tunnel into several logical channels.

X.509

The X.500 directory standards published by the ITU contain a subsection, X.509 [6.4.5], which sets out recommendations for an authentication services framework. X.509 defines both a detailed syntax for certificates and an operational protocol defining how a certificate is used for authentication.

Public-Key Cryptography Standards (PKCS)

PKCS is an X.509-compatible system that uses public key technology to specify details, such as encryption algorithms and key formats. The PKCS standards [6.4.6] consist of a series of documents published by RSA, covering the definitions of algorithm, message syntax, certificates, attributes, and other cryptographic details. PKCS #7 and PKCS #10, for example, are widely used for certificate enrollment requests.

6.4 Authentication, single sign-on

Kerberos

Kerberos [6.4.7] developed by Massachusetts Institute of Technology, is a widely used authentication system and an Internet standard. It is an open standard for distributed systems authentication. It relies on shared secret (or password) authentication by users to an authentication server that is called *Key Distribution Center (KDC)*. The KDC issues tickets to the users and grants them access to applications. The KDC concept provides optional delegation of access from one application service to another and optional interdomain trusts between groups of KDCs. As such, Kerberos is the only broadly implemented protocol to provide end-to-end confirmation of user identity and authentication across multiple application services in a distributed interaction scenario. Kerberos standard support is now relatively commonplace in UNIX as well as Windows environments. However while Microsoft Kerberos can interoperate with UNIX Kerberos, authorization compatibility is limited.

Security Assertion Markup Language (SAML)

When combined with XML-based remote procedure calls (RPCs) such as the Simple Object Access Protocol (SOAP), SAML [6.4.8] serves as a distributed authentication protocol between authentication and other security services. SAML allows loosely coupled security domains with heterogeneous systems and authentication methods to federate authentication. While SAML is much newer than other authentication methods, it is being adopted very rapidly by many authentication systems.

Authentication APIs

The next layer in figure 6.14 comprises the authentication APIs. Important APIs for authentication include the Generic Security Service (GSS) API, Java Authentication and Authorization Service (JAAS), Microsoft Security Support Provider Interface (SSPI) and CryptoAPI, the Java Cryptography Architecture, Intel's Common Data Security Architecture (CDSA) API, and Novell's Modular Authentication Service (NMAS).

Generic Security Service (GSS) API

GSS API is a standard set of generic programing interfaces designed for security services, including authentication, data integrity, and data confidentiality. GSS has been implemented with Kerberos on UNIX systems. Windows, however, doesn't support GSS. Thus, GSS has only limited reach even in Unix environments.

Security Support Provider Interface (SSPI) and CryptoAPI

Microsoft's SSPI is conceptually similar to GSS API, providing a generalized security framework that hides the details of authentication and cryptography from the application. CryptoAPI allows applications to invoke specific cryptographic functions without needing special knowledge of the algorithms. CryptoAPI invokes pluggable cryptographic service provider (CSP) modules. SSPI manages authentication processes and is the high-level interface to Kerberos, while CryptoAPI handles low-level cryptographic functions.

Java Authentication and Authorization Service (JAAS) and
Pluggable Authentication Module (PAM)

The Java Authentication and Authorization Service (JAAS) provides an interface to multiple forms of authentication, including passwords, Kerberos tickets, and certificates. It implements a Java version of the Pluggable Authentication Module (PAM) framework originally developed by Sun, which has gained favor among UNIX vendors and Open Group members. JAAS and PAM offer open and flexible frameworks for a growing number of UNIX platforms and Java-based applications.

Common Data Security Architecture (CDSA)

Initial work done by Intel, the Open Group's Security Working Group has continued to maintain and extend the CDSA specifications. Unlike CryptoAPI, CDSA is independent of an operating system. A Common Security Service Manager (CSSM) core provides the framework for plug-in security services that provide cryptographic, certificate storage, and authentication services. CDSA has support from platform vendors such as IBM, and Hewlett-Packard.

Novell Modular Authentication Service (NMAS)

NMAS is similar to PAM, CDSA, SSPI and offers a pluggable authentication interface. NMAS leverages the Novell eDirectory, and has been implemented in Novell's products as well as some third-party applications.

Internet and enterprise SSO services

On the top of the authentication layers (which are shown in figure 6.14) Internet and enterprise SSO services make the building blocks diagram complete.

SSO services enable users after being authenticated just one time, transparently granted access to a variety of permitted services and applications with no further login being required until after the user logs out. SSO usually provides identification, authentification and authorization services.

The following sections describe different web-based SSO approaches and technologies. The depicted SSO technologies are classified differently:

Microsoft Passport is a service provided only by Microsoft, but may be taken advantage of any Internet shop, such as e-bay. The *Liberty Alliance Project* is a technology initiative, just defining a set of specifications and has no intention to develop products or to offer SSO services. *Entrust GetAccess*, *RSA ClearTrust* and *Netegrity SiteMinder* are available independent SSO-products, which can be integrated in different enterprises' infrastructures. Finally *SAP Enterprise Portal SSO* and *IBM WebSphere/Tivoli SSO* are in SAP's respectively in IBM's middleware fully integrated SSO systems.

6.4.3 Microsoft .NET Passport

Intention and trade-offs

Microsoft .NET Passport [6.4.9] consists of a suite of services for authenticating (Microsoft calls it: signing in) users across a number of devices and Internet sites (applications). The Passport single sign-in service provides authentication for users by allowing them to create a single set of credentials that enable them to sign-in to any site that supports a Passport service. An example is the e-bay web site [6.4.x]. On the bottom of this web page is just a small button *Sign in,* where users are able to authenticate themselves against the e-bay site by pressing the button, using the Microsoft's Passport mechanism.

Passport can help providers allow customers to identify themselves across all of a web site's applications, so that users can go to the providers' web site, interact with all of their account information, pay bills, and get the kind of experience they want. The provider (or any enterprise) fulfils one of its critical infrastructure needs (authentication), and is able to build a deeper digital relationship with its customers. The provider continues to hold all of its customer's data; it simply relies on Passport to ensure that users identify themselves with the same username and password from visit to visit.

Users have the control over the amount of information they reveal to participating Passport sites. Those who want to have forms filled, or to take advantage of other specialized services, may choose to share all of their profile information. Those who prefer to be identified only by their Passport identity, and no personal information, can decline those services, or can create an account with nothing more than a username and password.

The challenge is to develop a balanced solution that provides the highest degree of privacy and security with the lowest impact on usability.

It is important to recognize that there are tradeoffs between these privacy and security priorities and the other things consumers want from their online experience, such as convenience and usability. Passport can provide a certain level of flexibility to make these tradeoffs desired by both businesses and users.

For example, some consumers want strict privacy – some even want anonymity – but few want to give up the kind of personalized services and custom features that web sites can only provide if they have certain types of personal information about their users. Consumers also say they want high levels of security, but not every Internet site warrants the same level of security as a banking transaction. Some applications could require users to create "strong" passwords, with eight or more characters that combine letters, numbers and symbols. However, strong passwords are hard for most computer users to remember and difficult for them to type.

Authentication Process and Single Sign-in

Passport uses the Kerberos security mechanisms with some extensions. Passport authentication messages are passed in the form of electronic tickets that are used to tell the accessed site that the user has signed in successfully. A ticket is simply a small

6 Security focus areas

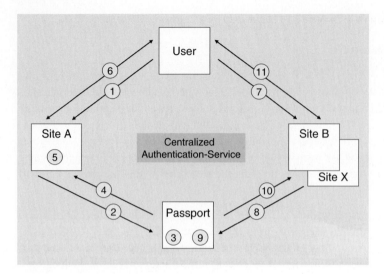

Figure 6.16 Passport single sign-in process

amount of data that tells at what time the sign-in occurred, when the user last manually signed-in and other information that is useful to the authentication process. Within the Passport system, these tickets take the form of cookies. Figure 6.16 shows the different steps of the authentication and single sign-in process.

Step 1: A user who has been registered at Passport.com and owns a Passport account wants to access a protected web page at site A. She or he clicks on the standard Passport sign in logo on the protected page to get a ticket.

Step 2: User is redirected to Passport.

Step 3: Passport checks user's cookie to see if the user already has an active ticket. As this is the first authentication no active ticket has been issued so far. Passport removes information that site A passed on the query string and redirects the user to a page that asks for the user's sign in name and password. After entering the correct information the process goes to step 4.

Step 4: The user is redirected back now to site A. Attached as cookies they bring two encrypted packets of information. The first cookie contains the authentication ticket information. The second contains any profile information that the user has chosen to share, and any operational information and unique identifiers that need to be passed. These packets are encrypted with a unique secret key that is shared between Passport and site A only.

Step 5: Site A decrypts authentication ticket and profile information, and signs the user into their site. Site A then takes this information and uses it to issue their own cookies. Now that site A knows the user has been authenticated by Passport, site A can take it from here and use the Passport User ID to look a user up in appropriate databases as well as perform authorization tasks. The profile information can be used to personalize the user's experience.

Step 6: User accesses the page, resource or service he or she requested from site A.

Step 7: The same user now wants to access site B. She or he clicks on the standard Passport sign in logo on the protected page of site B.

Step 8: User is redirected to Passport.

Step 9: Passport checks user's cookie to see if the user has an active ticket. In this case the user already has been issued an active ticket. Therefore Passport does not need to redirect the user to the sign in the page as described in step 3. Instead the user is redirected to site B immediately. Usually step 7, 8, and 9 will not be noticed at all by the user.

However site B has some choices to make about how to authenticate this user. Since the ticket contains the time that it was issued, it allows the referring site to decide how fresh the cookie needs to be in order to accept it. If the ticket meets the rules site B has chosen, the user is redirected back to the referring site along with the encrypted ticket and profile cookies. If the ticket is too old, the user is prompted to re-enter her or his credentials.

All participating sites can choose how old the ticket-granting-cookie can be before they will reject it. In addition, all participating sites have the option of requiring the user to reenter his or her password regardless of what cookies they have, and how fresh they are. By forcing a user to re-type credentials, the ability of someone, who does not know the user's password to access that user's information can be eliminated. Sites collecting sensitive information, such as financial services web sites, are encouraged to use this feature. It is unlikely that a site that only displays low security items such as localized news or weather would force the user to re-type his or her credentials.

Step 10: This step is identically to step 4 with regard to site B.

Step 11: User accesses the page, resource, or service requested from site B.

From the user's perspective any further accesses to sites X will occur in the same manner as described in steps 7 to 11. Her or his experience is the single sign-in regardless how many sites are going to be accessed.

Users may sign out of Passport by clicking the Passport sign-out logo on any participating site. Then all Passport cookies from all of the participating sites visited during the browser session are deleted from their computer.

Users can choose to be signed in to Passport automatically in the future. If a user checks the box authorizing the automatic sign-in feature, the user will not always see the Passport sign-in page and will not always have to type in his or her username and password while using that computer. Instead, the user will be able to use freely participating sites without having to input any information, and participating sites will receive the user's profile information consistent with the user's consent. To disable the automatic feature, a user simply has to select the Passport sign-out link at any participating site.

Additional Passport services

Security key

Passport offers an optional second layer of security that participating web sites can control. If a site has standard security needs, it can offer users an easy, straightforward online experience with the single user name and password in Passport. Sites with higher security needs can choose to require a secondary security key (a four-digit PIN in addition to a password) that must be entered before the user can complete a sensitive transaction or view confidential information. Unlike the password, this PIN cannot be stored on a computer; it must be presented by the user and passed over a secure, encrypted channel every time it is requested.

Passport express purchase (.NET Passport Wallet)

An optional adjunct to the single sign-in service is the Passport express purchase service. This service facilitates fast, easy online purchasing by allowing consumers to create a .NET Passport wallet, storing his or her billing and shipping information. With this service, consumers can make online purchases at any participating .NET Passport express purchase site by signing into their wallet and, with a few clicks, sending purchase information to the merchant, without having to retype their information. The data is sent using SSL encryption.

Kids Passport services

The Kids Passport Services give web sites, doing business in the United States, tools to help them comply with the parental consent requirements of the Children's Online *Privacy Protection Act (COPPA)*, which went into effect in April 2000. Parents can use the Kids Passport service to modify profile information their children can share with Passport participating web sites, subject to certain exceptions described in the Passport Privacy Statement. Parents can also choose a consent level to determine the extent to which participating Kids Passport sites collect, use, and share children's personal information.

Support of mobile devices

Passport provides support for Windows Mobile. Because mobile devices implement different browser technologies and are limited in terms of screen size, input and graphics capabilities, some Passport features are not supported on these devices in the current version. Nevertheless mobile users have access to key features like registration, single sign-in, sign-out.

Passport currently supports the following browsers: Microsoft Mobile Explorer (MME), HTML or WAP-mode, i-mode phones, WAP phones, HDML (Handheld Device Markup Language) phones.

Deployment

Enterprises that want to deploy and use Passport on their own web sites must sign the non-exclusive .NET Service Agreement. The standard .NET Service Agreement also includes a base service-level agreement (SLA). Sites with very high volumes may negotiate higher-level SLAs to meet their specific needs.

By signing the .NET Service Agreement, the participating site is committing to specific business guidelines that protect the personal information of Passport users and help ensure the integrity of the system.

For example, the contract states that all participating sites must post a privacy statement online and make it readily accessible to their users. Microsoft states to encourage strongly all sites to register with an independent, industry-recognized, privacy-assurance body such as TRUSTe.

Passport today is used as authentication service for Microsoft's MSN and Hotmail as well as for some other web sites.

Comments to .Net Passport

Passport strength is the balance and flexibility regarding security, privacy and usability for the most Internet applications and services excluding such which require a very high security level.

Customers often visit sites only occasionally, however many users cannot remember their logon credentials. If they fail three times to enter the information correctly, they must call e.g. a toll-free number to have their identity verified and to receive a new user name and password. The company's records show that many users simply give up at this point – and for those who continue, the company's support costs associated with the password reset are high. With Passport, the company may have an easy way to authenticate both new and repeat customers and stop losing sales from frustrated consumers, and the users can focus on their shopping and have a much better experience.

Nonetheless there are some current restrictions which limit the deployment of Passport as well as there are requirements for future Passport versions:

- Passport currently does not offer stronger forms of authentication such as multifactor authentication where the users must present something they have (such as a digital certificate, smart card or hardware token) as well as something they know (such as their PIN or password) to be strongly authenticated.
- More transparency for users and enterprises and the definition of control objectives as well as control activities examined by an independent auditing firm would help for more confidence in Microsoft's Passport services.
- Consumers cannot determine which private information should be transferred to what site.
- Companies which deploy Passport are not able to modify any Passport registration formats or authentication procedures. Existing authentication methods cannot be integrated or adopted unless deploying them in parallel. Passport cannot be deployed for non web legacy applications.

- Currently Passport cannot interoperate with any other existing authentication methods.

Customers and enterprises are still concerned about unauthorized people, who may be able to misuse or manipulate private data or enterprise assets. Therefore transparency and the examination of independent auditing are mandatory for common trust in Passport.

However Microsoft states that Passport will be adding support for *WS-Security* so that it can securely interoperate with other systems that support the WS-Security standard. By integrating these standards into its products and services, Microsoft will create a broad-based solution that will enable a host of federated security scenarios. In some of these scenarios, Passport becomes a node in a broader federation network.

In addition, Microsoft will be releasing new authentication technology code-named *TrustBridge*, which customers will be able to purchase and operate themselves. The TrustBridge technologies will provide customers with an integration point for their nodes in a broader federation system. TrustBridge will be deployed at the edge of the network and will speak WS-Security to the outside world. TrustBridge will talk to user directories within the customer organization that are based on Active Directory or a third-party Kerberos-based system. Because both Passport and TrustBridge will be speaking WS-Security, companies that deploy TrustBridge will have the technology necessary to federate with the Passport service if they choose to do so.

As Passport up to now has not been successfully deployed outside Microsoft's own services, a major change is probable and may result in new Identity Services, which may be more oriented on the Liberty Alliance approach.

6.4.4 Liberty Alliance project

The *Liberty Alliance Project* [6.4.10] represents a broad spectrum of industries united to drive a new level of trust, commerce, and communication on the Internet. Today one's identity on the Internet is fragmented across various identity providers like enterprises, Internet Portals, communities, business services. The result is cumbersome, the user experience is disappointing.

The federated network identity and single sign-on are key to solve this problem. The federated network identity approach is based on an open architecture and other than Microsoft's Passport not dependent on one company's technology and identity services. It is intended to position SSO services based on the Liberty standards in the market against Microsoft Passport.

Liberty objectives

The key objectives of Liberty are to
- enable consumers to protect the privacy and security of their network identity information,
- enable businesses to maintain and manage their customer relationships without third party participation,

- provide an open single sign-on standard that includes decentralized authentication and authorization from multiple providers,
- create a network identity infrastructure that supports all current and emerging network access devices.

These capabilities can be achieved when businesses affiliate together in circles of trust and on operational agreements that define trust relationships between businesses and in addition when users federate the otherwise isolated accounts they have with these businesses.

Federated network identity

Today, there are many islands of identity across the Internet. Every business connected to the Internet has an identity system for its employees. Most telecom companies, ISPs and other Internet networks (such as Yahoo! or AOL) also have systems for maintaining the identities of their users.

Federated network identity is the key to reduce this friction and realizing new business opportunities. In the new world of federated commerce, a user's online identity, personal profile, personalized online configurations, buying habits and history, travel and shopping preferences will be administered by the user and securely shared with the organizations of the user's choice.

Federated network identity means consumers and enterprises can allow separate entities to manage different sets of identity information. Account federation enables associating, connecting or binding a user's multiple Internet accounts within an affiliated group established between or among commercial and non-commercial organizations and governed by legal agreements.

Federated security is the ability for sites, services and applications to accept and recognize safely identities and authentication assertions issued by any one of a trusted set of partners.

Based on Liberty architecture and operational agreements there are circles of trust with which users can transact in a secure and apparently seamless environment as shown in figure 6.17.

From a Liberty perspective, the actors are the users, service providers, and identity providers. The service provider category includes any organization on the web today, e.g. Internet portals, retailers, transportation providers, financial institutions, entertainment companies, not-for-profit organizations, governmental agencies, etc.

Identity providers are service providers offering business incentives so that other service providers affiliate with them. Establishing such relationships creates the circles of trust shown in the figure. For example, in the enterprise circle of trust, the identity provider is leveraging employee network identities across the enterprises. Another example is the consumer circle of trust, where the user's bank has established business relationships with various other service providers allowing the user to wield his/her bank-

6 Security focus areas

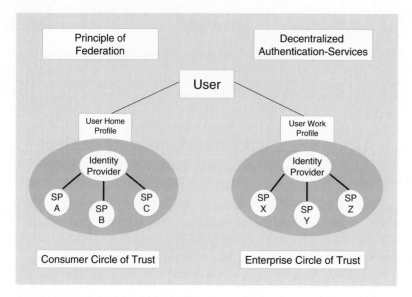

Figure 6.17 Liberty Alliance: federated network identity

based network identity with them. A single organization may be both an identity provider and a service provider, either generally or for a given interaction.

These scenarios are enabled by service providers and identity providers deploying Liberty-enabled products in their infrastructure, but do not require users to use anything other than today's common web browser.

Used techniques

Web Redirects

Liberty makes use of the HTTP command 302 *Temporary Redirect*. Such 302 web redirects work by placing the URI of another location in the Location field of an HTTP Response. The browser receiving such a response is obliged to perform an HTTP GET specifying the URI so conveyed in the HTTP response. This allows Liberty to create a communications channel between Identity Providers and Service Providers. During a Liberty web redirect, some private information about the user often travels in the HTTP message. This information needs to be protected. This is accomplished through the use of HTTPS.

SSL

SSL encrypts all HTTP communications between the client and server, so that even if an HTTP message is intercepted, the user information is protected. SSL has three main steps: the browser authenticates the server, the browser generates a session key, the server and the browser agree all further communications will be encrypted.

6.4 Authentication, single sign-on

SOAP and SAML

Liberty protocols exchange identity information through pre-existing protocols and languages, SOAP and SAML respectively, as well as web redirects. The SOAP envelope is a framework for expressing what is in a message, who should handle it, and whether it is optional or mandatory. SOAP also has encoding rules for exchanging application-defined datatypes, exactly what is needed in Liberty. SOAP also has Remote Procedure Calls (RPCs), which are used in Liberty.

SAML defines three types of assertions: authentication, attribute, and authorization decision. Liberty uses authentication assertions, which state that subject S was authenticated at time T by means M.

In summary, SAML authentication assertions are conveyed by either SOAP or web redirects in order to accomplish exchange of identity and authentication information.

Single sign-on process

In figure 6.18 and explanation one example scenario demonstrates the Liberty single sign-on processes from a user's perspective.

Step 1: At the Service Provider's web site, the user selects an Identity Provider for her or his identity authentication (or the Service Provider selects one for the user based on whatever approach is being used for introduction). He or she may press a button at the Service Provider's web site to select an Identity Provider, may fill in a form at the Service Provider's web site or may be requesting some resource and the Service Provider determines the Identity Provider from context. The mechanism that is used to transmit this information is an HTTP Request submitted by the user's browser.

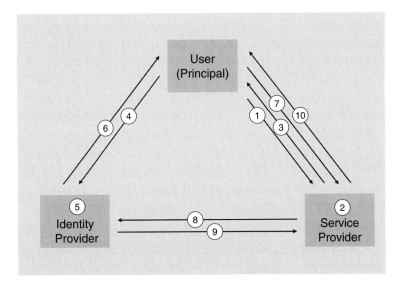

Figure 6.18 Liberty Alliance: single sign-on process

Step 2: The Service Provider determines the address of the Identity Provider and generates an alternate URI pointing at the Identity Provider.

Step 3: The Service Provider responds to the user's browser with an HTTP Response and an alternate URI in the location header field. The alternate URI field has a second, embedded URI pointing back to the Service Provider.

Now the Liberty protocol varies, depending on whether it is based on GETs, POSTs, or WML browsers. What will be explained here and onwards is the most common scenario, HTTP GETs.

Step 4: The user's browser performs an HTTP GET Request to the Identity Provider with the URI from the location field received in Step 3 as the argument of the Request.

Step 5: The Identity Provider processes the user's HTTP GET Request. If the user has not yet been authenticated by the Identity Provider, authentication occurs now.

Step 6: The Identity Provider responds with an authentication assertion, a SAML artifact, or an error. The response is conveyed using HTTP Redirect whose location header contains the URI pointing to the Service Provider (This has been extracted from the GET argument URI of Step 4).

Step 7: The user's browser obtains the artifact or assertion. The user sends an HTTP GET Request to the Service Provider using the complete URI taken from location field of the response received in Step 6.

Step 8: This step occurs only if the Step 6 response was a SAML artifact. (Recall that a SAML artifact is a small random number designed to point to SAML assertions. It is passed between sites using web redirects and embedding it in URL query strings.) The Service Provider now needs to get an authentication assertion corresponding to the artifact it received. The Service Provider sends a SOAP message to the Identity Provider, requesting the assertion.

Step 9: The step occurs only if the Step 6 response was a SAML artifact.

The Identity Provider processes the request, and responds with the corresponding assertion.

Step 10: The Service Provider sends an HTTP Response completing the user's original HTTP request in Step 1.

Comments to Liberty

The Liberty Alliance project offers the most open and standard-based approach and is designed as SSO platform for B2C, B2E and B2B equally.

As the Liberty Alliance Project's results are not products but specifications it will take some time those reliable products representing the latest specification will be available on the market. (Security specialists like Baltimore and Entrust probably will be among the first).

Liberty and web services-(WS)security both will deploy XML-based security like SAML, XML Signature, XML Encryption, XACML (Access Control), XKMS (Key Management) and therefore can be assumed as forward-looking and safeguarding technologies. However there are years to come and up to now there is no evidence whether major security holes can be avoided and whether the complex federation mechanism will work sufficiently in a mass market.

Though .NET Passport and Liberty represent different identity approaches and mechanisms the services may hopefully become interoperable within the next years.

6.4.5 Entrust GetAccess

Other than .NET Passport, the SSO service *GetAccess* from Entrust is targeted to the enterprise market and is designed to be integrated in an existing application environment with existing and different security mechanisms. And other than Liberty, GetAccess is not a set of specifications but a real service consisting of various components.

Portfolio

As the foundation of the *Entrust Secure Web Portal solution* [6.4.11], the *Entrust GetAccess* portfolio delivers a single entry and access point for user identification and entitlements across web portal applications.

Entrust GetAccess software centralizes security management and delivers the following services and features:

Identification, authentication and single sign-on

GetAccess provides *Single Sign-On (SSO)* for web resources and applications in a web site deployment. Once a user has identified him of herself to the GetAccess server, no further application layer authentication is needed. GetAccess will verify the user's credentials and inform the application of the user's identity.

GetAccess gives the flexibility to make use of a set of authentication mechanisms for deployment. Support is provided for authentication schemes including:
– Username/Password
– External LDAP directory
– X.509v3 digital certificates
– Tokens (including RSA SecurID)
– Windows Domain Authentication

Entitlements – authorization and roles-based access control

The GetAccess software delivers *Entitlements (authorizations)* via a *Roles-Based Access Control (RBAC)* model. This model uses the notion of roles as a layer of abstraction between users and the resources they need to access. Initially, an administrator can access the resources that need to be protected and define the roles that are needed to access each of those resources. Then, as users are created, they can be assigned roles appropriate to their relationship with and within the organization. Then GetAccess can calculate dynamically the resources that a user's roles allow him or her to access. This abstraction reduces the effort needed for an administrator to manage large numbers of users and privileges.

Dynamic resource menu

Once a user has been authenticated and authorized, GetAccess renders a personalized HTML menu that reflects the resources and applications for which the user is granted access. This allows users to navigate quickly through their applications without having to remember or bookmark various URLs. In addition, since this menu is dynamically generated, it will continue to give the user a real-time and up-to-date view of his or her privileges each time it is accessed. The resources displayed on this personalized screen will be recalculated with each access, reflecting all updates to his or her privileges.

Multi-domain access

As organizations merge, form partnerships with other organizations, and/or branch out into various brands, it becomes imperative to extend the same Identifications and Entitlements privileges across multiple Internet domains. However, due to an inherent limitation in the way cookies are implemented, they cannot be shared across multiple domains. And, since cookies are the primary containers for delivery of credentials to the browser, this is a substantial technical hurdle for providing cross-domain SSO and Entitlements.

GetAccess overcomes this hurdle, and provides multi-domain support for authentication, authorization, session management, real-time revocation, and logout.

Customizable look & feel

The HTML pages that GetAccess software generates are template driven, making it straightforward to change the look-and-feel of the implementation to match the rest of the site. Updating the pages that a user will see is easy by making the appropriate modifications to the provided templates.

Web-based & delegated administration

The GetAccess server ships with a browser-based administration tool. This tool can be used to manage all the users, roles resources, and other objects and parameters within the GetAccess server. Since this tool only requires a browser, there is no installation required on the administrators' machines. In additon an organization can allow administrators to be remote while being able to manage the security infrastructure.

GetAccess enables the delegation of administrative activity. The delegation model provides the possibility to give many different levels of administrative privileges to different delegated administrators.

6.4 Authentication, single sign-on

User self-service and automated provisioning

Self-service allows users to enroll themselves without any administrative intervention into the GetAccess server and dynamically receive appropriate privileges based on their relationship with the organization.

GetAccess is capable of leveraging an existing user management repository such as an LDAP directory or a Windows Domain infrastructure. A user that exists in the external directory can self-enroll and obtain a GetAccess account by presenting authentication credentials for that external directory. GetAccess validates these credentials against that directory and automatically creates a corresponding GetAccess account for this user if the authentication attempt is successful.

GetAccess also provides user self-service capabilities for maintaining their accounts. Authenticated users can manage their own accounts by selecting preferences and managing their passwords.

Non-web application integration

The GetAccess portfolio provides a toolkit that allows organizations to integrate client/server or other non-web applications into the GetAccess systems to leverage the Identification and Entitlements services that it provides. This API, known as CAAS (Client Authentication and Authorization Service), is implemented in Java and C++.

The CAAS provides a programmatic interface to GetAccess functionality. It can be used to authenticate users, obtain their credentials, request and enforce access control decisions, and verify the validity of user sessions. CAAS can also be used to build the same functionality for non-web environments that GetAccess software delivers for web applications.

APIs and extensions

In order to support the integration of GetAccess into enterprises environments, the product provides APIs that allow user management functions to be accessed programmatically. Implemented in Java, these APIs can be used to interface with other user management systems including ERP/HR systems and third-party administration tools. It can also be used to develop meta-tools allowing organizations to manage several infrastructure components, including the GetAccess server, from a single interface. Similarly, the APIs can also be used to accept real-time or batch updates from external systems.

There will always be scenarios where business requirements mandate modifications to some aspect of the behavior of the system. The GetAccess system has a variety of interfaces, called events that occur at defined points. Examples of events include successful log in, failed log in, password reset, etc. Developers or systems integrators can then create customized behavior by attaching extensions to the appropriate events. Extensions are compiled Java codes that extend core GetAccess functionality and allow a deployment to meet its functionality requirements.

6 Security focus areas

Wireless support

GetAccess provides Mobile Access capabilities with the delivery of the GetAccess Mobile Server. The Mobile Server plugs into the GetAccess environments and allows users to access the same applications and services that they can do with a browser, but by using wireless devices such as PDAs and mobile phones.

Architecture

The GetAccess architecture is designed to fit into traditional multi-tier enterprise application architecture. The appropriate services can be located across various hardware and software platforms of the DMZ and the Intranet tier as shown in figure 6.19.

Access service

It drives the user interface for log in, log out, account management, resource menu, and self-registration capabilities. The various servlets then interact with back-end components to provide the desired functionality. The Access Service is a client of the Authentication and Authorization Routing Service (AARS), Session Management Service (SMS), and Registry Service. It is accessed via HTTP or HTTPS by the end-user's browser.

The Identification and Authorization Service and Pluggable Authentication and Authorization Modules (PAAMs)

The GetAccess architectural framework allows the insertion of modular identification and authorization services specific to a particular authentication method into the overall

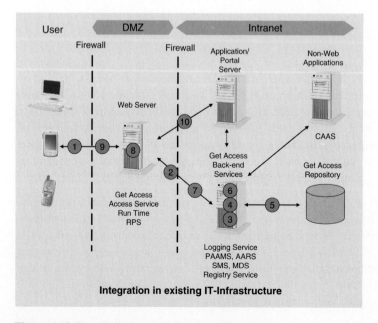

Figure 6.19 Entrust GetAccess enterprise SSO solution

architecture. These modules, called PAAMs, contain all the specific functionality for a particular type of authentication. This abstraction allows the rest of the GetAccess infrastructure to be deployed without needing specific knowledge of the internals of any particular PAAM. PAAMs have been developed by customers, third-party vendors for various authentication mechanisms and technologies.

PAAMs are called by the GetAccess Authentication and Authorization Routing Service depending on the authentication method the user is requesting.

Authentication and Authorization Routing Service (AARS)

The AARS plays several roles in the GetAccess infrastructure. It is responsible for accepting authentication requests during enrollment or log in, and forwarding them on to the appropriate PAAM for validation. If the authentication is successful, the AARS then communicates with the GetAccess SMS in order to have a new session generated for that user. It is also responsible for encrypting the user's credentials based on the random key generated for her or him at log in time.

The AARS abstracts all authentication and authorization logic away from the rest of the GetAccess architecture. The AARS is called by the Access Service and serves as a client of the various PAAMs, the Registry Service, and the SMS.

Logging and Audit Service

The centralized Logging Service provides logging capabilities by allowing an administrator to define, at a component level, the desired degree of details to capture in the log file. This feature allows deployment administrators and infrastructure managers to control the amount and types of information being gathered to manage risk and resources.

Session Management Service (SMS)

The SMS maintains a session table for all active user sessions in the systems. It is responsible for session creation (when users are authenticated) and session tracking (as users access various protected resources on the site).

Resource Protection Service (RPS)

The GetAccess Resource Protection Service, also referred to the GetAccess Runtime, is deployed as a web server plug-in and is responsible for performing all access control functions for protecting web resources. It examines each inbound web request to determine if the request is for a resource that is being protected. If the user's roles are insufficient to access the resource, the Resource Protection Service rejects the request by redirecting the user to an *Access Denied* page.

Data Repository and Registry Service

While GetAccess is leveraging external directories and databases for authentication and authorization information, it maintains its own repository for the purposes of storing data about secured resources and other system information. This repository also maintains GetAccess-specific data on users, including timeout values, failed and successful log in attempts, etc.

Multi-Domain Service (MDS)

GetAccess software uses a model of session credential storage and retrieval to facilitate the transfer of credentials across multiple Internet Domains. Once a user is authenticated to the primary domain, he or she can access secured resources on all primary and secondary domains without needing to re-authenticate. The state of the user's session will be tracked regardless of the domain he or she is in, meaning that an extended amount of time spent in applications on Domain B will not cause him to be timed out of Domain A. Similarly, user revocation by an administrator will also be enforced across all domains. Finally, if the user chooses to log out of the GetAccess system, the session will be removed from the central SMS, which means that access to any application in any domain will be denied.

Single sign-on process

When an unidentified user first logs into the GetAccess system, the system automatically collects and verifies the authentication information, entitles the user, creates a new session, and issues encrypted cookies that will serve as the user's credentials for the duration of the session.

The process is as shown in figure 6.19:

Step 1: User accesses the log in page. The Access Service renders a log in page pulling appropriate branding and other content from the appropriate HTML template. The user presents a username/password combination to the Access Service.

Step 2: The Access Service passes this information to the AARS for validation.

Step 3: The AARS determines that this is a request for authentication against the employee directory (stored e.g. in Active Directory), and forwards it to the LDAP PAAM.

Step 4: The Identification and Authorization Service takes the request and validates it against Active Directory. If the authentication is successful, the directory responds with the user's privilege information including group memberships and other user attributes. The Identification and Authorization Service returns the successful transaction to the AARS. It also passes on the user's entitlements as determined by Active Directory.

Step 5: The AARS then looks up the user's profile in the GetAccess repository. It determines if the user has any other entitlements and what the administrator-defined session limits are for that user.

Step 6: The AARS then requests the SMS for a new session. The SMS creates a session based on the timeout values provided by the AARS and generates a random, unique encryption key for that session. It returns this information to the AARS.

Step 7: The AARS uses the unique key to encrypt the credentials for that session. It packages these credentials into the response back to the Access Service.

6.4 Authentication, single sign-on

Step 8: The Access Service issues the encrypted credentials to the user's browser in the form of session cookies. These cookies are never written to disk, and are destroyed if the user closes the browser, or the user logs out of the GetAccess system.

Step 9: The user is then displayed by the RPS, the dynamic resource menu that lists those specific applications and resources to which he or she has been granted access.

Step 10: At this point, the log in process is complete. The user has been successfully identified and entitled. Credentials corresponding to the user's privileges have been issued to the browser, and the user has been presented with a tailored view of the resources to which he or she has access now. Those applications or services may be accessed via an application or portal server.

Comments to GetAccess

The Entrust GetAccess platform is suitable for an enterprise SSO solution.

As an integral component of the Entrust Secure Portal Solution, GetAccess delivers the authentication, authorization and SSO capabilities for portals with highly sensitive information and transactions.

GetAccess offers high flexibility for integration of the SSO services in existing security environments and provides rich authentication and authorization features. The Entrust GetAccess SSO solution is particularly suitable if medium or high authentication strenghts are required. The performance might be an issue in some implementations, because the abstraction of the related authentication, authorization and management processes results in some overhead.

6.4.6 Other SSO services

GetAccess is an enterprise SSO service, provided by Entrust, a company that has specialized and focused on security only. Its SSO service is application platform agnostic and therefore can be integrated in most modern application platforms. There are some other independent enterprise SSO services on the market, most worth to mention *RSA ClearTrust* [6.4.12] and *Netegrity Siteminder* [6.4.13]. In terms of functionality, flexibility, pricing and market reputation these services are comparable with Entrust GetAccess.

On the other hand there are the platform dependent enterprise SSO services that are designed and optimized only for their specific application platform environment. As examples *SAP Enterprise Portal* and *IBM WebSphere* are shortly depicted in the following.

SAP enterprise portal SSO

SAP Enterprise Portal provides end-to-end security to SAP applications and authentication/SSO based on user name and password or certificates. The portal server forwards the log on information to an external authentication mechanism. The external mechanism checks the data and returns authenticated user ID to the portal server, which assigns the external user name to the portal user name and issues a log on ticket.

With this ticket the user has single sign-on access to all applications that are accessible through the portal. Non-SAP applications can also use the ticket, which is digitally signed by the portal server. They can verify the ticket using a special library provided as part of the portal infrastructure. The Entrust GetAccess or RSA ClearTrust authentication mechanism can be integrated in the SAP Portal Server infrastructure and used as an external authentication mechanism.

The SAP Portal Server provides role-based access control, whereby the role information is stored in the portal content directory, which acts as a general object store for role definition, administration, and role data for page visualization. The portal management system assigns users to roles, roles to worksets, and worksets to iViews.

IBM WebSphere SSO

The WebSphere Portal Server provides authentication and SSO based on user name and password or certificates. The portal server forwards the log on information to authentication component such as WebSphere Application Server Security or web SEAL-Lite (a component of the Policy Director) or Netegrity SiteMinder or other authentication proxy server. The authentication proxy server can be integrated with WebSphere Application Server through its Trust Association Interceptor APIs. This provides a secure and uniform interface to WebSphere Portal Server. WebSphere security and the IBM authentication proxy servers are configured to use the portal LDAP directory to authenticate users. WebSphere Portal Server stores the various user informations: User ID, passwords, credentials including tokens, CORBA credentials. These credentials are available to portlets through a standard JAAS API, so that they can be passed to backend applications to achieve single sign-on.

WebSphere Portal Server provides role based access control. Administrators can define access control lists that manage access to each portlet. By replacing the access control system implementation, third party access control servers (such as IBM Policy Director or Netegrity Siteminder) may be used instead of the default Portal Server implementation.

6.4.7 Summary and recommendations

While some authentication methods and technologies like passwords, tokens, Kerberos, Passport are widely deployed, others like Certificates/PKI, SAML or Liberty are currently emerging. Determining when to adopt an emerging technology is a critical decision for an enterprise. If an enterprise launches its efforts too soon, it will suffer the painful and expensive lesson of deploying an immature technology; if it delays investment for too long, it runs the risk of being left behind by competitors that have made the technology work to their advantage.

The recommendations given in the following are distinguished in
- general statements representing some basic recommendations regarding common requirements and technology trends
- SSO evaluation considerations specifying roughly which SSO platform fits best for what business scenarios.

General statements

Enterprises first should look at the security classifications (public, private, sensitive, strictly confidential) and consider the global and local perspective for data and applications as well as the business risks in order to determine what strengths of authentication are required. Recommendations are:

- For routine applications User ID/password will probably remain the dominant identification/authentification mechanism for the next years.
- Large, complex enterprises may need to adopt multiple technologies for various required authentication strengths and various types of applications and security domains. Such general-purpose authentication systems should support multiple methods for determining identity, including username/encrypted password, X.509 certificates, and Kerberos.
- Medium strength authentication includes software based solutions such as software based PKI and software access tokens with sufficient strong password policies. In the long term PKI-based solutions are most flexible.
- High strength authentication should involve smartcards plus PIN and other hardware-enabled and PKI/certificate-based authentication methods including biometrics and hardware access tokens.
- Where to put the bar between high and medium strength authentication depends on the cost/risk factors involved with a particular application in a particular process environment.
- Enterprises should consider new approaches of user authentication, particularly for mobile business applications, e.g. RSA/Mobile or Entrust Mobile ID Server to provide SMS-based 2-factor authentication.
- As a prerequisite for efficient SSO systems enterprises should organize a centralized, policy-based management of all IT-resources.

SSO evaluation

Organizations can use Microsoft .Net Passport for B2C implementations if strong authentication is not a must requirement and there is no need to integrate this B2C application into the enterprises' existing non-Passport security framework as well as to interoperate with other authentification schemes.

The Liberty Alliance project is designed as SSO platform for B2C, B2E and B2B equally. However it will take several months or even longer until reliable products representing the full functionality will be available on the market. For enterprises therefore a long term migration path from an existing SSO platform like Entrust GetAccess or RSA ClearTrust to the more complex federation functionality is the appropriate way – if this functionality is required, e.g. providing partners access to Intranet resources.

The GetAccess, ClearTrust or SiteMinder SSO-platform is the right choice if enterprises need a general purpose identification and authentication/SSO system providing various medium or high authentication methods and if they need to integrate this platform into an existing infrastructure with heterogeneous security components and application environments. The decision which one of these 3 to prefer should be made in the context of the enterprises' infrastructure and specific requirements.

Integrated SSOs like SAP Enterprise Portal SSO or IBM WebSphere SSO are usually the first choice to apply in homogeneous SAP respectively IBM software environments. However integrated SSOs often have not the flexibility and functional richness compared to the above mentioned specialized SSOs. In other cases customers have heterogenous environments and want a unique SSO, which requires extensive integration to different environments. Even though integrated SSOs are capable to adopt other applications, often solutions based on independent SSO services are the better choice in the long term.

6.5 Web services and security

It is the goal that web services technology should enable enterprises to exchange mission-critical information both internally and externally. Web services can be built without significant incremental investment in hardware or software. Enterprises deploying these services therefore are realizing an immediate return on their investments. Moreover web services enable existing application investments to be leveraged with partners and customers. However, web services must operate in a trusted digital environment to reach these gains.

Web services security challenges and objectives

In many respects, the security challenges posed by web services are similar to those presented by first generation of web technology. The objective is the same: to create a convenient and trusted e-business environment, where enterprises can conduct cross-boarder communications, transactions and business processes.

The underlying challenges are the same:
– How to scale security to protect a widening set of resources against increasing points of vulnerability?
– How to manage user identities and verify who is on the other end of a network connection?
– How to exert fine-grained control over user access to sensitive resources?
– How to ensure the confidentiality and integrity of transactions and communications?

Providing a comprehensive model of security functions and components for web services requires the integration of currently available processes and technologies with the evolving security requirements of future applications. It demands unifying concepts, it requires solutions to both technological (secure messaging) and business process (policy, risk, trust) issues, and finally, it requires coordinated efforts by platform vendors, application developers, network and infrastructure providers, and customers.

The goal is to enable customers easily to build interoperable solutions using heterogeneous systems. For instance, the secure messaging model supports both public key infrastructure (PKI) and Kerberos authentication mechanisms as particular embodiments of a more-general facility and is capable of being extended to support additional security mechanisms. Integration through the abstractions of a single security model enables organizations to use their existing investments in security technologies while communicating with organizations using different technologies.

At the same time, every customer and every web service has its own unique security requirements based upon their particular business needs and operational environment. Within workgroup settings, for instance, simplicity and ease of operations are a top concern, while for public Internet applications the ability to withstand concerted denial-of-service attacks is a higher priority. A successful approach to web service security requires a set of flexible, interoperable security technologies that, through policy and configuration, enable a variety of secure web services scenarios [6.5.1].

6.5.1 Web services security standards and specifications

Web services security terminology

For better understanding of the web services security model some significant terms are explained as follows.

Security token

is a representation of security-related information and contains a set of related claims (assertions), e.g. X.509 certificate, Kerberos ticket, username/password, security tokens from SIM cards or smartcards.

Signed security token

is a security token cryptographically endorsed by an issuer.

Claim

is a statement about a subject either by the subject or by a relying party that associates the subject with the claim. Claims can be about keys potentially used to sign or encrypt messages. Claims can be statements the security token conveys. Claims may be used, for example, to assert the sender's identity or an authorized role.

Subject

of the security token is a principal (e. g. a person, an application or a business entity) about which the claims expressed in the security token apply. As the owner of the security token the subject possesses information necessary to prove ownership of the security token.

Web service endpoint policy

Web services have complete flexibility in specifying the claims they require in order to process messages. These required claims and related information refer to the Web Service Endpoint Policy. Endpoint policies may be expressed in XML and can be used to indicate requirements related to authentication (e. g. proof of user or group identity), authorization (e. g. proof of certain execution capabilities), or other custom requirements.

Claim requirements

can be tied to the whole message or elements of messages, to all actions of a given type or to actions only under certain circumstances. For example, a service may require a requester to prove authority for purchase amounts greater than a stated limit.

Intermediaries

As SOAP messages are sent from an initial requester to a service, they may be operated by intermediaries that perform actions such as routing the message or even modifying the message. For example, an intermediary may add headers, encrypt or decrypt pieces of the message, or add additional security tokens. In such situations, care should be taken so that alterations to the message do not invalidate message integrity, violate the trust model, or destroy accountability.

Actor

is an intermediary or endpoint (as defined in the SOAP specification) which is identified by a URI and which processes a SOAP message. Neither user nor client software (e. g. browsers) are actors.

Web services security model

Web services can be accessed by sending SOAP messages to service endpoints identified by URIs, requesting specific actions, and receiving SOAP message responses (including fault indications). Within this context, the broad goal of securing web services breaks into the subsidiary goals of providing facilities for securing the integrity and confidentiality of the messages and for ensuring that the service acts only on requests that express the claims required by policies (authentication and authorization).

Secure Socket Layer (SSL) along with the de facto *Transport Layer Security (TLS)* is used to provide transport level security for web services applications. SSL/TLS offers several security features including authentication, data integrity and data confidentiality. SSL/TLS enables point-to-point secure sessions.

IPSec is another network layer standard for transport security that may become important for web services. Like SSL/TLS, IPsec also provides secure sessions with host authentication, data integrity and data confidentiality.

Today's web service application topologies include a broad combination of mobile devices, gateways, proxies, load balancers, demilitarized zones (DMZs), outsourced data centers, and globally distributed, dynamically configured systems. All of these systems rely on the ability for message processing intermediaries to forward messages. Specifically, the *SOAP message* model operates on logical endpoints that abstract the

6.5 Web services and security

physical network and application infrastructure and therefore frequently incorporates a multi-hop topology with intermediate actors.

When data is received and forwarded by an intermediary beyond the transport layer both the integrity of data and any security information that flows with it may be lost. This forces any upstream message processors to rely on the security evaluations made by previous intermediaries and to trust completely their handling of the content of messages. What is needed in a comprehensive web service security architecture is a mechanism that provides end-to-end security. Successful web service security solutions will be able to leverage both transport and application layer security mechanisms to provide a comprehensive suite of security capabilities.

The following web services security model demonstrates how these goals can be achieved:

- A web service can require that an incoming message proves a set of claims (e.g. name, key, permission, capability, etc.). If a message arrives without having the required claims, the service may ignore or reject the message. The required claims and related information are referred as policy.
- A requester may also be a web service, which can send messages with proof of the required claims by associating security tokens with the messages. Thus, messages both demand a specific action and prove that their sender has the claim to demand the action.
- When a requester does not have the required claims, the requester or someone on its behalf can try to obtain the necessary claims by contacting other web services. These other web services, referred as security token services, may in turn require their own set of claims. Security token services broker trust between different trust domains by issuing security tokens.
- This model is illustrated in figure 6.20, showing that any requester may also be a service, and that the Security Token Service may also fully be a web service, including expressing policy and requiring security tokens.

Typical message flow:

Step 1: Requester (web services client) sends request for token to security token service.

Step 2: Security token service sends back the requested token.

Step 3: Web services client adds token to SOAP message.

Step 4: Web services client signs and sends message to web service.

Step 5: Validation of client's token by security token service.

Step 6: Web service sends response to web services client.

The security token service might be *Kerberos, PKI,* or a *username/password* validation service. Indeed, a Kerberos service ticket granting service might be accessed through the Kerberos protocols using operating system security functions. Once the client (web service client) gets the tokens it wants to use in the message, the client will embed

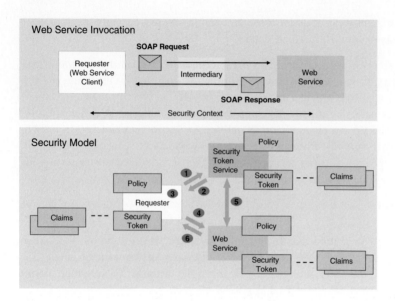

Figure 6.20 Web services Security model

those tokens within the message. The client should sign the message with a piece of data that only she or he knows.

The server (web service) will be able to deduce the signature in a number of ways. If the client is using a *Username type token* for authentication, the client should send a hashed password and sign the message using that password. The server will be able to verify that the client sent the message if the signatures it generates for the message match the signatures contained in the message. When using *X.509 certificates*, the message can be signed using the private key. The message should contain the certificate in a certificate-type token. When using X.509, anyone who knows the X.509 public key can verify the signature. Finally, when using a Kerberos-ticket, the message could be signed or encrypted with a session key embedded in the Kerberos ticket. Because the Kerberos ticket will be encrypted with the key of the receiver, only the receiver will be able to decrypt the ticket, discover the session key, and verify the signature.

This general messaging model subsumes and supports several more specific models such as identity-based-security, access control lists, and capabilities-based-security. It allows use of existing technologies such as X.509 public-key certificates, Kerberos shared-secret tickets and even password digests. It also provides an integrating abstraction allowing the system to build a bridge between different security techniques. The general model is sufficient to construct higher-level key exchange, authentication, authorization, auditing, and trust mechanisms.

XML related security standards

The web services standardisation will be pushed ahead by software vendors (mainly IBM, Microsoft) and standardization organizations such as *W3C, WS-I, OASIS, UDDI.org* [6.5.2].

Like XML is a major enabler of web services, *XML security* is the basis of the web services security standards. Developed mainly by W3C and industry consortia, XML security today consists of:

XML Signature

defines an XML scheme for cryptographically authenticating data. The authenticated data may consist of a complete document, individual elements in an XML document, or an external data object referenced by an XML document.

XML Encryption

defines an XML scheme for encrypting data. The encrypted data may consist of a complete XML document, individual elements in an XML document, or an external data object referenced by an XML document.

XML Key Management Specification (XKMS)

defines trusted web services for managing cryptographic keys, including public keys. The specification consists of services used by a party relying on a cryptographic key (location and validation) and services used by the holder of a cryptographic key (registration, revocation, reissue and key recovery). An important objective of XKMS is to shield applications from the complexity of the underlying PKI. This is accomplished by delegating the details of digital certificate processing to a separate web service.

Security Assertion Markup Language (SAML)

is a framework for specifying and sharing 'trust assertions' in XML. A trust assertion can be any data used to determine authentication and authorization of any subject (people, application) such as credentials, credit ratings, approved roles, and so on. SAML is important for interoperability and is designed to support interoperable authentication and authorization services.

XML Access Control Markup Language (XACML)

is a language for defining how policy information related to access control is expressed and transferred. By writing rules a policy author can flexibly and selectively define which web services can exercise what access privileges for which XML documents.

Security framework and specifications

As web services may be part of cross company and cross boarder orchestrated processes a series of *Web services security specifications* [6.5.3] has been worked out with regard to message based collaboration and covering issues such as privacy, policy, trust among partners and federations. This work was initiated by IBM and Microsoft and supported by security specialists, such as Verisign and RSA Security. Currently these specifications are not taken over by standardization organizations and therefore the standard status is not yet given.

The figure 6.21 illustrates the web services security framework and specifications.

6 Security focus areas

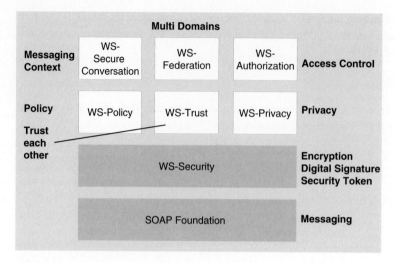

Figure 6.21 Web services security framework

This set of specifications includes a message security model (WS-Security) that provides the basis for the other specifications. Layered upon are the policy (WS-Policy), the trust (WS-Trust) and the privacy (WS-Privacy) models. These initial specifications provide the foundation on which secure interoperable web services across trust domains can be established.

On top of this foundation the secure conversation (WS-Secure Conversation), the federated trust (WS-Federation) and the authorization (WS-Authorization) models expand the deployment scenarios.

The combinations of these security specifications will enable the interoperability of secure web services. The following descriptions explain shortly the purposes and functions of the specificied security models.

WS-Security

WS-Security provides a general-purpose mechanism for associating security tokens with messages. No specific type of security token is required by WS-Security. It is designed to be extensible (e.g. support multiple security token formats). For example, a requestor might provide proof of identity and proof that they have a particular business certification.

WS-Security describes extensions to SOAP messaging to provide quality of protection through message integrity and message confidentiality, and defines how to attach and include security tokens within SOAP messages. The specification specifies binary encoded security tokens (e.g. X.509 certificates). These mechanisms can be used independently or in combination to accommodate a wide variety of security models and encryption technologies.

Moreover, WS-Security describes a mechanism for encoding binary security tokens. The specification describes how to encode X.509 certificates and Kerberos tickets as well as how to include encrypted keys. It also includes extensibility mechanisms that can be used to describe further the characteristics of the security tokens that are included with a message.

WS-Policy

WS-Policy describes how senders and receivers can specify their requirements and capabilities.

WS-Policy is fully extensible and does not place limits on the types of requirements and capabilities that may be described; however, the specification identifies several basic service attributes including privacy attributes, encoding formats, security token requirements, and supported algorithms.

This specification defines a generic SOAP policy format, which can support more than just security policies. This specification also defines a mechanism for attaching service policies to SOAP messages.

WS-Trust

WS-Trust covers the model for establishing both direct and brokered trust relationships including third parties.

The specification describes how existing direct trust relationships may be used as the basis for brokering trust through the creation of security token issuance services. These security token issuance services build on WS-Security to transfer the requisite security tokens in a manner that ensures the integrity and confidentiality of those tokens.

In addition the specification describes how several existing trust mechanisms may be used in conjunction with this trust model.

The trust model explicitly allows for delegation and impersonation.

WS-Privacy

Organization creation, managing, and using web services will often need to state their privacy policies and require that incoming requests make claims about the sender's adherence to these policies.

By using a combination of WS-Policy, WS-Security, and WS-Trust, organizations can state and indicate conformance to stated privacy policies. This specification describes a model for how a privacy language may be embedded into WS-Policy description and how WS-Security may be used to associate privacy claims with a message. Finally, this specification describes how WS-Trust mechanisms can be used to evaluate these privacy claims for both user preferences and organizational practice claims.

WS-Secure Conversation

WS-Secure Conversation describes how a web service can authenticate requester messages, how requesters can authenticate services, and how to establish mutually authenticated security contexts.

In addition the specification describes how to establish session keys, derived keys, and per-message keys.

The specification also describes how a service can securely exchange context (collections of claims about security attributes and related data). In order to accomplish this, the specification, built upon the concepts of security token issuance and exchange mechanisms, is defined in WS-Security and WS-Trust. Using these mechanisms a service might, for example, support security tokens using weak symmetric key technology as well as issue stronger security tokens using non-shared (asymmetric) keys.

WS-Secure Conversation is designed to operate at the SOAP message layer so that the messages may traverse a variety of transports and intermediaries. This does not preclude its use within other messaging frameworks. In order to increase the security of the systems, transport level security may be used in conjunction with both WS-Security and WS-Secure Conversation across selected links.

WS-Federation

This specification defines how to construct federated trust scenarios using the WS-Security, WS-Policy, WS-Trust, and WS-Secure Conversation specifications. For example it describes how to federate Kerberos and PKI infrastructures.

Moreover, a trust policy is introduced to indicate, constrain and identify the type of trust that is being brokered.

This specification also defines mechanisms for managing the trust relationship.

WS-Authorization

This specification describes how access policies for a web service are specified and managed, in particular how claims may be specified within security tokens and how these claims are to be interpreted at the endpoint.

It is designed to be flexible and extensible with respect to both authorization format and authorization language. This enables the widest range of scenarios and ensures the long-term viability of the security framework.

Standardization outlook

The major players in the field of web services have shown a strong interest to cooperate in developing security standards. They all have recognized that web services can only gain broad acceptance with adequate mechanisms to guarantee privacy as well as confidentiality and integrity of transactions.

Agreements on standards probably will get much more difficult as the attention turns to more complex extensions like federated identity and trust and the compliance with other specifications such as from Liberty Alliance.

The Liberty Alliance rolled out, end of 2003, the following phase (phase 2) of its federated identity specifications, which enables identity functions for web services and provides the foundation for the *Liberty Identity Web Services Framework*.

While phase 1 was about federated identity for single sign-on as depicted in a previous section, phase 2 at a high level is about permissions-based attribute sharing.

The web services framework from Liberty Alliance provides a way of delivering identity-based web services that can make web services more secure and private and represents a standard way to identity-enable these web services by identifying all the players in a secure, trusted manner.

Liberty Alliance also has introduced a Services Expert Group to develop interoperable service specifications that utilize the Liberty Identity Web Services Framework and address the needs of specific industries, applications, and business models. These specifications are called Identity Service Interface Specifications (ID-SIS).

The standardization on the one hand must regard a high degree of freedom in order to be flexible, e.g. incorporating different security techniques, defining attributes, policies, etc., on the other hand it means that many definitions about semantic contexts have to be agreed upon in a concrete environment.

Unfortunately WS-Federation and WS-Trust are not compliant with the Liberty Alliance specifications, because Microsoft and IBM, the main promotors of the WS specifications, are not members of the Liberty Alliance. As a consequence at least for some years industry must live with different standardization approaches.

Relation to today's security techniques

This web services security model is compatible with the existing security models for authentication, data integrity and data confidentiality in common use today. As a consequence, it is possible to integrate web services-based solutions with other existing security models:

Transport security

Existing technologies such as secure sockets (SSL/TLS) can provide simple point-to-point integrity and confidentiality for a message. The web services security model supports using these existing secure transport mechanisms in conjunction with WS-Security (and other specifications) to provide end-to-end integrity and confidentiality in particular across multiple transports, intermediaries, and transmission protocols.

PKI

At a high level, the PKI model involves certificate authorities issuing certificates with public asymmetric keys and authorities, which assert properties other than key ownership (for example, attribute authorities). Owners of such certificates may use the associated keys to express variety of claims, including identity. The web services security model supports security token services issuing security tokens using public asymmetric keys. PKI is used here in the broadest sense and does not assume any particular hierarchy or model.

Kerberos

The Kerberos model relies on communication with the Key Distribution Center (KDC) to broker trust between parties by issuing symmetric keys encrypted for both parties and introducing them to one another. The web services model has been built upon the core model with security token services brokering trust by issuing security tokens with encrypted symmetric keys and encrypted testaments.

Note that while the models are compatible, to ensure interoperability, adaptors and/or common algorithms for signatures and encryption will need to be agreed upon.

Existing models for federation, authorization (including delegation), privacy and trust are less common and more ad hoc. Specifications to address these security properties are identified, but may be still subject of discussion.

Often the existing trust models are based on business agreements. An example of this is the UDDI web service. In UDDI, there are several participants who provide a Universal Business Registry through an agreement to support a set of APIs. Rather than defining a single model for *trust* through the requirement of a specific authentication mechanism, the *trust model* in UDDI gives the responsibility for authentication to the node, which is the custodian of the information. That means, each implementation of the UDDI web service has its own authentication mechanism and enforces its own access control policy. The trust is between operators, and between the requester and the operator that is the custodian of its information.

6.5.2 Web services security scenarios

Web services are likely to be implemented incrementally, first within an enterprise and then expanding outward as standards and technologies allow.

The development may be anticipated as shown in the following:

Phase one: intra-enterprise

Enterprises will initially use web services internally, mainly for EAI (Enterprise Application Integration) and for increasing visibility and productivity of selected business processes, e. g. delivery and payment status and process. For example, an enterprise may integrate its web-based shipping and legacy accounts payable systems in order to track order delivery so that it can bill in real time and predict cash flow more accurately. One of the advantages of starting internally is that it is relatively easy to ensure that chosen technologies and standards are available, secure and compatible.

Phase two: extra-enterprise with selected partners

As web services are successfully utilized internally, enterprises will likely extend them to partners and suppliers with which they have already negotiated agreements. Enterprises will transform existing applications to a web services platform to automate the processes that implement e.g. a supply chain relationship. A supply chain management application, for example, could utilize web services components to publish automatically and execute orders, query and consolidate shipping capacity, and aggregate and schedule production needs among various participants in the enterprise's value chain. During this phase, transaction protocols and security standards will become critical to the success of web services enabled applications.

Phase three: partner communities

As the breadth of companies deploying web services grows, so will rise the potential for more sophisticated interactions. During this phase, enterprises will likely use web services to automate the negotiation of business agreements within a set group of partners, suppliers, and customers. For example, an enterprise might post request for proposals and quotes to its extended community of suppliers, receive their responses, and, based on that information, negotiate terms dynamically. This phase is far more dynamic than the earlier phases, performing logic that may vary over time and virtually eliminate the need for human intervention, unless exception handling.

Phase four: dynamic collaboration

The most promising phase in the evolution of web services will improve on previous phases by enabling not only B2B process execution and negotiation with existing partners, but also the dynamic search, identification, and involvement of new business partners. Once potential partners are identified, web services-enabled applications will negotiate the terms of the operating relationship between enterprises that may never have worked together, execute the resulting agreements, and even enable billing and payment for services and products. Achieving this level of service will require widespread agreement on a wide range of standards, as well as global directories that enable anonymous but reputable and legitimate participants to locate easily and reliably for collaboration.

According to the phases mentioned previously the figure 6.22 illustrates the different scenarios of secured web services.

The diagram shows a business process represented through a workflow and implemented by orchestrated web services. On the one hand these web services may represent some business process objects and on the other hand provide the connections to enterprises' applications and resources as well as to customers and partners whenever this is required dependent on the workflow.

As examples of the previously depicted phase 1, web services messages (arrows marked with 1 in figure 6.22) are shown executed on the same application server. In these cases web services invoke other web services, connect to a WSDL-wrapped existing standard or legacy application or provide access to a database.

As example of phase 2 and 3, selected partners and customers may also be integrated in the workflow, deploying web services technology (arrows 2, 3). Though the enterprise may have already negotiated agreements and policies with their business partners, the security impact concerning authentication, confidentiality, integrity and non repudiation is much stronger as web services communicate via the Internet and http-protocol bindings pass the firewalls without control.

6 Security focus areas

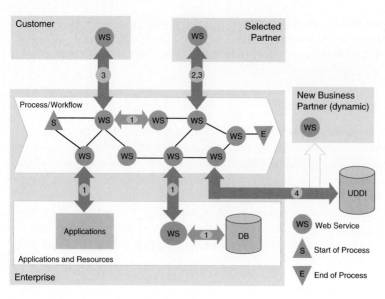

Figure 6.22 Web services deployment phases

As mentioned in phase 4, a dynamic collaboration between partners who never before had business relationships, might be required (arrow 4). This is indeed the most valuable scenario, but with regard to security and trust, it is certainly the most sophisticated one. Trust between these partners must be achieved dynamically by standardized negotiations and agreements.

6.5.3 Web services deployment example

The deployment example in this section shows the way web services security technologies can be applied in business processes. Figure 6.23 illustrates a mortgage application process. This mortgage process has been extracted from a RSA Security White Paper, *Web Services Security* [6.5.4], but the illustration is different in figure 6.23.

The mortgage application consists of checking the user's credit rating, the user's access rights to access a property database, to verify the property's details and finally to sign a contract.

Step 1: An applicant fills out an online mortgage application form and hits the submit button. The web services application now begins the process.

Step 2: Before the mortgage application service can interact with other web services, it must be able to authenticate itself to those services. This will be accomplished by presenting a digital certificate that has been issued by a trusted third party. Providing an interface to a public key management system, the *XKMS* server retrieves the mortgage company's digital certificate.

Step 3: The mortgage application service now queries a *UDDI* directory, asking to be connected to any of the three nationally known credit rating firms with whom the mort-

6.5 Web services and security

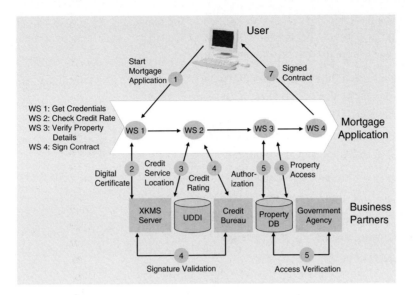

Figure 6.23 Web services business example

gage company does business. The UDDI returns the name of one firm and indicates that requests must be digitally signed.

Step 4: When the mortgage application service submits its signed request, the credit bureau accesses the XKMS server to validate the requester's *PKI* credentials. The XKMS server responds that the credentials are valid. The credit bureau then answers the mortgage company's request with an attribute assertion stating that the applicant has the highest credit rating.

Step 5: Having verified the applicant's credit-worthiness, the mortgage application service now needs to validate the details of the property in question by checking a property data-base maintained by the appropriate government agency. Before granting access however, the database company checks to verify that the mortgage company has contracted to access this resource – and then returns a *SAML* authorization assertion.

Step 6: The mortgage application service submits a property query, with a WS-Security header containing the authorization assertion issued in step 5. A response is returned with the indication that the property fits the description provided by the applicant and is free and clear of legal and financial claims.

Step 7: Having obtained the necessary assurances about the applicant and the property, the mortgage application issues a signed contract, approving the mortgage loan. *XML-Signature* and *XML-Encryption* ensure the integrity and confidentiality of this document.

6.5.4 Vendors and products

The implementation of web services security is still in the evolving phase.

Nevertheless the basic building blocks are offered by the major players now or will be provided in the near future. More complex security scenarios – such as federation – will probably raise more discussion and open issues.

The following basic building blocks are more or less available with products of the vendors listed in this section below:

- Secure socket layer (*SSL/TSL*) for channel confidentiality
- Web Services Description Language (*WSDL*) for integrity
- *SAML* for authentication and authorization
- *XML-Encryption* for granular document confidentiality
- *XML-Signature* for granular integrity and non-repudiation
- *Web Services Security* (authentication, encryption and signature)
- *XKMS* (key management)
- *XACML* (access control)

Companies are expected to announce more detailed web services security roadmaps as standards evolve. The features, known so far, are described below.

Microsoft .NET

Microsoft has implemented SSL and XML security as foundations of the .NET Framework.

In addition Microsoft currently is developing a set of technologies code-named *TrustBridge*, [6.5.5] which embrace WS-Security and other WS standards, and enable applications to use credentials created on a wide range of systems, including Active Directory, Microsoft .NET Passport, and other products that support WS-Security (for example, IBM WebSphere products).

TrustBridge will be able to federate with other enterprise or Internet-based authentication systems using the WS-Security approach. This will enable enterprises, which have chosen to interoperate with the Passport system, to allow their users signing in with their existing credentials at Passport-participating sites.

Microsoft development tools and the .NET Framework provide basic support for the WS-Security and will add further support for these new interoperability standards so that developers can build applications that use WS-Security and related specifications from the WS-Security roadmap.

IBM Tivoli

The actual version of the WebSphere Application Server offers web services features that include a UDDI service, a Web Services Gateway (which addresses web services communication capabilities issues through Service Mapping, Import and Export Mapping, Transformation, and UDDI publication and lookup features), and an implementation of the WS-Security specification that includes digital signature support and identity propagation capability [6.5.6].

Tivoli Access Manager (TAM, [6.5.7]) offers the new web services federated identity management interfaces that enable customers to plug in support for identity standards, including out-of-the box support for the XML Key Management Specification (XKMS).

In addition to an implementation of the WS-Security specification, Tivoli extends Access Manager's federated identity management interface support to include additional advanced federated capabilities. Web Services Trust Proxy, Trust Broker and Security Token Service, new components of the Tivoli Access Manager, will offer trust brokering with external trust providers, such as Microsoft's Windows based Trust-Bridge federation technology, allowing companies to automate the process of entering into trusted business relationships. IBM plans to support a broad range of brokering methods, such as Microsoft TrustBridge, Kerberos tokens, Public Key Infrastructure credentials, SAML and other means of delegated trust that develop in the future.

Additionally, Tivoli Access Manager will implement cross-enterprise, federated identity management that includes validating and asserting cross-enterprise credentials, generating cross-enterprise federated identity tokens, such as Kerberos tokens, SAML, PKI and securely linking or mapping external identities to internal identity definitions. Added capabilities will consist of an Identity and Credential Mapping service, for handling identity translations between companies, and an Identity Profile Service, for managing attribute profiles of users from trusted organization within the federation. Tivoli also plans to provide fine-grained authorization for SOAP transactions in web services environments. This new feature will allow businesses to control access to web services applications based on a user's identity and associated roles and entitlements.

SAP NetWeaver

With reference to SAP's White Paper *Security: Secure Business in Open Environments* [6.5.8], the security infrastructure of mySAP Technology delivers security features for heterogeneous business environments. That means it protects business transactions and information within applications from unauthorized use by addressing the key security issues of authentication, authorization, privacy, non-repudiation and integrity:

– User administration with a unified user store enables to manage user roles and authorizations.
– Secure system management includes authentication and encryption mechanisms.
– Digital signatures provide security and non-repudiation on the application level by attaching trust information to the data itself.
– Trust relationship management offers authentication, single sign-on, and impersonation mechanisms, as well as integration of public key infrastructures.
– An audit framework enables to perform detailed checks on existing security mechanisms to ensure the integrity of business transactions.

It is on SAP's roadmap to offer a WS-security compliant framework as part of the Web Application Server (WAS) of the Netweaver platform.

Entrust Secure Transaction Platform

The Entrust Secure Transaction Platform [6.5.9] is a new security framework for defining how to integrate foundation security services into web services applications. This platform will allow integrating and deploying security services that add identification, privacy, entitlements and verification to make web services transactions trusted transactions.

The identification service enables organizations to control centrally, which identities are trusted for automated web services transactions so that each web services application does not have to manage these issues independently.

The entitlement service provides the centralized administration of access entitlements as well as interfaces that allow applications to check those entitlements.

The verification service confirms the integrity and accountability of transactions through centralized digital signature and timestamping services.

The privacy service encrypts information so that only designated entities can access that information.

Entrust provides four methods of integrating security into web services applications:
– The Security toolkit integration is the traditional method; developers include the security functionality directly into their applications.
– The Direct Integration allows web services applications to call out directly to the foundation security services delivered by the Entrust Secure Transaction Platform. This platform offers web services interfaces to application developers.
– The SOAP Firewall Integration provides a method to deliver transparent security. SOAP Firewalls sit in the flow of information on a network. They look for specific application-level messages and transform those messages as they pass by through the firewall. The SOAP Firewall can perform a variety of security actions on behalf of the application.
– The application server plug-in integration is a similar concept to that of the SOAP Firewall. It provides security on behalf of web services, however runs directly on the application server that also executes the business logic of the web services application.

6.5.5 Summary and recommendations

Enterprises that consider a web services implementation need to make security an integral part of their IT-strategy and planning efforts. One way to reduce the risk and complexity of deploying this new technology is to start with an application that can be secured easily using existing capabilities. This is mostly the case with intra-enterprise applications, i.e. web services deployment across the enterprise perimeter (phase 1 in section 6.5.2). Even with selected partners conventional security mechanisms can be deployed, for example, point-to-point interactions between two companies can be authenticated and protected using VPN or SSL sessions (phase 2).

6.5 Web services and security

Web services will be a de facto standard for application deployment and particularly for application integration. Therefore it is important that enterprises move to understand this technology. Application integration today often managed by point-to-point *spaghetti* connections will successively be replaced by hub- and spoke-technologies and especially deploying web services.

Ad hoc business process implementations will become essential and help companies to stay competitive being able to react fast to changing market conditions and requirements. More complex, multi-partner web services deployment (phase 3 and 4) should be approached cautiously. It will require large-scale commitments of resources to security techniques, including PKI. On the other hand, companies that already have implemented PKI should be encouraged to use the embedded mechanism to implement even more complex web services deployments.

It can be assumed that companies that have decided web services deployment strategically will need PKI sooner or later, while companies with existing PKI environment are in a better position to deploy enhanced web services soon.

7 Outlook

The development of our society and economy is determined by ethical and social issues, by the desires of individuals, by economic and business needs, by political, legal and regulatory issues and, finally, by the evolution of technologies.

Analysts regularly study these developments and their impact, with the result that a variety of future scenarios are drawn up and published nearly every month.

The author does not have the intention either of commenting on these predictions or of describing any other view of the future. Instead, some of the main trends in the field of information and communication technology will be considered in the light of their relationship with the issues addressed in this book. These are namely *Mobility, Web Services* and *Security*.

7.1 Trends in information and communication technology

In terms of the way future business solutions will evolve and gain widespread acceptance, four trends in the information and communication field are of crucial significance:

– Convergence of networks
– Virtualization of services
– Always-on society
– Intuitive user experience

Convergence of networks

The ability to digitize any content, such as text, data, voice, graphics, photos, video or multimedia, is a crucial prerequisite if networks are to converge to form a worldwide IP network. Technologies such as voice over IP and the implementation of the IP protocol stacks within various access technologies, as shown in figure 7.1, will enable this convergence to progress gradually.

Convergence is significant for carrier backbone and access networks (wireline and wireless) as well as enterprise networks. In enterprise networks, even the next generation of PBX will be IP-enabled.

7.1 Trends in information and communication technology

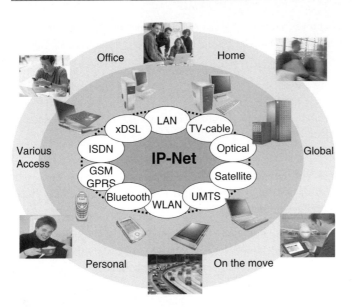

Figure 7.1 Convergence of networks

This convergence is the only answer to the problem of increasing network complexity and is driven mainly by the cost reductions it promises and the advantage of seamless communication.

The unifying transport layer is the Internet. The integration of real-time communication with IT applications will drive the replacement of circuit-switched architectures by packet-switched IP switches and routers. Real-time *SIP (Session Initiative Protocol)* will play a key role in assuring seamless voice communication in wireless and wireline IP networks. During the transitional phase, gateways will transform the traditional protocols. Reliability and quality of service issues may arise but should be solved by 2007.

VPN services will become still more important. These provide flexible access to enterprises and make it possible to set up virtual and secure communication paths within an all-embracing, open network.

Mobile devices will support the IP protocol stack and IP proxies will complement WAP gateways. In addition, enhanced mobile technologies will make it possible to develop more intelligent mobile devices that provide new services representing considerable consumer value.

Moreover, converged networks will also foster peer-to-peer communication that will also be employed in many business applications, such as distributed processing, distributed storage services or decentralized collaboration.

Virtualization of services

The need for mobility and globalization, increased cost pressures and competition, as well as the emergence of new technologies will increasingly force enterprises to virtualize their organizations and services. If they are to adapt quickly and flexibly to new market requirements, companies must concentrate on their core competencies. There is a tendency to organize other activities within virtualized environments.

Models such as outsourcing and offshoring form part of this trend and are successfully exploited today. However, in the long term, technologies such as web services, grid services, service-oriented architectures, software agents and the business-on-demand paradigm will drive the virtualization of services to a new level that will result in major changes to today's business solutions.

Today's standard packages will become modularized and more specialized and new competitors will arise offering best of breed services. The concept of a purely linear value chain will be replaced by more complex networks of services.

Future business solutions will be characterized by dynamic, ongoing changes in the interactions between partners and customers. Semantic web services will bring about plug & play service modules and automated service creation. The virtualization and outsourcing of services as well as business process outsourcing will become the norm for every enterprise. Thanks to these changes, companies will gain the flexibility that will allow them to react in real time, trim supply chains and inventories, improve customer satisfaction and avoid unpleasant surprises.

Always-on society

The term *always-on* or *connected society* was created by Gartner to refer to the prediction that more than 75% of EU and US citizens will have the option of immediate access to e-services for over 80 percent of their nonworking time by 2007. The always-on society will evolve as a consequence of widespread, easy access to sufficient wireless network bandwidth coupled with the availability of mobile devices capable of exploiting this bandwidth at affordable network fees.

The trend towards mobility will become an integral part of society, influencing the actions and attitudes of the majority of citizens. Widely accepted applications such as instant messaging, location-based and context-aware services as well as electronic payment or ticketing based on mobile phone accounts will drive this trend.

Furthermore, in the always-on world, a mobile device will become a personal companion in a variety of leisure situations, such as communication, entertainment, information, traveling and learning.

Personal mobile devices will increase in processing power, while their networking capabilities and battery capacity will also improve. As a result, personal devices will evolve to become advanced personal application platforms. The combination of computing and networking will allow the development of autonomous peer-to-peer applications. Such applications will be deployed in numerous fields, such as messaging, games, communities, dating and media piracy.

As far as business solutions are concerned, the always-on society implies a redefinition of the concepts of work and leisure. Such a society will reinforce the tendency to move from *fixed time* to *anytime* and from *fixed place* to *anywhere* working scenarios. Networking and computing capabilities will mean that there is no longer any clear divide between the leisure and working worlds. However, this development will bring about new challenges for enterprises: increased security requirements, more event-driven working style, more dynamic and flexible tasks and team creation.

Intuitive user experiences

Devices, networks, and applications have all grown in complexity over recent years. Users are close to the point at which they will reject new developments which fail to offer simplicity of use. It is therefore generally accepted that user experiences must be improved significantly by means of smarter devices and applications and through the deployment of innovative human interface technologies. Personalized, intuitive, learning interfaces must adapt to the user's needs, the current situation, the requested services and applications. The individualization of content and services must increasingly meet the user's personal preferences.

The result will be the development of smart applications that are aware of the user's context and take account of his or her profile, preferences, working processes and workflows or leisure situations, the current location, the communication device and capabilities. These applications may even recognize the user's habits and emotions.

Multimodal interfaces will add speech, pen and handwriting recognition to the traditional pointer and keyboard interfaces. New concepts for vision and touch-based interaction will emerge. Multimodality will allow users to use multiple input and output modes in an intuitive way. For example it will be possible to combine voice commands, predictive text input, keypad use and graphics in the same interaction. In some scenarios, a range of sensors may permit context-sensitive interaction with the environment, taking account, for example, of light, noise, or movement conditions, wellness, etc.

The user's experience is undoubtedly a key focus of attention for future-oriented business solutions and is crucial for the acceptance of innovative technologies and applications.

7.2 Relationship with mobility, web services and security

It is a remarkable fact, and one which may be unique in the history of IT, that all of the major software vendors (middleware and applications) have joined together in supporting a new architecture (SOA) and technology (web services). Furthermore, all of the vendors are currently boosting their efforts to significantly enhance the mobility and security features of their platforms.

Web services

As far as web services are concerned, it is worth noting that the market leaders (IBM, Microsoft, SAP) are obviously intensifying their cooperative efforts. They will probably pursue this avenue of development, both in their own interests and in the context of their customers' requirements. This will also strengthen the positions of the three market leaders and will place their competitors in a difficult position.

At the same time, SOA will undoubtedly provide impetus in the market for innovative solutions and services and this will create new opportunities for niche players offering highly specialized or innovative services. This means increasing competition for SAP, Microsoft and other standard software vendors, while simultaneously giving SAP the opportunity to offer its own modularized software modules, packaged as web services that can be used regardless of the underlying platform.

As far as the enterprise is concerned, a web service is a virtual service. Its functions are defined by the WSDL descriptions. The requester of a web service has no need to know the programming model chosen to implement the service.

Multiple service providers may offer identical functionality in their web services, which, however, may differ in terms of their operational suitability, e.g. whether they can meet defined business policies, such as the requirement that all data to be exchanged has to be encrypted. Consequently, the use of a service-oriented architecture demands an infrastructure which identifies the most suitable web service in terms of the technical and business-related aspects that are relevant to the requester. This infrastructure, which is called the *service bus,* is currently the subject of discussion by experts and will be of crucial importance for the virtualization of services.

This and today's other debated but as yet unresolved web services issues, such as security, federation, distributed transactions, business process languages and accounting, should be solvable at the technical level by 2006 at the latest. However, the software vendors, standards organizations and industry consortia may have different perspectives and pursue divergent interests – the different approaches to federation and trust standards proposed by WS-I and the Liberty Alliance being only one example here. It is difficult to predict how these disagreements may hinder the deployment and diffusion of web service based business solutions.

However the changes that will arrive in the near future will be significant and enterprises need to keep a careful eye on developments in the light of their own specific situations. It seems that the time window available to make the appropriate architectural and technological decisions will be limited.

IT service providers will also have to realign their portfolios. Enterprises require consulting services in order to decide how to deal with web services (particularly external web services) and need to define a web services strategy. It is also clear that solution architects who are able to help enterprises migrate towards forward-looking, service-oriented architectures will be in great demand. Furthermore, IT service providers will be in a position to create new business opportunities by providing *trusted web services.* In this role, they will act as trusted mediators by offering selected business processes based on web services.

Mobility

Mobility is a megatrend and enterprises will sooner or later face the challenges of mobile business solutions. When planning and implementing secure mobile solutions, two key aspects should be borne in mind.

First, mobile solutions should be based on proven, standards-oriented infrastructures and easily integrable, modular building blocks that enable step-by-step implementations. Reusable web services integrated in enterprises' portal architectures are the best way to achieve economic targets while also securing the agility and flexibility that are required in order to stay competitive. Centralized applications using browser clients are easy to manage and often the most promising solution. However, intelligent mobile clients offer more flexibility and may therefore predominate in the long term. This may also come about as a result of the second aspect that needs to be mentioned here.

This second aspect concerns the always-on society and its implications for the concepts of leisure and work. The strict separation of leisure and work will disappear in an always-on society. This fact will have consequences for mobile device capabilities, as well as for applications and platforms.

Users will have access to both the network operator's portal and the enterprise portal and will also be able to connect directly to web services via the Internet. A possible configuration is shown in figure 7.2.

The diagram depicts the variety of applications that users may choose depending on their leisure activities and business tasks. The kind of device illustrated here will typically be used by mobile knowledge workers. It offers the functional integration of a variety of applications. Some application areas may be relevant for both business and leisure, such as payment, location-based services, MMS, e-learning, etc.

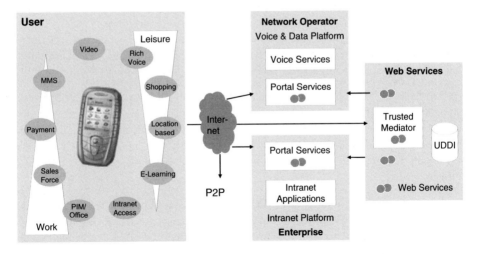

Figure 7.2 Leisure and work platforms

7 Outlook

From the individual user's perspective, it is possible to distinguish between four different ways of benefiting from network services: access to the enterprise portal, access to the network operator's portal, direct access to third-party web services or web services provided by trusted mediators and, finally, *peer-to-peer (P2P)* communication and services.

The greater the volume of available data services or services with digitized content, the closer the architectures of enterprises' and network operators' platforms will grow and the greater the extent of service overlap will be. Whatever the source, service-oriented architectures will evolve and make it possible to offer both home-grown and third-party web services.

The consequence of this will be keener competition in the field of service-oriented application platforms. For example, horizontal services, such as location-based, push, MMS, PIM, and PKI/authentication services could be offered by network operators on behalf of enterprises, at least in the case of SMBs. On the other hand, independent IT service providers, which play the role of trusted mediators providing best-of-breed web services, could offer these services to enterprises and even compete with the network operators by offering enhanced services to their subscribers.

These areas of competition will drive the widespread deployment of web services and service-oriented architectures, provided that this is not blocked by other influences, such as regulatory requirements or disagreements concerning standardization.

Intelligent mobile devices provide the prerequisite for P2P computing. By avoiding centralized overhead, P2P might also become a valuable application model for business. However, we currently lack the relevant experience in this field. Instant messaging, data exchange and distribution, and alerts/notifications could act as example applications.

Security

In an always-on world comprising mobile access to enterprise resources, network operators' services and third-party web services, the triple A challenge (Authentication, Authorization and Accounting) will take on a new dimension.

On the one hand, VPNs play an essential role by providing secure channels for business applications. On the other, however, password access methods neither provide the required security level nor are easy to handle when access to a dozen or more resources may be required. A reliable PKI environment offering a single sign-on facility seems to be the only reasonable answer, at least in the case of corporate applications requiring Intranet access.

Confidential information such as private keys is best stored in tamper-resistant modules. Smartcards and SIM cards are both based on a tamper-resistant chip technology that integrates hardware and software protection measures and offers a very high security level. Moreover, these media are state of the art, portable, standardized and interchangeable across different devices. This means that users can carry their private keys with them in the same way as a credit card and use them in different devices.

As described in chapter 6, the smartcard is a multifunctional security tool for a whole range of enterprise security applications, e.g. for building admission control, user authentication and authorization for network and application access, and digital signatures for signing e-mails or as proof of origin for electronic documents. These combined capabilities make the smartcard an ideal electronic identity tool, for example in the form of employee or citizen cards that comprise a multitude of different applications.

Meanwhile, SIM cards, which are based on the same processor technology and ISO standard (7816), are currently used primarily as tokens to authenticate subscribers to their network operators. However, the WAP standard 1.2/2.0 has introduced the Wireless Identification Module (WIM). WIM provides a dedicated specification for users' security tokens which includes private keys and user certificates as well as cryptographic functions.

WIM itself is defined as a smartcard application and can either be accommodated in software form on the network operator's SIM card or be implemented as a separate card, the *WIM card* (with a SIM form factor), which can also be issued by a non-carrier service provider or by an enterprise. In the latter case, the WIM card may be used in a second SIM-type slot provided on some mobile devices. In UMTS networks, the SIM card will be replaced by a *Universal SIM card (USIM)* which is both upwardly compatible and even offers additional security features based on the latest chipcard processor technology (e.g on-chip crypto-controller capable of generating private keys inside the chip).

With reference to the leisure and work configurations illustrated in figure 7.2, the combined deployment of smartcard and USIM/SIM/WIM technology in business scenarios with high security requirements will constitute a forward-looking solution.

This type of security solution is presented in figure 7.3.

The solution requires the enterprise to possess an underlying PKI infrastructure. Enterprises with multi-channel (wireline and wireless) business provisioning strategies will be forced to harmonize their wireline and wireless security architectures in order to protect their investment through future-proof designs. In particular, separate security infrastructures for web and WAP should be avoided as these will increase costs and reduce economies of scale.

Figure 7.3 illustrates just such a harmonized security architecture, providing authentication, integrity and non-repudiation based on certificates and digital signatures with web and current WAP/SIM or future IP/USIM technology.

In a personalization process compliant with the PKI standard, employees' private keys and certificates are to be stored in the smartcard's file system as well as in the appropriate WIM area. Either the enterprise or a network operator or another trusted service provider generates keys as well as trust center/certification authority certificates and distributes the private keys and certificates to the hardware tokens (smartcard, WIM) and the public key to directories. Responsibility for personalization depends on whether WIM is implemented as an application on the SIM card (carrier's responsibil-

7 Outlook

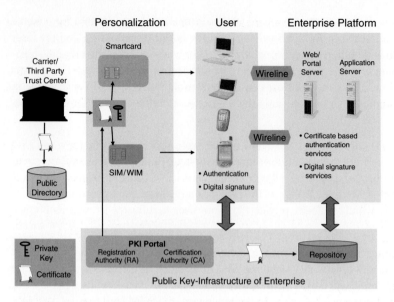

Figure 7.3 Smartcard and SIM card based security

ity), whether the enterprise takes responsibility itself or prefers to outsource this task to a specialized, trusted service provider.

In most cases, users are assigned different private keys for authentication and encryption. In advanced security solutions, the authentication key is generated directly on the smartcard/USIM by the users themselves and then initiated via their PCs once they have been registered by a local registration authority. The encryption key, which is generated and administrated by a trust center, can then be securely downloaded to the smartcard/USIM. This type of advanced solution will bring about a further significant reduction in administrative effort.

From the user's perspective, this chipcard-based solution obviates the need to use dozens of passwords and different procedures for authentication, digital signatures, etc. From the enterprise's point of view, it is ultimately, despite the need to invest in a PKI infrastructure, a cost-saving solution that offers a high level of security for a variety of mobile devices in a world in which these can be expected to be used for both leisure and business purposes.

The Universal Personal Communication Module

As a final thought with regard to the medium-term future, the author would like to spend some time considering the idea of the *Universal Personal Communication Module (UPCM)*.

As discussed in chapter 4, the divergence of wireless devices will increase. Many more intelligent smartphones, PDAs, laptops, tablet PCs, portable TVs, etc. will penetrate the market. GPRS/UMTS, WLAN and Bluetooth networks are complementary technologies that will co-exist throughout the next decade. New business and leisure application scenarios will emerge. Personalization will be a key factor in permitting the fast and simple use of these applications. Identification, authentication and, in some cases, digital signatures and encryption will become mandatory in order to make use of any service. This will demand the provision of the appropriate attributes, keys and certificates, which users will want to carry with them in the same way as credit cards and which they will want to be able to employ regardless of the type of device they happen to be using.

Considering these aspects (device and network independence, security and personalization) and given the continuing miniaturization of memory, processor and communication chips, the fascinating idea of a new communication module becomes conceivable: the UPCM.

This UPCM would combine security and network technologies coupled with PIM and additional personal attributes and files in a single module. As figure 7.4 illustrates, it could be plugged into any device via a standardized interface, for example via the CF card port. When the card is inserted, the device operating system would automatically recognize the UPCM and perform the necessary configuration and activation operations. Optionally, the UPCM might be equipped with a fingerprint sensor meaning that it could only be activated by the authorized UPCM owner's finger press.

Before this idea can become a reality, device manufacturers and network operators must agree upon a UPCM standard which, though it might not be very different to the USIM standard, would also have to specify a standardized device interface and agree on selected communication interfaces and standards (GPRS, UMTS, Bluetooth, WLAN 802.11 a, b, g, i, etc.).

Such a UPCM could be offered by device manufacturers or network operators. The SIM/USIM functionality could either be integrated or a separate card could be inserted in the UPCM.

As shown in figure 7.4, the proposed UPCM architecture resembles that of modern chipcards, comprising CPU, RAM, ROM, EEPROM/Flash, and crypto-controller. It will be tamper-resistant to permit the storage of various keys and certificates and will be equipped with PIM software which can be synchronized with the user's PC. It will also contain the standardized device interface as well as the integrated GPRS/UMTS, Bluetooth and WLAN communication modules.

The UPCM clearly offers a number of advantages compared with today's communication and security components:

- A single component comprising both security and communication functionality that can be used in conjunction with all types of mobile devices (laptops, tablet PCs, PDAs, smartphones) to replace today's multiple pluggable security and communication components which often differ between device classes.
- Regardless of the mobile device and the current network environment, the user can conveniently connect to any network or network resource thanks to the integrated, certificate-based authentication methods.

7 Outlook

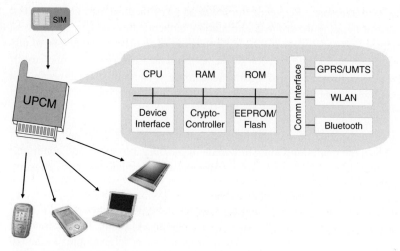

Figure 7.4 Universal Personal Communication Module

- Regardless of the employed mobile device, users' personal data (PIM) and files are available locally on the UPCM. Users' personal attributes are also stored since these may be relevant for online or offline applications.
- Users always carry their UPCM (CF card size) with them and can use it in any other device provided it has a UPCM interface.
- The UPCM is tamper-resistant, i.e. the over-the-air downloading of keys, applications and data is secure. This provides considerable flexibility in terms of the use of different service providers and applications as well as in terms of the capability of the currently used device.
- Enterprises reduce costs because they have to purchase, personalize and administer only one instead of a number of different security and communication components.
- Device manufacturers will be in a position to design cheaper devices without equipping each device with security and communication components. The design of device and security/communication technologies can be decoupled, thus accelerating development.

It will be exciting to see how industry responds to the increasing security and communication challenges and whether it will be possible to standardize modules such as the UPCM.

7.3 Summary and conclusion

Recently, research conducted by Gartner has revealed that security is the number one IT-related issue worrying CIOs, ahead of EAI/middleware, messaging and portals, and that it will remain the key issue up until 2006. At the same time, web services, the number 5 technology issue in 2003, will climb to second position in 2006.

7.3 Summary and conclusion

Increasingly, information is becoming an organization's most important asset. It does not matter what form it takes. However the information is stored, transmitted or processed, the need for protection is of paramount importance in order to provide business continuity and minimize any potential damage. Security as a horizontal technology is embedded in every component of e-business solutions and is only as reliable as its weakest link. Both mobile applications and the deployment of web services will usher in the development of a new range of crucial security challenges.

Web services and service-oriented architectures constitute a new paradigm for IT-based business support. This will bring about significant change, greater competition and accelerated application development. It will also confront IT managers with the question of how to deal with these changes. In addition, the web services model creates a kind of two-level programmability which in turn offers greater flexibility in designing and changing business processes. Enterprises and IT service providers will therefore have to redefine their business relationships and responsibilities.

The mobility megatrend will permanently influence both social life and business activities. According to Meta Group, application mobilization will become a key enterprise challenge and develop into the greatest consumer of resources and business effort. Unfortunately, organizations often do not adopt the correct approach until they have already failed in their first attempt. One example is the introduction of PCs and the client/server architecture, with some organizations taking 20 years to solve the resulting problems.

The first step towards adopting mobility in an enterprise has to be the establishment of a mobility policy. This policy may include deployment rules, purchase rules, ownerships, budget responsibility, selection of device types, vendor selection, standards, sanctions, etc. It is quite clear that most enterprises can justify selective mobilization today.

Though mobility, security and web services are undoubtedly disparate technologies with independent technical implications and histories, they must be considered together in the context of the overall changes of paradigms, architectures and business needs that will be witnessed over the next decade.

In the light of these developments, the important message for CIOs and other IT experts and decision-makers is:

Bring together all the knowledge you possess concerning these three areas of technology, align the security, mobility and application policies, set up your business solutions on the basis of proven, standards-oriented infrastructures using easily integrable modular building blocks and elaborate a transitional plan that leads towards a service-oriented architecture and that takes account of your enterprise's business risks, the mobility requirements, web services integration and forward-looking business process management.

CIOs have never before been faced with such a critical shift of circumstances, one that brings with it such a range of challenges and risks. However, taking the right decisions now and transferring these to the safeguarding of their business solutions may also represent the greatest opportunity they have ever had.

References

Foreword

[F1]   MÜNCHNER KREIS, Tal 16, 80331 München
        http://www.muenchner-kreis.de/index_e.htm

Chapter 2

[2.2.1] GSMWorld. http://www.gsmworld.com/index.shtml

[2.2.2] WAP Forum. http://www.wapforum.org/what/technical.htm

[2.2.3] UMTS Forum. http://www.umts-forum.org/servlet/dycon/ztumts/umts/Live/en/ umts/Home

[2.2.4] 3GPP. http://www.3gpp.org

[2.2.5] Wireless Ethernet Compatibility Alliance. http://www.wirelessethernet.org/

[2.2.6] Bluetooth. www.bluetooth.org

[2.2.7] GPRS and 3G wireless applications. Professional developer's guide, by Cristoffer Andersson, Publisher John Wiley & S Inc, 2001, ISBN 0-471-41405-0

Chapter 3

[3.1.1] IT-Lösungen im e-Business. by Lothar Gläßer, Publicis Corporate Publishing, 2003, ISBN 3-89578-203-3

[3.1.2] ebXML. http://www.ebxml.org

[3.1.3] OASIS. http://www.oasis.org

[3.1.4] RosettaNet. http://www.rosettanet.org/RosettaNet/Rooms/DisplayPages/LayoutInitial

[3.1.5] W3C. http://www.w3c.org

[3.1.6] XML. http://www.xml.org

[3.1.7] XML inclusions. http://www.w3.org/TR/2002/CR-xinclude-20020917/

Chapter 4

[4.3.1] WAP 2.0. http://www.wapforum.org/what/technical.htm

[4.3.2] Palm OS. http://www.palmsource.com/palmos/

[4.3.3] Windows Mobile. http://www.microsoft.com/windowsmobile/default.mspx

[4.3.4] Symbian OS. http://www.symbian.com

[4.3.5] Nokia, Series 60. http://www.forum.nokia.com/main/0,6566,010_40,00.html

[4.3.6] Research in Motion, BlackBerry. http://www.rim.com

[4.3.7] J2ME. http://java.sun.com/j2me/

[4.3.8] .NET Compact Framework. http://msdn.microsoft.com/mobilty/ prodtechinfo/ devtools/netcf/

[4.3.9] Windows Mobile development tools. http://msdn.microsoft.com/library/ default.asp?url=/library/en-us/dnppcgen/html/devtoolsmobileapps.asp

[4.3.10] IBM Enterprise mobile applications. http://www-3.ibm.com/software/ pervasive/enterprise/

[4.3.11] SAP Mobile Infrastructure. http://www.sap.com/solutions/mobilebusiness/

[4.3.12] Extended Systems Mobile Enterprise Applications. http://www.extended systems.com/ESI/Products/Mobile+Data+Management+Products/ Mobile+ Application+Development/MAP+Features.htm

[4.3.13] Mobility Solutions Fujitsu Siemens. http://www.fujitsu-siemens.com/ mobility/

[4.4.1] Mobilelife Portal. https://www.siemens-mobilelife.de

Chapter 5

[5.2.1] Global XML Web Services Architecture (GXA). http://msdn.microsoft.com/ library/default.asp?url=/library/en-us/dngxa/html/understandgxa.asp

[5.2.2] WS-I Organization. http://www.ws-i.org/

[5.2.3] W3C, Web services standards. http://www.w3c.org/2002/ws/

[5.2.4] WS-CAF. http://www.oasisopen.org/committees/tc_home.php? wg_abbrev=ws-caf

[5.2.5] OASIS FWSI. http://www.oasis-open.org/committees/tc_home.php? wg_abbrev=fwsi

[5.3.1] OASIS WSDM. http://www.oasisopen.org/committees/tc_home.php? wg_abbrev=wsdm

[5.4.1] SAP NetWeaver. http://www.sap.com/solutions/netweaver/

[5.4.2] Microsoft Web services. http://msdn.microsoft.com/webservices/

[5.4.3] WebSphere & Web services. http://www-106.ibm.com/developerworks/ ibm/library/i-services.html

Chapter 6

[6.1.1] Computer emergency response team. http://www.cert.org

[6.2.1] Computer Security Handbook. 4th edition, by Bosworth, Kabay, Publisher John Wiley & S, Inc. ISBN 0-471-41258-9

[6.2.2] Siemens Business Services. http://www.siemens.com/index.jsp?sdc_p= po1050773fcls2mu2&sdc_sid= 6108248724&sdc_bcpath=10501

[6.2.3] Fraunhofer Gesellschaft. http://www.sit.fraunhofer.de/english/hps1/

[6.3.1] WAP standards. http://www.wapforum.org/what/technical.htm#Approved

References

[6.3.2] WLAN Protected Access. WI-FI Protected Access Finally Arrives, Business Communication Review, May 2003

[6.3.3] Bluetooth Security White Paper. http://www.bluetooth.com/upload/24Security_Paper.PDF

[6.3.4] Security on Pocket PC. http://www.microsoft.com/windowsmobile/resources/whitepapers/security.mspx

[6.3.5] Security on Palm. White Paper: Handheld Security for the Mobile Enterprise, 2002 Palm, Inc.

[6.4.1] IDC Report. E-World Survey and Internet Commerce Market Model, 2002

[6.4.2] RADIUS. http://www.ietf.org/rfc/rfc2138.txt?number=2138

[6.4.3] TSL/SSL. http://www.ietf.org/rfc/rfc2246.txt?number=2246

[6.4.4] SSH. http://www.ssh.com/solutions/secureshell.html

[6.4.5] X.509. http://ietf.org/html.charters/pkix-charter.html

[6.4.6] PKCS. http://www.pkcs.org/

[6.4.7] Kerberos. http://www.ietf.org/rfc/rfc1510.txt?number=1510

[6.4.8] XML Security, SAML. http://www.nue.et-inf.uni-siegen.de/~geuer-pollmann/xml_security.html

[6.4.9] Microsoft .NET Passport. http://www.microsoft.com/net/services/passport/

[6.4.10] Liberty Alliance Project. http://www.projectliberty.org/index.html?faqs/index.html~content

[6.4.11] Entrust GetAccess. http://entrust.com/getaccess/index.htm

[6.4.12] RSA ClearTrust. http://www.rsasecurity.com/products/cleartrust/index.html

[6.4.13] Netegrity SiteMinder. http://www.netegrity.com/products/index.cfm?leveltwo=SiteMinder

[6.5.1] Web Services Security by Mark O'Neill et al., Publisher McGraw-Hill/Osborne 2003, ISBN 0-07-222471-1

[6.5.2] UDDI, OASIS. http://www.uddi.org, http://www.oasis-open.org/home/index.php

[6.5.3] Web services security specifications. http://msdn.microsoft.com/library/default.asp?url=/library/en-us/dnglobspec/html/wssecurspecindex.asp

[6.5.4] RSA Security, White Paper Web services security. http://www.rsasecurity.com/solutions/web-services/whitepapers/WSS_WP_0802.pdf

[6.5.5] Microsoft Trustbridge. http://www.microsoft.com/presspass/press/2002/Jun02/06-06TrustbridgePR.asp

[6.5.6] IBM WebSphere, WS-Security. http://www-106.ibm.com/developerworks/webservices/wsdk/

[6.5.7] IBM Tivoli Access Manager. http://www-306.ibm.com/software/tivoli/products/access-mgr-e-bus/

[6.5.8] SAP, Secure Business in open Environments, http://www.sap.com/solutions/netweaver/brochures/

[6.5.9] Entrust Secure Transaction Platform. http://www.entrust.com/stp/index.htm

Index

.NET Compact Framework 67
.NET Enterprise Servers 118
.NET Enterprise Services 43
.NET framework 30, 117
.NET Passport Wallet 164
.NET-managed components 42
2.5 generation (2.5G) technologies 21
3 generation mobile networks 20
3 Generation Partnership Projects (3GPP) 21
3G rich voice service 85
3G/UMTS service classes 85
802.11 LAN standards 22
802.11 WLAN working group 22
802.11b standard 23
802.11g standard 23

A

AARS (Authentication and Authorization Routing Service) 174-175
ABAP (SAP's object-oriented programming language) 111
access control 154
accessibility 54
ACID (Atomicy, Consistency, Isolation, Durability) 94
Active Server Page (ASP) 36
ad hoc business processes 104
ad hoc networks 24
ad hoc processes 48, 115
ADO.NET 31
Advanced Encryption Standard (AES) 143
agile enterprise 11
always-on 55
always-on connectivity 18
always-on society 200
amazon.com 118
anti-virus software 127
anti-virus strategy 127
application development 28
application gateway 127
application server 38, 42, 57, 118, 149
application-to-application communication 89
ASP (Active Server Page) 36

ASP.NET 31
ASP.NET mobile web applications 70
atomic transaction 99
Atomicy, Consistency, Isolation, Durability (ACID) 94
attacks 122
authentication 40, 127, 152-153
Authentication and Authorization Routing Service (AARS) 174-175
authentication APIs 159
authentication methods 154
authentication protocols 157
Authentication, Authorization and Accounting (triple A challenge) 204
authorization 40, 153
automatic failover 43
availability 125

B

B2B (business-to-business) 50, 102
B2C (business-to-consumer) 50, 102
B2E (business-to-employee) 50, 102
B2E applications 77
banking services 62
BAPIs (proprietary SAP interfaces) 113-114
BEA 99
BEA WebLogic 43, 94
best-of-breed applications 115
BIM (Business Information Management) 63
binding 91
biometric authentication 157
biometric devices 157
BizTalk 100, 113
BlackBerry 66
Bluetooth 23, 143
Bluetooth Special Interest Group 24
Boston Consulting Group 86
BPEL (Business Process Execution Language) 46, 48, 100, 107

BPEL4WS (Business Process Execution Language) 46, 100
BPM (Business Process Management) 45, 106, 114, 118
BPM modeling and simulation tools 107
BPML (Business Process Modeling Language) 99
BPO (Business Process Outsourcing) 108
BREW 66
business activity 99
business agility 105, 107
business continuity 133
Business Information Management (BIM) 63
business integration 44, 120
business logic tier 35
business process design 120
business process engine 45
Business Process Execution Language (BPEL4WS, BPEL) 46, 100
business process integration 104
Business Process Management (BPM) 45, 106, 114, 118
Business Process Modeling Language (BPML) 99
Business Process Outsourcing (BPO) 108
Business Web 11
business-to-business (B2B) 50, 102
business-to-consumer (B2C) 50, 102
business-to-employee (B2E) 50, 102
bus-oriented topologies 44

C

C# programming language 31
CA (Certification Authority) 128
CAAS (Client Authentication and Authorization Service) 173
CDC (Connected Device Configuration) 67
CDMA (Code Division Multiple Access) 20

213

Index

CDSA (Common Data Security Architecture) 160
Cell of Origin (COO) 21
CERT (Computer Emergency Response Team) 121
Certicom movianCrypt 148
Certicom movianVPN 148
Certicom Trustpoint Client 148
certificates 128
Certification Authority (CA) 128
challenge/response 156
Checkpoint VPN-1Secure Client 148
Chemical Industry Data Exchange (CIDX) 114
Children's Online Privacy Protection Act (COPPA) 164
cHTML (compact HTML) 19, 66
CIDX (Chemical Industry Data Exchange) 114
circles of trust 167
claim 181
CLDC (Connected Limited Device Configuration) 67
Client Authentication and Authorization Service (CAAS) 173
client/server paradigm 15
Code Division Multiple Access (CDMA) 20
collaboration services 41
COM+ 31
Common Data Security Architecture (CDSA) 160
Common Object Request Broker Architecture (CORBA) 44, 90
communication/presentation tier 35
component software models 29
Computer Emergency Response Team (CERT) 121
Computer Security Handbook 126
confidence 13, 48
confidential access 148
confidentiality 125
Connected Device Configuration (CDC) 67
Connected Limited Device Configuration (CLDC) 67
connected society 200
convenience 54
convergence of networks 198
convergence on IP networks 25
COO (Cell of Origin) 21
COPPA (Children's Online Privacy Protection Act) 164
CORBA (Common Object Request Broker Architecture) 44, 90
CORINA (Corporate Remote Intranet Access) 150
CRM (Customer Relationship Management) 44, 55, 63
cross-enterprise solution architectures 46
CryptoAPI 159
Customer Relationship Management (CRM) 44, 55, 63

D

dangers and vulnerabilities 122
data encryption 128
Data Repository and Registry Service 175
DCOM (Distributed Component Object Model) 90
demilitarized zone (DMZ) 140
Denial-of-Services (DoS) 123
Dense Wavelength Division Multiplexing (DWDM) 17
desaster recovery 133
device profiles 66
DHCP (Dynamic Host Configuration Protocol) 151
digital certificates 40, 128, 157
digital passport 152
digital signature 128
discovery 91
Distributed Component Object Model (DCOM) 90
Distributed Network Architecture (DNA) 43
DMZ (demilitarized zone) 140
DNA (Distributed Network Architecture) 43
Document Object Model, tree-oriented (DOM) 34
Document Type Definitions (DTDs) 34
DOM (Document Object Model, tree-oriented) 34
DoS (Denial-of-Services) 123
DTDs (Document Type Definitions) 34
DWDM (Dense Wavelength Division Multiplexing) 17
Dynamic Host Configuration Protocol (DHCP) 151
dynamic load balancing 43

E

EAI (Enterprise Application Integration) 44, 190
e-business and mobile business architectures 57
ebXML 32, 46
Eclipse 111
e-commerce 63
EDGE (Enhanced Data Rates for GSM Evolution) 21
EJBs (Enterprise JavaBeans) 30, 42-43
E-learning 53
Electrical and Electronics Engineers (IEEE) 22
electronic identity 152
emergency 52
end-to-end secure application platform 143
end-to-end security 53, 124, 134-135, 143, 149
Enhanced Data Rates for GSM Evolution (EDGE) 21
Enhanced Observed Time Difference (E-OTD) 22
Enterprise Application Integration (EAI) 44, 190
Enterprise JavaBeans (EJBs) 30, 42-43
enterprise portal 58
Enterprise Resource Planning (ERP) 44, 55, 63
Enterprise Services Architecture (ESA) 109
entitlements (authorizations) 171
Entrust GetAccess 171
Entrust Secure Transaction Platform 196
Entrust Secure Web Portal solution 171
Entrust VPN client 148
E-OTD (Enhanced Observed Time Difference) 22
ERP (Enterprise Resource Planning) 44, 55, 63
ESA (Enterprise Services Architecture) 109
ETSI (European Telecommunications Standards Institute) 20
Everyplace Toolkit for WebSphere Studio 71
Everyplace WebSphere Studio 71
Extended Systems Mobile Solutions Platform 73
eXtensible Markup Language (XML) 15, 32
eXtensible Stylesheet Language (XSL) 33
eXtensible Stylesheet Language Translation (XSLT) 62

F

fashion phones 26
federated network identity 167
federated security 167
firewalls 127, 149
fleet management 52, 62
FOMA (Freedom of Mobile Multimedia Access) 21
forward-looking e-business solution architectures 28
F-Secure 148
FWSI (Framework for Web Services Implementation) 100

Index

G

Gartner 86, 200, 208
GDS (Global Distribution Services) 63
General Packaged Radio System (GPRS) 17, 84, 141-142
Generic Security Service (GSS) API 159
GetAccess single sign-on process 176
Global Distribution Services (GDS, Amadeus, Sabre, etc) 63
Global Positioning System (GPS) 22
Global System for Mobile Communications) (GSM) 17, 84, 141-142
Global XML Web Services Architecture (GXA) 46, 96
Glück & Kanja Technology AG, CryptoEx Volume 148
GPRS (General Packaged Radio System) 17, 84, 141-142
GPS (Global Positioning System) 22
Graphical User Interface (GUI) 28
grid computing 13
grid services 13
GSM (Global System for Mobile Communications) 17, 84, 141-142
GSS (Generic Security Service) 159
GUI (Graphical User Interface) 28
GXA (Global XML Web Services Architecture) 46, 96

H

High Speed Circuit Switched Data (HSCSD) 21
holistic security solution 129
house of e-business security 124
HSCSD (High Speed Circuit Switched Data) 21
HTML (HyperText Markup Language) 16
HTTPS (HTTP secure) 141, 143, 168
hub-and-spoke topologie 44
HyperText Markup Language (HTML) 16

I

IBM 97, 100, 112, 118, 184, 201
IBM Tivoli 194
IBM WebSphere 43, 94, 112
IBM WebSphere Business Integration 46

IBM WebSphere Everyplace family 70
IBM WebSphere SSO 178
IBM's Eclipse 29
ICC (Integrated Circuit Card) 129, 156
identity 152
identity management 153
identity providers 167
Identity Service Interface Specifications (ID-SIS) 189
IDocs (SAP proprietary interfaces) 114
IDS (Intrusion Detection Systems) 127
ID-SIS (Identity Service Interface Specifications) 189
IEEE (Electrical and Electronics Engineers) 22
IEEE 802.11i 142
i-mode 19
Information Security Management System (ISMS) 130
infotainment 53
instant couponing 52
Integrated Circuit Card (ICC) 129, 156
integration brokers 44
integration server 38, 44, 57, 118, 149
integration services 41
integration tier 35
integrity 125
intelligent mobile clients 64
intermediaries 182
intrusion 127
Intrusion Detection Systems (IDS) 127
intuitive user experiences 201
IP devices 142
IP spoofing 123
IPsec 182
ISMS (Information Security Management System) 130
ISO 17799 130
IT paradigm shifts 14

J

J2EE (Java 2 Enterprise Edition) 30, 67, 111
J2EE application server 103, 118
J2EE architecture 31
J2ME (Java 2 Micro Edition) 66-67
J2ME Web Services Specification (JSR 172) 68
J2SE (Java Standard Edition) 67
JAAS (Java Authentication and Authorization Service) 160
Java 2 Enterprise Edition (J2EE) 30, 67, 111

Java 2 Micro Edition (J2ME) 66-67
Java API for parsing XML documents (JAXP) 44
Java Authentication and Authorization Service (JAAS) 160
Java Community Process (JCP) 31, 112
Java Connector Architecture (JCA) 44, 113
Java Database Connectivity (JDBC) 31, 44
Java Mail 43
Java Messaging Services (JMS) 43
Java Metadata Interface (JMI) 106, 113
Java Naming and Directory Interface (JNDI) 43
Java Portlet Standard JSR 168 113
Java programming language 31
Java Server Page (JSP) 31, 36, 43
Java servlets 37, 43
Java Standard Edition (J2SE) 67
Java Transaction Services and APIs (JTS/JTA) 43
Java world 30
JavaBeans 43
JAXP (Java API for parsing XML documents) 44
JCA (Java Connector Architecture) 44, 113
JCo (SAP Java Connector) 112
JCP (Java Community Process) 31
JDBC (Java Database Connectivity) 31, 44
JMI (Java Metadata Interface) 106, 113
JMS (Java Messaging Services) 43
JNDI (Java Naming and Directory Interface) 43
JSP (Java Server Page) 31, 36, 43
JSR 109 (web service for J2EE) 103
JSR 172 (J2ME Web Services Specification) 68
JTS/JTA (Java Transaction Services and APIs) 43

K

Kerberos 159, 183, 190
Key Distribution Center (KDC) 159, 190
Kids Passport services 164
knowledge management 41

L

laptops 64

215

Index

leisure and work platforms 203
LFS (Location Fixing Schemes) 22
Liberty Alliance Project 166
Liberty Alliance Single sign-on process 169
Liberty Identity Web Services Framework 188
lifecycle management 111
lingua franca 16, 32
Linux 27, 66
localization 54
location finding 52
Location Fixing Schemes (LFS) 22
location-based services 41, 51, 62-63, 85
location-dependent shopping services 62
logging and audit service 175
long-running transaction 94

M

machine-to-machine telematics applications 52
Managed Mobile Device (MMD) 74
managed security services 134-135
man-in-the-middle attacks 124
master data management 111
m-butler 81
MDS (Multi-Domain Service) 176
message brokers 44
Meta Group 119, 209
microbrowser 37, 59
micropayment services 63
Microsoft 97, 100, 112, 117, 184, 201
Microsoft .NET 31, 94, 112, 161, 194
Microsoft Biztalk 46
Microsoft COM+ components 42
Microsoft Message Queuing (MSMQ) 113
Microsoft Mobile .NET 69
Microsoft Office 2003 118
Microsoft Windows Server 43
middleware 9, 102, 118
MIDlets 67
MIDP (Mobile Information Device Profile) 67
MMC (Multimedia Memory Card) 74
MMD (Managed Mobile Device) 74
MMS (Multimedia Messaging Services) 18, 50
mobile access 37
mobile application categories 50
mobile application platforms 57

mobile commerce 53
mobile communication 52
mobile control and monitoring 52
mobile controls 70
mobile device evolution 25
mobile device platforms 63
mobile devices 25, 144, 199
mobile end-to-end security 139
mobile enterprise applications 75
mobile entertainment 53
mobile field service 81
mobile Healthcare Life Portal 84
Mobile Information Device Profile (MIDP) 67
mobile information server 69
mobile information services 52
mobile internet 16
mobile intranet applications 51
mobile intranet/extranet access 85
mobile location technologies 21
mobile office 51, 62
mobile Outlook manager 69
mobile phones 25, 64
mobile sales force automation 79
mobile security 137
mobile travel services 62
mobile videophony 86
Mobile Web Form 70
mobile workforce 62
mobile workplace 62
mobility 9, 47, 198, 203
monitoring 52
monolithic application paradigm 15
mortgage application process 192
MQSeries (WebSphere Business Integration) 113
MSMQ (Microsoft Message Queuing) 113
Multi-Domain Service (MDS) 176
Multimedia Memory Card (MMC) 74
Multimedia Messaging Services (MMS) 18, 50
multitier application architecture 35
mySAP Business Intelligence 111
mySAP Business Suite 110
mySAP Enterprise Portal 111
mySAP ERP 110
mySAP Mobile Business 111
mySAP Smart Business Solutions 110
mySAP solutions 109
mySAP technology 71, 110

N

Netegrity Siteminder 177
NetWeaver 71
NetWeaver platform 109
network evolution 16

network identity 152, 166
NMAS (Novell Modular Authentication Service) 160
non-repudiation 126
Novell Modular Authentication Service (NMAS) 160

O

OASIS (Organization for the Advancement of Structured Information Standards) 46, 96, 107, 112, 184
Object Management Group 90
object-oriented programming 29
offshoring 200
OLAP (Online Analytical Processing) 106
on-demand computing 13
one-factor authentication 153
Online Analytical Processing (OLAP) 106
Open Mobile Alliance 18
open source software 13
Organization for the Advancement of Structured Information Standards (OASIS) 46, 96, 107, 112, 184
outsourcing 120, 200

P

P2P (peer-to-peer) 204
PAAM (Pluggable Authentication and Authorization Module) 174
packet filter 127
packet sniffers 123
Palm OS 27, 65
PAM (Pluggable Authentication Module) 160
Passport single sign-in process 162
password attacks 123
passwords 155
PDAs 25, 64
peer-to-peer (P2P) 204
peer-to-peer communication 199
Personal Information Management (PIM) 26, 62, 77
personal mobile devices 200
personalization 55
personalization services 40
Petroleum Industry Data Exchange (PIDX) 114
physical break-ins 124
PIM (Personal Information Management) 26, 62, 77
PKCS (Public-Key Cryptography Standards) 158
PKI (Public Key Infrastructure) 40, 129, 157, 189
platform interoperability 103

Index

Pluggable Authentication and Authorization Module (PAAM) 174
Pluggable Authentication Module (PAM) 160
Pocket PC 65
points of interest 52
policy 124
portal engine 39
portal server 38, 57, 118, 149
portlets 39, 106
pre-payment services 63
presentation services 39
privacy 125
process monitoring 77
professional IT service provider 120
proprietary SAP interfaces (BAPIs) 113-114
proxy server 127
Public Key Infrastructure (PKI) 40, 129, 157, 189
Public-Key Cryptography Standards (PKCS) 158
publishing 91
publishing services 41
push/notification services 62

Q

QoS (Quality of Services) 61, 84

R

Radio Frequency Identification (RFID) 76
RADIUS (Remote Access Dial-in User Services) 158
RAS (Remote Access Server) 141, 148
RBAC (Roles-Based Access Control) 171
RC4 encryption 143
reachability 54
real-time enterprise 11, 104
Remote Access Dial-in User Services (RADIUS) 158
Remote Access Server (RAS) 141, 148
remote control 52
Remote Function Calls (RFCs) 114
repair and telematics applications 52
Research in Motion (RIM) 27, 66
Resource Protection Service (RPS) 175
RFCs (Remote Function Calls) 114
RFID (Radio Frequency Identification) 76
RIM (Research in Motion) 27, 66
risk analysis 131

risk assessments 133
risk management 132
Robust Security Network (RSN) 142
Roles-Based Access Control (RBAC) 171
RosettaNet 32, 114
RPS (Resource Protection Service) 175
RSA ClearTrust 177
RSN (Robust Security Network) 142
runtime environment 42
runtime services 42

S

Sales Force Automation (SFA) 55, 62
SAML (Security Assertion Markup Language) 159, 169, 185, 193
SAP 99, 112, 201
SAP .NET connector 112
SAP Business Warehouse (SAP BW) 113
SAP BW (SAP Business Warehouse) 113
SAP enterprise portal SSO 177
SAP Exchange Infrastructure (SAP XI) 111, 113
SAP Exchange Integration 46
SAP Java Connector (JCo) 112
SAP Mobile Engine (SAP ME) 71-73
SAP Mobile Infrastructure (SAP MI) 71
SAP NetWeaver 94, 108, 195
SAP R/3 enterprise 109
SAP Web Application Server 71, 111
SAP XI (SAP Exchange Infrastructure) 111, 113
SAP's object-oriented programming language (ABAP) 111
SAX (Simple API for XML) 34
SCM (Supply Chain Management) 44, 55, 63
SD Card/Multimedia Memory Card (SD/MMC) 74
SDK (Software Development Kit) 146
SD/MMC (SD Card/Multimedia Memory Card) 74
seamless mobile travel services 78
secure access 148
secure network channel 140
Secure Shell (SSH) 158
Secure Socket Layer (SSL) 128, 182
security 9, 12, 48, 198, 204
security analysis 132

Security Assertion Markup Language (SAML) 159, 169, 185, 193
security awareness 48
security focus areas 121
security goals 124
security policy 126, 131
security portfolio 135
security roadmap 132
security service provider 135
security services 40
security strategy 13, 48, 133
Security Support Provider Interface (SSPI) and CryptoAPI 159
security techniques 124, 126
security token 181
security token services 183
Series 60 operating system 26
Series 60 platform 65
service bus 202
Service-Oriented Architecture (SOA) 9-10, 48, 89, 93, 106, 109, 116, 202
services/resources tier 35
Session Initiative Protocol (SIP) 199
Session Management Service (SMS) 174-175
SFA (Sales Force Automation) 55, 62
SGML (Structured Generalized Markup Language) 15, 32
Short Message Service (SMS) 18, 50
short-duration transactions 94
Siemens Business Services 74, 81, 135, 150
Siemens Corporate Card 156
Siemens' Xelibri family 26
SIG (Special Interest Group) 23
SIM cards 156, 205
Simple API for XML (SAX) 34
Simple Object Access Protocol (SOAP) 35, 118, 169
Single Sign-On (SSO) 40, 128, 138, 152-153, 171
Single Sign-On standard 167
SIP (Session Initiative Protocol) 199
Slammer Worm 134
Small and Medium Business (SMB) 114
smart clients 64
Smart Device Programmability for Visual Studio .NET 69
smartcards 129, 156, 204
smartphones 25, 64-65
SMB (Small and Medium Business) 114
SMS (Session Management Service) 174-175

217

Index

SMS (Short Message Service) 18, 50
SOA (Service-Oriented Architecture) 9-10, 48, 89, 93, 106, 109, 116, 202
SOAP (Simple Object Access Protocol) 35, 48, 90, 118, 169
SOAP message 182
Software Development Kit (SDK) 146
Special Interest Group (SIG) 23
SSH (Secure Shell) 158
SSL (Secure Socket Layer) 128, 182
SSL/TLS protocol 141-143
SSO (Single Sign-On) 40, 128, 138, 152-153, 171
SSO services 160
SSPI (Security Support Provider Interface) 159
strong authentication 153
Structured Generalized Markup Language (SGML) 15, 32
Sun 99
Supply Chain Management (SCM) 44, 55, 63
supply chain optimization 76
surveillance 52
Swing 31
Symbian OS 65

T

tablet PCs 64
TAM (Tivoli Access Manager) 195
tamper-resistant 129
tamper-resistant modules 204
TC (Trust Center) 128
TCP/IP devices 147
TDMA (Time Division Multiple Access) 21
TDOA (Time Difference of Arrival) 22
Time Difference of Arrival (TDOA) 22
Time Division Multiple Access (TDMA) 21
Tivoli Access Manager (TAM) 195
TLS (Transport Layer Security) 128, 182
TLS/SSL 141-143, 158
tokens 155
tracking 52
tracking and logistics 76
tracking services 62
transport encryption 128
Transport Layer Security (TLS) 128, 182
transport security 189
travel assistance services 77
travel services 52

Trend Micro Office Scan 148
Trend Micro PC-cillin 148
triple A challenge (Authentication, Authorization and Accounting) 204
trust 48, 124, 126
Trust Center (TC) 128
TrustBridge 166, 194
trusted web services 202
two- or three-factor authentication 153

U

UDDI (Universal Description, Discovery, and Integration) 35, 91, 118
UDDI.org 184
UMTS (Universal Mobile Telecommunication System) 20, 84, 141-142
unified messaging 52
Unified Resource Locator (URL) 59
unified web/WAP platform 61
Universal Description, Discovery, and Integration (UDDI) 35, 91, 118
Universal Mobile Telecommunication System (UMTS) 20, 84, 141-142
Universal Personal Communication Module (UPCM) 206
Universal SIM card (USIM) 205
universality 54
UPCM (Universal Personal Communication Module) 206
URL (Unified Resource Locator) 59
user ID 40
user management 39
username type token 184
USIM (Universal SIM card) 205
utility computing 13

V

value of mobile applications 53
value of mobility 55
Virtual Private Nerworks (VPN) 127, 141-142, 150
virtualization of services 199
viruses 123
Visual Studio .NET 29, 68
Visual Studio .NET Development Environment 69
Voice eXtensible Markup Language (VoiceXML) 62
VoiceXML (Voice eXtensible Markup Language) 62
VPN (Virtual Private Nerworks) 127, 141-142, 150
VPN dial-in 150

VPN GPRS 151
VPN internet 150
VPN services 199
VPN WLAN 151

W

W3C (World Wide Web Consortium) 46, 96, 112, 184
WAP (Wireless Application Protocol) 18, 37, 58, 141
WAP 1.1 141, 145
WAP 1.2 142
WAP 1.2.1 145
WAP 2.0 58, 145
WAP architecture 58
WAP browser 37, 58, 141
WAP devices 141, 145
WAP forum 18, 58
WAP gateway 59, 141-142, 149
WAP server 59
WAP standard 141
WAP wireless protocol stack 59
WAS (Web Application Server) 195
W-CDMA (Wideband-CDMA) 20
WDP (Wireless Datagram Protocol) 19, 37, 59
Web Application Server (WAS) 195
web redirects 168
web server 36, 149
web service broker 91
web service endpoint policy 181
web service for J2EE (JSR 109) 103
web service provider 91
web service requester 91
web service security 13
web services 10, 43-44, 47, 88, 198, 201
web services and security 180
Web Services Choreography Interface (WSCI) 99
Web services Composite Application Framework (WS-CAF) 100
web services deployment example 192
Web Services Description Language (WSDL) 35, 89, 118
Web Services Distributed Management (WSDM) 107
web services extended standards 95
Web Services Flow Language (WSFL) 100
Web Services for Remote Portals (WSRP) 103, 106
Web Services for Remote Portlets (WSRP) 113
web services impacts 101

218

Index

Web Services Interoperability Organization (WS-I) 97, 112, 184
web services management 107
web services paradigm 10, 89, 103, 108
web services security 138
web services security model 182
web services security scenarios 190
web services security specifications 185
web services security standards 181
web services security terminology 181
web services standards 95, 118
web services technology 9
web-based e-business 15
web-based e-business paradigm 16
webpads 64
WebSphere application server 118, 194
WebSphere Business Integration (MQSeries) 113
WebSphere Everyplace Access 71
WebSphere Everyplace Connection Manager 71
WebSphere product family 118
WECA (Wireless Ethernet Compatibility Alliance) 23
Wideband-CDMA (W-CDMA) 20
WiFi (Wireless Fidelity) 23
WIM (Wireless Identity Module) 145
WIM card 205
Windows CE .NET 65
Windows Forms 31
Windows Mobile 27, 65, 69
Windows Server System 2003 118
Wireless Access Point (WLAN AP) 142
Wireless Application Protocol (WAP) 18, 37, 58, 141
Wireless Datagram Protocol (WDP) 19, 37, 59
Wireless Ethernet Compatibility Alliance (WECA) 23
Wireless Fidelity (WiFi) 23
Wireless Identity Module (WIM) 145
Wireless LAN (WLAN) 22

Wireless Markup Language (WML) 19, 66
wireless session protocol 19
Wireless Session Protocol (WSP) 59
Wireless Telephony Applications (WTA) 19, 60
Wireless Transport Layer Security (WTLS) 59, 128, 141, 145
WLAN (Wireless LAN) 22
WLAN AP (Wireless Access Point) 142
WML (Wireless Markup Language) 19, 37, 59, 66
WMLScript 19, 59
WMLScript Crypto 145
workflow engines 10, 45, 107
World Wide Web Consortium (W3C) 46, 96, 112, 184
WPKI standard 146
WS-Addressing 98
WS-Attachments 98
WS-Authorization 188
WS-CAF (Web services Composite Application Framework) 100
WSCI (Web Services Choreography Interface) 99
WS-Coordination 99
WSDL (Web Services Description Language) 35, 89, 118
WSDM (Web Services Distributed Management) 107
WS-Federation 188
WSFL (Web Services Flow Language) 100
WS-I (Web Services Interoperability Organization) 97, 112, 184
WS-Inspection 97
WSP (Wireless Session Protocol) 59
WS-Policy 187
WS-PolicyFramework 97
WS-Privacy 187
WS-Referral 98
WS-ReliableMessaging 98
WS-Routing 98
WSRP (Web Services for Remote Portals) 103, 106
WSRP (Web Services for Remote Portlets) 113
WS-Secure conversation 187
WS-Security 98, 166, 186
WS-Transaction 99
WS-Trust 187
WTA (Wireless Telephony Applications) 19, 60

WTA server 60
WTLS (Wireless Transport Layer Security) 59, 128, 141, 145
WTLS Class 1 145
WTLS Class 2 145
WTLS Class 3 145

X

X.509 158
X.509 certificates 184
X.509 standard 152
XACML (XML Access Control Markup Language 185
xAPPS 109, 115
XHTML 66
XHTML browsers 26
XKMS (XML Key Management Specification) 185, 192
XLANG 100
XLink 34
XMI (XML Metadata Interchange) 113
XML – the Lingua Franca of the Internet 32
XML (eXtensible Markup Language) 15, 32
XML Access Control Markup Language (XACML) 185
XML document 33, 89
XML encryption 185, 193
XML for analysis (XMLA) 106
XML Key Management Specification (XKMS) 185, 192
XML Metadata Interchange (XMI) 106, 113
XML related security standards 184
XML scheme 34
XML security 185
XML signature 185, 193
XML web services 34, 44, 47, 68, 97
XML.Org 33
XML/XSLT engine 62
XMLA (XML for analysis) 106, 113
XPath 34
XPointer 34
XSL (eXtensible Stylesheet Language) 33
XSL processor 33
XSLT (eXtensible Stylesheet Language Translation) 62

Georg Berner

Management in 20XX
What will be important in the future – a holistic view

August 2004, approx. 240 pages, 141 coloured
illustrations, 17.3 cm x 25 cm, hardcover
ISBN 3-89578-241-6
Approx. € 39.90 [D] / sFr 60.00

The whole world is witnessing radical economic changes. Traditional markets are stagnating; global markets are emerging. Business processes are becoming more mobile, more flexible, and much more streamlined. The boom companies of yesterday have disappeared from the scene. Such an environment calls for innovative ideas – for new ways of doing business, for new products and services, and for a totally new world.

To survive, companies will have to be resilient and yet adaptable. To turn their visions into reality, they will have to act as well as react. Growth will come to only those companies that can identify demand and apply the right technological know-how to create tangible customer benefit. Development, marketing, and sales departments must arrive at the right strategies, just as corporate organization, production, and logistics managers must devise and implement the best possible processes.

The book lays out some remarkable scenarios and ambitious visions for the future. It helps readers to formulate ideas and plot new directions for their business and points out the changes needed to meet challenges that lie ahead. The new role people will play in the evolving world of business also receives attention in this book that is at once informative and inspiring.

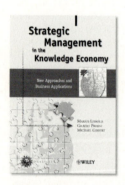

Leibold, Marius; Probst, Gilbert; Gibbert, Michael

Strategic Management in the Knowledge Economy
New Approaches and Business Applications

2002, 353 pages, 17 cm x 25 cm, hardcover
ISBN 3-89578-168-1
€ 49.90 [D] / sFr 75.00

Due to the dramatic shifts in the knowledge economy, this book provides a significant departure from traditional strategic management concepts and practice. Designed for both advanced students and business managers, it presents a unique combination of new strategic management theory, carefully selected strategic management articles by prominent scholars such as Gary Hamel, Michael Porter, Peter Senge, and real-world case studies.

On top of this, the authors link powerful new benchmarks in strategic management thinking, including the concepts of Socio-Cultural Network Dynamics, Systemic Scorecards, and Customer Knowledge Management with practical business challenges and solutions of blue-chip companies with a superior performance (Lafite-Rothschild, Who's Who, Holcim, BRL Hardy, Kuoni BTI, Deutsche Bank, Unisys, Novartis).